Homeland of the
Buddha

Homeland of the
Buddha

A guide to Buddhist holy places of India and Nepal

John Tosan McKinnon

Pada Print
P.O. Box 7027, Nelson 7042, New Zealand

To Diane,

My companion for life and on many Asian journeys;
and Shugen Sensei, for many years of guidance
and compassion.

If this one day in a lifetime of a hundred years is lost,
When will you ever get your hands on it again?

EIHEI DOGEN 1200–1253

ISBN **978-0-9941131-0-8 (full colour print)**
      978-0-9941131-1-5 (black & white print)
      978-0-9941131-2-2 (MOBI colour)
      978-0-9941131-3-9 (ePub colour)
      978-0-9941131-4-6 (PDF ebook colour)

DESIGNED BY Mark Watson/Highlux Design. www.highlux.co.nz.

PUBLISHED BY Pada Print

www.homelandofthebuddha.com

Contents

7 Introduction

17 Varanasi

23 Sarnath

37 Bodhgaya

61 Rajgir

75 Nalanda

83 Patna

93 Vaishali

105 Kesariya & Pava (Fazilnagar)

109 Kushinagar

117 Gorakhpur

125 Being First: the Buddhist Archaeologists

139 Lumbini

149 Tilaurkot: Nepalese–Kapilavastu

165 Ramagrama

169 Piprahwa: Indian–Kapilavastu

179 Shravasti

197 Sankasya

203 Suggested tour

206 Glossary

211 Acknowledgements

213 Bibliography

214 About the author

Introduction

THIS book is a guide for those visiting the major sites of Buddhism which lie on the great plain of the Ganges in India and Nepal. The main emphasis is the life of the Buddha; how each location was significant during his time; and how that history came to be known in the modern world. It is also useful for those who seek to know where and how the Buddha taught, two and a half thousand years ago. Although it discusses some aspects of what the Buddha taught, it does not seek to be a book about Buddhism.

HOW TO USE THIS BOOK

What's outlined is a tour to all the sites, suggesting where to travel and what to do on a daily basis. For geographic reasons, the tour starts in Varanasi and ends in Agra sixteen days later. The direction of travel, the number of days and what to do each day is based on the author's experience over several visits to the region. Sixteen days is an ideal amount of time to visit all the significant Buddhist sites. It could be extended or shortened and some sections deleted, if you wished. The book does not detail hotels or restaurants, or how to travel (although having your own transport is the ideal), as information about these ever-changing essentials are readily obtainable elsewhere. There are no footnotes or references, apart from a bibliography and glossary, as it is meant for the general reader rather than the specialist.

A chapter is devoted to each site. The first section of each chapter summarises the reason why the place has Buddhist significance and details how the Buddha, and other individuals contributed to our knowledge of that place. The 'Today' section of each chapter summarises what the modern traveller can see in each place, in the sequence that they experience them.

TRAVEL OR PILGRIMAGE?

Every visitor to India is changed, no matter how much, or how little, they may be cosseted by luxury, or how little they are attuned to the realities of life which India forces on them. It is a truism that India alters the way people think about themselves and their lives. In that sense any

FACING PAGE
Seated Buddha, Myanmar Temple, Lumbini.

travel to India is a pilgrimage. How much more so therefore, when your travel is directed to walking the same paths as one of the world's greatest teachers and more so, if your intent is towards self-awareness. Whatever your intention, you can anticipate as you head to India, that the one who returns will be different from the one who left. When touring the homeland of the Buddha, we all carry the metaphorical staff of a pilgrim.

Who was the Buddha and where did he live?

Separating fact from legend is difficult for any heroic figure, and much more so when that individual lived two and half thousand years ago at a time before written records. Many claims relating to the Buddha are obviously mythical, but within those stories are aspects of Buddhist wisdom which support other more verifiable teachings of the Buddha. We can never know absolutely details of the Buddha's life but there is sufficient historical and archaeological evidence to support much of the literature and thus flesh-out the personality of a remarkable person.

It is important to appreciate that the Buddha was definitely not a mythical figure, but a real human individual, with all the joys and aches that being human involves. He was not a god and during his life he strongly discouraged those who sought to place him beyond the human realm. As a youngster and young man he lived the 'normal' life of a privileged young person of his time. He married and had a child and then unceremoniously left them, to set out on a quest for personal realization. Years of effort led him to attain a state of supreme awareness which we describe (inadequately), as enlightenment. Appreciating that this change could be realised by others and that it would be transformative, was his teaching for the next forty five years. The enlightened state does not separate that person from being human, so like everyone else, Gautama suffered the human indignities of old age, of sickness and of death.

The Buddha lived all his life in the plain of the Ganges, that vast outwash of flatland created by rivers rushing southwards from the Himalaya— 'the abode of the gods'. He was born in what we now call Nepal, and lived the vast majority of his life, in India. During his time the area was a collection of developing princely states and early democracies, sparsely populated. Now, this region is amongst the most densely inhabited on the planet. During his time, the vast majority of people were farmers, living their lives tied to the endless cycle of seasons and harvest.

SPIRITUAL LIFE IN THE BUDDHA'S TIME

The Buddha lived during a time of considerable political and religious ferment. The Aryan peoples from central Asia, the future Buddha's ancestors, had invaded India about twelve hundred years prior to his birth. They brought with them the religious certainties of Vedic gods:

Gods, who for the most part, were focused on the needs of an agricultural society. They also brought the beginnings of India's caste system—a social structure which sought stability by allocating one's position in society according to birth. At the top of the social pyramid were the Brahmin priests, whose demands on the populace for expensive sacrifice and ritual, became increasingly resented by the time of the Buddha.

A few hundred years before his birth, the rural society which had been little changed for the previous thousand years, was transformed by new iron-age technology. Jungle was more readily cleared, allowing the fertile soil to produce surplus food, and thus wealth. The Ganges plain region became the centre of Indian civilisation. Small city states developed, and with them differing forms of governance, and the rise of occupations which were not agricultural. As trade expanded around the region, rich city-bound merchants and bankers did not fit easily into the traditional caste system. The power of this group, brought about significant social tension as they challenged the status of Brahmin priests and the kshatriyan (warrior caste) rulers who dominated Aryan society.

By Gautama Buddha's time these minor principalities had shuffled the territories to become the sixteen mahajanapada, or 'great footprint' of the tribe. The Buddha was known and respected by many rulers of 'the sixteen'. Despite their affection, his teachings on nonviolence were largely ignored when they sought to dominate another region. During Gautama's life, no one state prevailed, but shortly after his death the kingdom of Magadha gradually subjugated the others to eventually become India's first empire, the Mauryan.

ABOVE
Bowing to the Bodhi Tree, Bodhgaya Temple.

As well as societal upheaval, it was also a period of religious tumult. Dominating the spiritual lives of most people were the gods and spirits of their own village or town. These were mostly malevolent deities

9

whose worship helped deflect disease or disaster such as flood or famine. Imposed on these ancient beliefs were Aryan demands for sacrifice and ritual to the new gods, such as Indra and Brahma.

With ritual, fire and sacrifice, Brahmin priests claimed ability to control the forces of nature. Without their knowledge of Sanskrit mantras (formulaic prayers), and exact details of each ritual, the universe would cease to exist.

Sanskrit had been the language of the original Aryan invaders, but by the Buddha's time it was a language known only by priests. A part of this world-sustaining ritual was animal sacrifice. As society became increasingly urbanised, the provision of sacrificial animals was difficult to maintain, and was expensive. Validated by hundreds of years of tradition, Brahmin priests and their rituals were inflexible. This unwillingness to change did not fit well with the upheaval occurring in society. These tensions of the Buddha's time, continue to reverberate today.

ABOVE
**An offering of
lotus flowers.**

Reflecting the religious uncertainties of the time, wandering religious seekers, or shramanas, were commonplace. Their aim was to escape the apparently endless cycle of birth and rebirth, the prevailing belief of the time. With few or no possessions they begged for a living, walking from place to place seeking spiritual relief. Large numbers of shramanas placed a burden of care upon the householder community. This responsibility most householders accepted willingly, as they envisaged personal benefit from feeding and housing these wandering spiritual seekers.

Most seekers were genuine, but as you might expect, some were dropouts or runaways, who had little interest in personal development. Concerned about the economic burden placed on householders by large numbers begging for their living, the rulers of Rajagriha and Shravasti passed laws requiring individual shramanas to demonstrate that they did indeed provide spiritual benefit to the general citizens.

At times they gathered into groups around a special guru to debate the relevance of a particular philosophy. Many practiced extreme austerities, starving or abusing their bodies, which they saw as a source of impurity and religious distraction.

Foremost of the shramana groups during the Buddha's time, was that of the Jains. Led by their historical founder, Mahavira (Great Hero), Jain groups attracted support from householders and rulers which competed with the needs of the Buddhist community. There is no evidence that Mahavira and the Buddha ever met, although they lived at the same time and travelled throughout much the same region. Nor is there evidence of the two groups confronting each other with more than words.

Several spiritual disciplines of that period continue to this day. Of them, only Buddhism spread its teachings beyond India to become a universal belief system. Jainism and the worship of local deities remained as beliefs of the Indian sub-continent, with limited international influence. Brahmanic beliefs slowly evolved to become Hinduism which meaningfully influenced the culture of South East Asia.

Today, depending on the season, and your perspective, the region where those religious strivers preached is either a sun-baked desert of intolerable hardship, or a vast swathe of green, and immensely fertile, rice-paddy. It is a region of few trees, most of them umbrella-form acacia; picturesque, but offering little relief from the punishing sunlight of modern Bihar. For the Buddha, the sun of two millennia ago was no less exhausting, particularly for a walking mendicant, no matter how enlightened. At his time, there were few people and a great deal of dense jungle, home to numerous tiger, leopard and elephant—and that's just the animal hazards. Banditry was rife, as were the unseen menaces of malaria and other diseases. Most 'roads' were unpaved tracks between towns. There were no bridges across the multitude of rivers, which for three months during the monsoon, were transformed into impassable torrents. When you consider the perils of that age, it's a wonder the Buddha survived his eighty years.

The Buddha, and his early group of followers, were a rag-tag bunch of wanderers, itinerant, except during the rainy season. Walking from town to town, without fixed occupation, they begged for a living. Permanent monastic settlements happened later in the Buddha's life. Until his death, the Buddha was for the most part a nomad, spending nine months of the year on the road.

Favoured places, where he was well known, were visited many times. Most of these locations were separated by days of arduous travel, a significant demand for single passage, let alone a lifetime of multiple journeys. During his forty five years of ministry, the Buddha roamed an area of the Gangetic plain roughly the size of England.

WHEN DID HE LIVE?

ca. 500–400 BCE

All traditions agree that the Buddha became enlightened at the age of thirty five and that he lived for eighty years. However, the year of his birth and death, have been subject of vigorous debate, since earliest times. For scholars, the generally preferred dates are 484–404 BCE, while some Buddhist traditions prefer a hundred or so years earlier. Scholars can debate absolute dates, a generalist choosing to support a 'middle way', can reasonably assume that the historical Buddha lived in the period from ca. 500–ca. 400 BCE.

AND WHAT WAS HIS BIRTHDAY?

Theravadan traditions are confident that the Buddha was born, became enlightened and died on the full moon day, in the month of Visaka (April/May) in the appropriate year. East Asian Mahayana Buddhists claim these events happened on the 8th day of respective months: April (birth); December (death); and February (enlightenment).

The life of the Buddha – a summary

There was a person who lived in north India, around the 5th century BCE, who is widely regarded as one the world's great souls. We refer to him as 'The Buddha'. Most Buddhist traditions refer to him as Siddhartha—he whose aim is accomplished—but in life, he was mostly called 'Gautama' which was his clan name. His father was a noble of the Sakya people from Kapilavastu, now in modern Nepal. In the literature, Gautama-Siddhartha is usually referred to as a prince.

ABOVE
Sujata offers curds to the starving Gautama, Karma Kargyu Temple, Bodhgaya.

Prior to his birth, it was predicted that Siddhartha would either be a great religious teacher or a cakravartin, a world-ruler. Seeking to distract him from the religious life his father indulged the young prince with all worldly pleasures. Siddhartha grew up, to marry a cousin, Yasodhara and they had a son together. Despite his life of privilege, the young man was troubled and, as the story goes, his attitudes were questioned when one day he met on the highway, an old man; a sick man; a dead man; and a monk. Legend relates that this was his first experience of such things—not a likely story—but sufficient to demonstrate that Siddhartha was confronting life's great existential questions. Why is there old age and disease, and why death?

In later life the Buddha was to refer to old age, sickness and death as 'the divine messengers.' Messengers who are all around us and who we tend to ignore. It is said that Gautama was twenty nine when he first became aware of the divine messengers. As a consequence, he was deeply troubled and sought answers that would satisfy him.

Abandoning his wife and new-born son, he initially sought out a series of spiritual teachers, none of whom could provide the answers he needed. He then joined a group of renunciates and for years practised extreme austerities. Anyone who visits India has seen their modern equivalents—religious enthusiasts who starve, beat, deny and otherwise abuse their physical bodies in a search for spiritual transcendence. For six years, Gautama pursued physical austerities which bordered on madness. Eventually, near to death from starvation, he came to realise that a life of extreme physical denial was a religious dead end. He took food, rested and restored his health. And in response, his five companions of the time abandoned Gautama as a turncoat, a shramana who lacked resolve.

At modern Bodhgaya, Siddhartha then sat in meditation under a peepal tree, resolving not to leave until he was enlightened. It is said, that he sat unmoved for six days and nights, assailed by the demon Mara who enlisted his host of beauteous daughters to distract the aspiring Buddha. Although tempted, Gautama strengthened his resolve and eventually reached a state that is called enlightened. That word has different implications for different people. Suffice to say that he realised in a deeply profound way the true nature of human existence and of reality—not that these are separate things—and at that moment, he became The Buddha, the 'awakened one'.

ABOVE
Ashokan lion pillar, Vaishali.

Accepting the task of communicating his insight, he sought out his former companions. In the deer park of Sarnath, near Varanasi he located them and preached his first sermon. 'Turning the Wheel of the Dharma' set in motion the Dharma, or teachings, of the Buddha. For the next fifty years the Buddha travelled the plains of the Ganges teaching. His charisma and teaching attracted an increasing group of followers, the Sangha, or community of Buddhist practitioners. Amongst them were kings and courtesans, the rich and the poor. At the age of eighty the Buddha died at Kushinagara. He had entered the realm of parinirvana, beyond the world of constant rebirth.

After the death of a spiritual teacher, there is a strong tendency, for his followers to create a glorified record of their deceased master so that conflicting religious dogmas can be overwhelmed, and their own devotee-status enhanced. The Buddha was treated no differently. He had spent a lifetime pointing out the futility of ritual, and the uselessness of a personality cult directed at a spiritual leader. Despite a lifetime of actively discouraging this practice, the Buddha, while alive, was revered and honoured in a form akin to worship. It is not surprising, that following his death he became an object of more intense ritual worship and the recipient of a huge personality cult—a cult which thrives in our own times. Nevertheless, Buddhist religiosity is not in conflict with and does not detract from, the Buddha's primary teaching which was to 'understand the cause of suffering and how suffering can be relieved'. A teaching, as relevant today as it was two and a half thousand years ago.

Sites of Buddhist pilgrimage

THE GREAT FOUR AND THE EIGHT

There are in total, eight major sites of Buddhist pilgrimage on the Ganges plain, four of them are believed to have been suggested by the Buddha.

There are four places, Ananda, which the believing man should visit with feelings of reverence and awe.

Which are the four?

- *The place at which the Tathagata was born*
- *The place at which the Tathagata attained enlightenment*
- *The place at which the Tathagata preached the first sermon*
- *The place at which the Tathagata passed away.*

The four places suggested by the Buddha are:

- **Lumbini**; where he was born, in southern Nepal
- **Bodhgaya**; where he became enlightened, in Bihar state, India
- **Sarnath**; where he preached the first sermon, just north of Varanasi
- **Kushinagar**; where he died, in Uttar Pradesh, India

The Buddha died around 404 BCE. Within two hundred years of his death, four other places became important sites of pilgrimage as well. Collectively these are the eight great sites of Buddhist pilgrimage. This book describes them all.

The other four are:

- **Rajagriha**; where he preached many important sermons and where he subdued the wild elephant Nalagiri. (Now known as Rajgir, in Bihar)
- **Vaishali**; where he received the gift of honey from the monkey, near Patna in Bihar
- **Shravasti**; site of 'The Great Miracle', in Uttar Pradesh, near the Nepalese border
- **Sankasya**; where he descended from Trayastrimsa heaven after preaching to his deceased mother

THE DECLINE OF BUDDHISM

By the 12th century Buddhism had died out in India. Multiple factors led to this decline: the loss of royal patronage; the development of Tantric Buddhism which had less community appeal; revival of a more dynamic Hinduism; and the Muslim conquest all contributed.Over time, monuments and great cities which had thrived in Buddhist times became overgrown or were converted into Hindu shrines. For most sites, their original name and significance were forgotten.

During the eighteenth century, early European explorers became aware of similarities in design and sculpture of numerous jungle-clad monuments from Mumbai to the Ganges, but just who or what they signified was a total blank. Time had induced a collective amnesia, so that even the name 'Buddha' was unknown in the land of his birth. However, despite the hazards of history, two important locations had continued as places of worship right to modern times. These were Bodhgaya, the place of enlightenment, and Kushinagara where the Buddha died. Their relationship to Buddhism had been forgotten, but the fact that they were in some way spiritually significant had been retained.

Although Buddhism had withered in India it had flourished and spread elsewhere. Burma and Ceylon were particularly important in the modern 'discovery' of Buddhism. In both countries, Buddhist monks had retained knowledge of their spiritual origins so that European scholars and amateur archaeologists were gradually able to piece together the history of the Buddha, his faith and its genesis on the plains of north India. By the end of the 19th century the broad principles of Buddhism, the history of the Buddha's life and the location of the most significant sites had been identified.

For the modern visitor, it is a rare privilege to experience places where the Buddha lived and taught. With the right-attitude, travelling through his homeland will hopefully bring greater understanding of his message of hope, and its significance. *Homeland of the Buddha* seeks to untangle the various threads of history and belief of this great person, the historical Buddha.

ABOVE
The Parinirvana Temple, with the stupa behind, Kushinagar.

15

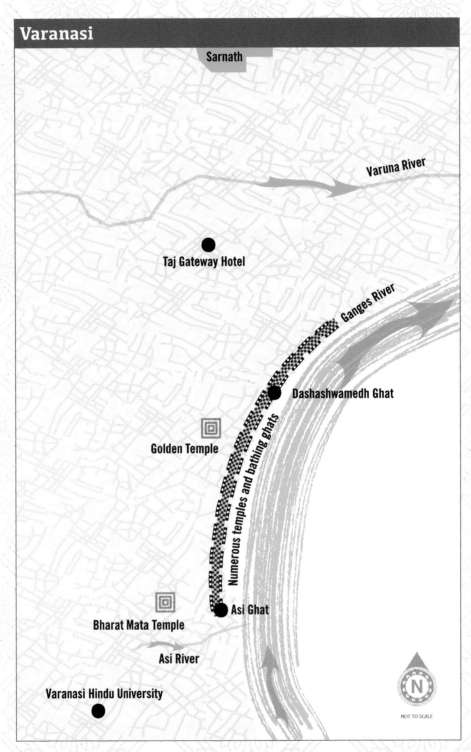

Varanasi

Sarnath

Varuna River

Taj Gateway Hotel

Ganges River

Dashashwamedh Ghat

Golden Temple

Numerous temples and bathing ghats

Asi Ghat

Bharat Mata Temple

Asi River

Varanasi Hindu University

N

NOT TO SCALE

CHAPTER ONE

Varanasi

HISTORY

VARANASI claims to be the oldest continuously inhabited city in the world, an antiquity confirmed by any walk through the old town. City of 'lights', 'religion', 'learning' and 'history', it is undoubtedly the religious capital of the world's most religion-obsessed country.

The Rig-Veda, written around 1300 BCE, referred to it as Kashi—*the Luminous one* an allusion to its historical status as a centre of culture and learning. Hindus believe that it was founded by Lord Shiva thousands of years before the generation of that document, and that the ancient city lies on his trisula, or trident. It is believed that on this spot Lord Shiva and his consort Pavarti, stood at the very first instant when time began. Thus, it has been a site of Hindu pilgrimage since before recorded history and a place where many Hindu temples were constructed.

Traditionally, Hindu temples are showered with offerings of the faithful. Such wealth attracts attention for those with little respect for an infidel religion. When Qubt-ud-din Aibak, the founder of the Delhi Sultanate, came here in 1194 he destroyed a thousand temples and carried away 1400 camel loads of gold, silver and precious stones. Varanasi was sufficiently rebuilt, to catch the imagination of Mark Twain, who declaimed:

ABOVE
Hindu devotee, Varanasi riverbank.

> *Benaras is older than history, older than tradition, older even than legend and looks twice as old as all of them put together.*

VARANASI AND THE BUDDHA

The Buddha came here. So did the founder of the Jain religion, Mahavira—a contemporary of the Buddha. But Varanasi is, and always has been, overwhelmingly a Hindu town and, as far as we know, it was not a place where the Buddha lingered.

Today's Varanasi

THE OLD CITY

Now, in addition to religion, it is a city noted for its crafts—especially the weaving of fine cotton and brocade-silks, perfumes, ivory and sculptures. The old city is crammed with temples and holy men of every persuasion, dress, undress and shade of belief. Saints and shysters; diseased, dying and departed; rich-man, poor-man, beggar-man, thief—they are all here in a colourful crush of humanity. It recalls Bruegel's medieval Europe of five hundred years ago, only a sight more colourful. If you can tolerate the crowds and the noise, this is a wonderful city to experience.

At Varanasi, even in the dry season, the river is several hundred metres wide. It flows directly northward towards the Himalaya, 500 kilometres distant. This abrupt change in direction is interpreted by Hindus as symbolising the transition from death to rebirth in a new body and it is why this section of the river is particularly holy. The city is built on the western bank, above a continuous series of stone steps, the ghats. Some are much more sacred than others and it is to these that Hindu pilgrims come to immerse themselves in Mother Ganga.

At the ghats, people wash themselves and their clothes, or perform personal puja (ritual) ceremonies to the river. At two public sites the dead are burned on huge pyres of wood. For a Hindu, to die in Varanasi is to be released from the cycle of rebirth. Such is the sanctity of this city, that

LEFT
Hindu sadu with his portable shrine, Varanasi.

BELOW
Dusk on the Varanasi ghats.

ABOVE

Cremation wood: Manikarnika Ghat, Varanasi.

the dying are brought here from all over India. It has probably been always thus. In narrow lanes approaching the burning ghats one frequently meets bodies being carried on their last journey. Swathed in red or white, lying on simple bamboo litters, each body is placed with their feet in the holy water for a few moments before being burned. It takes three hours and about 200 kilograms of wood to complete the process. Each day several hundred cremations are performed.

In the great Hindu epic, the Mahabarata, King Yudhisthira says:

Each day death strikes—and we live as though we were immortal.
This is the greatest wonder.

And one of the great wonders of contemporary India is the way death and life are made obvious, to even the most casual visitor. This is never more so than at Varanasi.

BOAT TOUR ON THE RIVER

It is quite appropriate that the first tour suggested on this Buddhist journey, is wholly Hindu. Boarding a rowboat for a journey on the Ganges, is a voyage literally, about life and death. The boatmen will take you downstream adjacent to the ghats which team with life, and at the burning ghats, with death.

In the evening, you have also come for a show. The event is to view the evening aarti (fire ceremony) at Dashashwamedh Ghat. Of all the great spectacles in India this daily event is right at the top. On seven marble plinths, facing the river, young Brahmin priests offer evening praise and worship to Mother Ganga. The aarti ritual has been performed on this river-edge for thousands of years. It's a ceremony that helps sear the spiritual seal of India into every sinew of this ancient land. In similar form, you can see this rite throughout India, but at Dashashwamedh it is done with more than a touch of modern pizzaz. Clad in a shimmer of golden silk, each priest is part of a splendid corps de ballet. In sequence they offer water, fire, incense and yak-tails in a wonderfully choreographed religious spectacle. Floodlights and loudspeakers add, rather than detract as attested by the devotion of thousands of Hindu devotees, who clap and chant their praise of this mighty river's deep currents.

Walking in the old city is a much less advertised tourist attraction. It will inevitably have elements of the unexpected which reveal the vitality of this great city. The unplanned nature of tourism is reality everywhere in India, but more so in the City of Light.

The Bharat Mata (Mother India) temple exemplifies 'Amazing India'. A modern non-devotional temple, it celebrates the land of India as a goddess. It expresses the serious importance women and female gods in Hinduism. Conventional Hindu temples have images of deities, carved in stone or splendidly gilded and bejewelled. But here, the image of Mother India takes the form of a marble-relief-map of an undivided India from the high plateau of Tibet and the Himalaya, to the tip of Cape Cormarin —all to scale both vertically and on the flat.

ABOVE
Evening *aarti* at Dashashwamedh Ghat, Varanasi.

Nearby Varanasi Hindu University has a vast museum with an appealing collection of Indian miniature paintings; Hindu and Buddhist statues; and a wine cup inscribed to both the Emperor Jahangir and his great, great, great, great grandfather, the central Asian astronomer, Ulug Beg. Boasting India's highest shikara (spire), the University temple is a further expansion of the mysteries and glories of Hinduism.

Sarnath Town

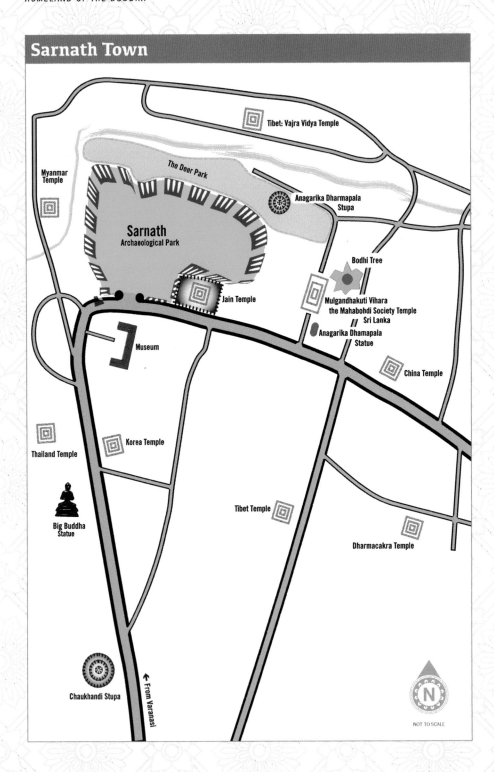

Tibet: Vajra Vidya Temple

The Deer Park

Myanmar Temple

Anagarika Dharmapala Stupa

Sarnath
Archaeological Park

Bodhi Tree

Jain Temple

Mulgandhakuti Vihara
the Mahabohdi Society Temple
Sri Lanka

Anagarika Dhamapala
Statue

Museum

China Temple

Thailand Temple

Korea Temple

Big Buddha
Statue

Tibet Temple

Dharmacakra Temple

Chaukhandi Stupa

← From Varanasi

N

NOT TO SCALE

CHAPTER TWO

Sarnath

SARNATH is revered by Buddhists as the place where the Buddha preached his first sermon and where his disciples collected as a group to become the first Sangha. Today it is a 'Buddhist town' but Jains also make pilgrimage here. And, although few Hindus visit, the name Sarnath derives from an ancient title for Shiva, Sagarnath: *Lord of the Deer.*

SARNATH AND THE BUDDHA

After Sakyamuni became enlightened, he stayed several weeks in Bodhgaya savouring the experience. He was faced with a dilemma: either to retire from the world as a fully enlightened being or to teach his experience to others. He knew that it would not be easy to put into words his transcendent experience and to offer a doctrine which challenged people's instincts. Nevertheless, he chose to teach, and thus change the history of the world and the lives of millions. For almost fifty years he traversed the plains of the Ganges, a region that came to be known as 'the Buddha holy land'.

WHO TO TEACH, AND HOW?

Many villagers readily accepted the Buddha's teaching. He recognised them as practical people used to seeing results from their labour. As a group, they responded readily to a teacher who insisted that they verify for themselves the effects of what he taught.

More difficult were the shramanas, or wandering ascetics. The Buddha saw them as worthy because most were genuine spiritual seekers. However, they sought enlightenment in a very different manner from that practiced by the Buddha. Many, such as the Jains, were fixated on extremes of self-mortification while others spent their time in endless philosophic debate. Topics such as the existence of 'an eternal soul', 'enduring existence after death' or the 'presence of an unchanging eternal

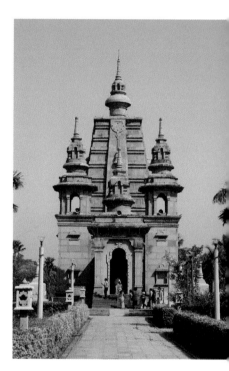

ABOVE
The Mahabodhi Society Temple, Sarnath.

self (atman)' were constantly under discussion by the shramanas, but formed no part of the Buddhas formal teaching. He saw such topics as a distraction for his students whom he taught to experience reality from their own directly observable experience.

Many shramanas focussed on subjects which could not be verified. For example, to agonise endlessly over 'What is life?', misses the fundamental dilemma of how to make your own life work. The Buddha equated such an approach to the prevarication of:

> ... a warrior injured in battle with a poisoned arrow, who refuses treatment until all his questions are answered: 'Who shot the arrow? What was his name, his family, his caste? What kind of feathers are in the arrow—and, what kind of gut in the bow-string?'

As the warrior's life fritters away, his problem would not be solved by answering such questions. He simply needed to pull the arrow out.

The Buddha's style of teaching was direct and pragmatic. Brahmin teachers used priestly Sanskrit that was not understood by the common people. The Buddha taught in local language so that people could more readily identify with his message. He would alter his style of teaching depending on the degree of understanding and receptivity of his audience. By using stories, parables, ideas and metaphor he sought to lead his listeners to way of practice that avoided unhelpful beliefs and attitudes. Such practice leads to the realisation that Nirvana is a way of experiencing this life, and that Nirvana is not a place in some imaginary future existence.

Remarkably, the Buddha insisted that he did not teach 'absolute Truth', claiming that his concepts were to be used by each follower to determine for themselves, the true nature of existence. Literal interpretation of the Gautama's words he regarded as a form of blindness, a blindness which could be rectified by directing attention towards genuine self-awareness.

MEETING THE ASCETICS

Having made a decision to teach 'trainable men' Sakyamuni resolved to reveal his understanding to the five ascetics with whom he had practiced during the six years of wandering in the wilderness. Hearing that they were in the region of Varanasi he set off to find them.

It was a long way. He had to walk 250 kilometres to the densely forested region around Sarnath known then as Risipatana Mrgadava—'the game-park of the 500 risis (holy men)'. One account relates that on the banks of one river he encountered a ferryman who would not provide transport without payment. Being without money the Buddha 'went through the sky like the king of birds'. On hearing this story King Biimbisara of Magadha, is said to have abolished the ferry-fee for ascetics.

The current name, Sarnath, is derived from a jataka (legendary pre-Buddha) tale, meaning 'Lord of the deer'. One day the Buddha, in the guise of a deer, offered his life to a king who was about to kill a doe. The king was so impressed he created a sanctuary for deer. Thus, Sarnath is frequently referred to as 'the deer park'. Spotted deer used to roam the whole archaeological site, but are now confined to a smaller region north of the Mahabodhi Society temple.

Arriving at the deer park, Siddhartha's former companions saw him coming. They resolved to remain seated, not to offer greeting and to reject him as a luxury-seeking backslider, someone they saw as a loser, who had given up a life of denial for one of ease. However, as the Buddha approached they were so moved by his presence they all rose and invited him to sit and talk with them. Just where in Sarnath, this encounter took place is a matter of considerable dispute.

ABOVE
Buddha and his disciples, Burmese shrine, Sarnath.

THE FIRST SERMON

It was the 'second watch' of the night—midnight to four AM when he preached the First Sermon, a teaching known as 'Turning the Wheel of the Dharma'. We do not know exactly what the Buddha said in his first sermon. His later style was to speak informally about principles of his teaching rather than offer lists of detailed doctrine, but that is not how the 'First Sermon' is portrayed in the literature.

At the start of this first sermon, he advised against practicing extremes of lifestyle. The Buddha lived and preached, a life of moderation. His 'Middle Way' was at variance with much religious teaching of the time. His own early experience had been a life of comfortable luxury: the life of a pleasure seeker. When this proved unsatisfactory he had endured years of painful self-mortification, which was equally unrewarding.

> Two extremes there are, O monks,
> which he who strives after enlightenment must avoid.
> Which two?
> A life addicted to pleasure which is vulgar and worthless,
> and a life given to self-mortification which is painful and equally profitless.

Throughout his life the Buddha constantly insisted that the primary purpose of his teaching was to overcome human suffering. His first sermon declares that suffering exists, that is has a cause and that it can be overcome by following his defined eight-fold path. Tradition relates that Gautama then expounded two lists of essential statements—*The Four Noble Truths* and *The Eightfold Path*.

The Four Noble Truths

The 'Four Noble Truths', baldly enunciate fundamental principles of Buddhism.

Suffering exists.
Suffering has a cause.
The cause is desire (or attachment)
There is a way to overcome suffering

That suffering, dukkha, is universal to human experience seems self-evident. Dukkha is usually translated in English as 'suffering', but in Buddhism the understanding of this is more subtle than physical pain or distress. The root meanings of dukkha in Sanskrit include 'not fitting well' and 'uneasiness'. The 'suffering' referred to in the Noble Truths includes a spectrum of human dis-ease, from physical pain, to a feeling of disquiet and a sense that life is awry. By focusing on dukkha, Gautama was addressing the unease and dissatisfaction, inherent in human life, even when it might appear that all is well. His solution to this pervading human ill is expressed as:

The Eightfold path

Right Understanding
Right Thought
Right Speech
Right Conduct
Right Livelihood
Right Effort
Right Mindfulness
Right Concentration

Such a skeletal outline of the Buddha's teaching sits uneasily with Gautama's later method of explaining his doctrines in a much more discursive way. It is likely that the first sermon was indeed much more expansive than what we are told. In any case, it was sufficiently compelling for the five former companions to accept the Buddha-way and become the first members of his Sangha. The Buddha remained for his first rainy season in Sarnath, and it was from here that the Buddha and his companions set forth to change the lives of individuals and the world. And it was from Sarnath that he first challenged the ritualistic teachings of Brahmanism, the dominant religion of the time. After that initial rainy season, he was not to return to Sarnath for another thirty-six years.

THE EARLY COMMUNITY

This small early community were called by Gautama, 'Sakyaputra shramanas'—sons of Sakya, wanderers. In the earliest years of his mission, they did not live in monastic communities, but travelled widely, becoming 'men and women of the four quarters' except in the season of rains. Those earliest groups had few formal rules, relying on the positive changes wrought by following the Buddhist path for social harmony. Later, as the Sangha grew and became more residential, instances of disharmony required greater regulation. With widely disparate small groups, it could not have been easy to maintain community discipline. In the record, there are numerous instances where the Buddha intervened to solve disputes.

A feature of Buddha's teaching was its all-inclusive nature. As he once remarked about himself, that he was not 'tight fisted about the Truth'. It was his view that teachings should be offered to all, as the dharma belonged to everyone. There should be no discrimination on the basis of caste or gender or membership of a particular religious group. He specifically urged his disciples to share their understanding with others, and he encouraged them to travel widely 'for the benefit of many'. This injunction, early in his ministry, led to widespread acceptance of his teachings on the plains of the Ganges, and subsequently beyond the subcontinent.

ABOVE
**Seated Buddha,
Sarnath Museum,
5th century CE.**

THE EMPEROR ASHOKA AND SARNATH

Ashoka came to Sarnath around 250 BCE, raising the Dharmarajika Stupa and another of his pillars. The pillar still stands but has been fractured. It carries three inscriptions. The first, by Ashoka admonishes the monks to avoid schism but has no other comment about the Sarnath site; the second from the Kushan period around 160 CE refers to the 40th year of King Ashvaghosha; and the third is a Gupta inscription mentioning an early teacher.

On top of his column, Ashoka placed India's most famous image. Carved from a single block of highly polished sandstone, four vigorous lions sit back to back. When Xuanzang came here in 636 CE he found Ashoka's pillar and its lions intact, protecting a thriving community of 1500 monks. Sometime later, the pillar was split, probably by lightning, and these magnificent lions, who had roared out the truth of the Buddha's dharma for at least a thousand years fell fifteen metres to the ground.

They sustained little damage and were buried by time, only to resurface during the excavations by the English archaeologist Oertel in 1904. The capital is now in the Sarnath museum and this image of Ashoka's magnificent lions is the State Symbol of modern India. The base of the capital has a frieze of animals, each separated by the Dharmachakra (the Wheel of the Dharma)—a symbol which flutters at the centre of every Indian flag.

THE EMPEROR KANISHKA

During Kushan times (c 100 BCE–180 CE) another great Emperor, Kanishka added temples and viharas (monasteries) to Sarnath. The Kushans came from central Asia. By the time of Kanishka, the fifth ruler, their empire extended through modern day Uzbekistan, Afghanistan and Pakistan into the north western part of India. Initially the Kushans adopted Greek and Persian artistic and religious traditions, which merged with those of India as the empire expanded.

Kanishka was tolerant of all religions and certainly gave support to Buddhism. At Peshawar he built a multi-storeyed stupa that was a marvel of the ancient world. Xuanzang describes it as being around 180 metres high, *'covered in jewels'.* When the Kaniskha stupa was excavated in 1908 by a British group they discovered at its base a gold casket containing three bone relics thought to be those of the Buddha. These relics were transferred to Mandalay, modern Myanmar, where they are still housed. Kanishka convened the Kashmir 4th Buddhist Council. This meeting helped define the Mahayana school of Buddhism which spread throughout central Asia to China and beyond. Without Kanishka's help, Buddhism may not have spread so widely.

It was from the Kushan winter capital at Mathura that a new school of vigorous Buddhist art arose influenced by Hellenistic images from Gandhara and the sensuality of India. And it was during Kanishka's reign that the first images of the Buddha in human form were made. In the Gandhara region of modern Pakistan these early figures of Buddha were strongly influenced by the art of Greece, while those which originated around his winter capital of Mathura expressed the sensuality of India.

The Guptas (4th–6th century) built the impressive Dhamek stupa and contributed great artworks. The most sublime is that of the Preaching Buddha, now in the Sarnath museum. The Buddha is depicted in typical Gupta style—a serene meditative face, draped in gracefully transparent robes, backed with a nimbus surmounted by flying apsaras (celestial beings). With his hands, he makes the pravartana-mudra signifying the Turning of the Wheel of the Law. Xuanzang was so impressed that he had a sandalwood copy made, the fourth of his seven famous images that were carried in a grand procession around Xi'an on his return to China in 645.

The two Chinese monks, Faxian (4th century.) and Xuanzang in the 7th, were impressed by the religious activity of Sarnath. The latter describing the main shrine, 'the Hall of Fragrance' as a pyramidal structure '... *two hundred feet high, surmounted by a golden amra (mango) fruit.'*

DESTRUCTION: MEDIEVAL AND MORE RECENT

Support for Buddhism dropped in later centuries. The devastation of Sarnath by the Muslim invader Mahmud of Ghazni, in 1017, was a final deathblow to a religion already in decline because of Hindu renaissance.

The region became deserted, and the monuments became an ideal source of building material for nearby Varanasi.

Today, little remains of the Dharmarajika stupa, constructed by Ashoka. In 1794 it was quarried to the ground by Jagat Singh, the Diwan (Chief Minister) of the Banaras Rajah. Singh was in search of materials for a new housing colony, Jagatgunj, which today is crammed between the modern city's two major rail stations. During this demolition a green-marble relic casket was discovered, containing human bones, pearls, gold leaf and other jewels. Singh knew value when he saw it, so kept the jewels and consigned the relics to the Ganga. Unfortunately they were probably relics of the Buddha. The casket survived and is now in the Kolkata museum.

This action might have gone unnoticed but for the English Commissioner of Banaras whose report in the 1798 'Asiatick Researches' attracted attention of English 'orientalists'. Preliminary excavations were done but were no defence to the unsympathetic officials of the Public Works Department. In 1837 they used 'fifty to sixty cartloads' of the Chaukhandi stupa as foundations for the first iron bridge in Banaras, and for good measure, heaved some forty bas-reliefs and statues of the Buddha, collected by General Cunningham, into the river Varna as flood protection. A more sympathetic administration, and excavations by the Archaeological Society of India, revealed, and protected, the Sarnath that we see today.

Today's Sarnath

The Chaukhandi stupa is the first monument obvious to visitors arriving at Sarnath. It is thought to be the place where the Buddha and his soon-to-be, disciples first met. Scholars argue about the exact location of events in Sarnath. What's described here is the generally accepted religious-geography.

The large brick mound of Chaukhandi seen today, was raised by the Guptas and partially restored by the British. On top is a 16th century monument erected by the great Mughal Emperor Akbar. It records a critical time in the history of the Mughals when his father Humayun was endeavouring to suppress the rebellion of Sher Shah Suri. In a series of dismal battles Humayun lost the Indian empire and was only able to regain it fifteen years later. Just why Akbar should build a monument to what was effectively a military disaster by his father is a mystery. The Persian inscription on the Mughal monument does not clarify:

As Humayun, king of the Seven Climes, now residing in paradise, deigned to come and sit here one day, thereby increasing the splendour of the sun, so Akbar, his son and humble servant, resolved to build on this spot a lofty tower reaching to the blue sky.

THE MAHABODHI SOCIETY TEMPLE—THE MODERN MULGANDHAKUTI VIHARA

The restoration of modern Sarnath owes much to the charismatic
Ceylonese monk Anagarika Dharamapala. He founded the Mahabodhi
Society whose focus was to restore the sacred Buddhist sites of India to
the care of the Buddhist community. One of his projects was the construction of this temple. It resembles in style, the more famous Bodhgaya
monument.

At the entrance, to the right of the walkway, is a statue of Dharmapala,
standing sternly with his arms folded in front. In 1933, at the age of
seventy, he died here in Sarnath. His body was cremated, and his ashes
interred, in a small stupa which stands a few hundred metres away at the
rear of the temple, inside the gates of the deer park.

On the interior walls of the temple are stylish paintings of significant
events in the Buddha's life. Painted by a Japanese artist over a four year
period, most are well known and easy to recognise. Less common is the
depiction of the Buddha's encounter with the notorious murderer, Angulimala who confronts his intended victim in a fiery halo of digits. This
encounter took place in Shravasti, where Angulimala had a penchant for
making a necklace from the fingers of his victims.

The temple is usually crowded with groups of Buddhist pilgrims. They
come mostly from Sri Lanka, Thailand, Myanmar, Vietnam and Japan
and are a constant feature of travel throughout the Buddhist lands. Usually accompanied by a monk in the robe of appropriate national colour,
their devotion makes modern Buddhism palpable.

THE TAXILA BUDDHA RELICS

On the day the temple was opened, relics of the Buddha were enshrined under the main statue. That was in 1931. These relics had been brought from Taxila, now in Pakistan. They had been placed in a Taxila stupa around 250 BCE by the Emperor Ashoka as part of his distribution of relics throughout the empire. There is harmony in this return of the Buddha's bones to the site of his original teaching after an absence of more than two thousand years.

Near the Mahabodhi Temple is a descendent of the original Bodhi tree of Bodhgaya, planted here by Anagrika Dharmapala in 1921. It was brought here from the tree in Anuradhapura, Sri Lanka. That tree had originally been taken to the 'resplendent island' by Ashoka's daughter Sanghamitra.

THE SARNATH MUSEUM

(Hours: Daily 10.00–5.00, closed Friday and public holidays).

A principal delight of any Sarnath visit is the museum. Here are displayed some of India's greatest sculptures. Ashoka's Lion Capital was erected around 250 BCE. It stood atop the column almost two thousand years, before falling and then being rescued. It's appropriate that such a majestic work, standing more than two metres tall, is the state symbol of India and that the spoked-wheel chakra—wheel of the Dharma—which forms a base, holding up the lions, is at the centre of India's flag. It is an outstanding example of Mauryan art.

The Gupta period (320–500 CE) is known as 'the Golden Age' of India. Ruling from Pataliputra (modern Patna) a succession of rulers created a society with high standards of civil control, a mostly peaceful time when the arts, science and technology flourished. During Gupta rule, Sarnath became a prominent centre of Buddhism. The Sarnath School of Art was renowned for its sculptural simplicity and elegance, producing exquisite images of the Buddha carved from lovingly polished sandstone. The efforts of those talented artists are on display here.

BELOW:
Tibetan monk, Sarnath.

A clue to Gupta identification is their 'transparent' treatment of clothing and their use of finely polished sandstone. The Sarnath museum has the best collection of sculpture from this time, all of it excavated from the Sarnath site. The image of the preaching Buddha is stunning. Carved in warm oatmeal-sandstone he is seated in full lotus position, with his hands in the dharmachakra, or teaching mudra. His calm, relaxed posture and gentle smile project a serenity which few images of any age or religion can match. This statue was found in the vicinity of the ruined Dharmarajika stupa in 1905.

ABOVE
Pilgrims at Mahabodhi Temple, Sarnath.

Immediately preceding the Guptas, were the Kushans, Central Asian nomads. Their 'storm trooper' style of sculpture (several examples in the museum) forms a striking contrast to the later sensitivity of the Guptas. One of them in the main gallery is from the Mathura school. Donated by the 2nd century monk Bala, the sculpture depicts a massive standing bodhisattva with his right hand in the abhayamudra gesture of reassurance. For this statue, it is an appropriate gesture, as hanging over him is an equally massive umbrella of sandstone, which threatens to crush the worshippers below.

One stele depicts the four great and the four secondary places of pilgrimage. It is rare to find all eight on a single piece. The 'great' are: the birth, enlightenment, first sermon and death. While the 'secondary' are: the subjugation of the mad elephant, the monkey's gift of honey, the miracle at Shravasti and the descent from Trayastrimsa heaven.

Another notable late-Gupta statue is of the Saviour-goddess Tara who stands in a nearby gallery. Her name derives from the Sanskrit root 'tar' (to cross). As the Shakti (feminine energy) of the Buddha of Compassion, it is her job to help devotees to cross the 'Ocean of Existence'. Full breasted and bejewelled, she stands in relaxed anticipation of pleas for her assistance.

Sarnath archaeological site

THE SARNATH MAIN ARCHAEOLOGICAL SITE

The Sarnath main site has impressive remains from Ashokan and later times. Sarnath's first, and most important stupa, was erected by the Emperor to commemorate the Buddha's first sermon.

Ashoka's Dharmarajika stupa, was initially 14 metres in diameter. It was enhanced and enlarged several times before being mined to ground level by Jagat Singh in the 18th century.

Xuanzang saw the stupa intact and beside it noted the presence of 'the wheel-turning' Buddha statue now in the museum, a location confirmed by the British excavation. Nowadays, a flat brick base is all that remains of former glory.

Facing the stupa, Ashoka erected a 15 metre Ashokan column. Xuanzang commented that the pillar was erect with its capital intact in 656 CE, describing it as '... *bright as jade. It is glistening and sparkles with light.*' Segments of the fractured column are enclosed by a steel grill near to its original location. It bears an inscription exhorting the Sangha not to become divided and if schism develops, for those monks or nuns to be expelled.

Immediately to the west of the pillar is an apse-shaped Ashokan temple. Because this is a very early structure and has its open end directly facing the pillar, is thought likely to have been built by the emperor. Later shrines of this type commonly contain a stupa or statue in the apse. At the Sarnath apse-temple fragments of a column with surmounting chakra (Wheel of the Dharma), were found. This leads some scholars to believe that Ashoka's temple was built to commemorate the site of the Buddha's first sermon.

Immediately adjacent to the column is Mulagandhakuti temple, where the Buddha spent his first rainy season after enlightenment. Almost every ancient Buddhist monument seen today, was expanded and enlarged by later dynasties. That was true for this temple, which originally would

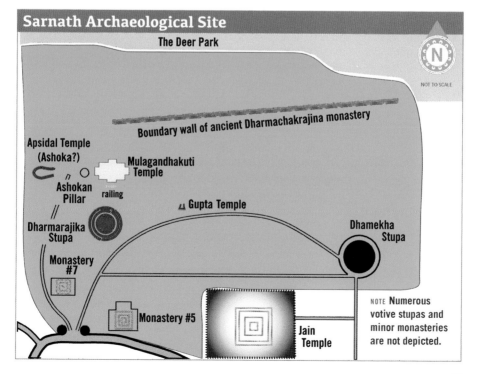

Sarnath Archaeological Site

The Deer Park

N

NOT TO SCALE

Boundary wall of ancient Dharmachakrajina monastery

Apsidal Temple (Ashoka?)

Mulagandhakuti Temple

Ashokan Pillar

railing

Gupta Temple

Dharmarajika Stupa

Dhamekha Stupa

Monastery #7

Monastery #5

Jain Temple

NOTE Numerous votive stupas and minor monasteries are not depicted.

have been a wooden structure. Mula means 'root' or 'base' and Gandha-kuti, 'fragrant hut'. So this is the original 'Fragrant Hut', or name given to each place where the Buddha dwelt. 'Fragrant' because his disciples gave flowers and burned incense in his honour.

The Buddha's original hut was later expanded to contain five chapels, with statue-niches in the surrounding walls. Today it is still an impressive brick structure with stone columns. Xuanzang describes it as more than sixty metres high, topped with '... a golden-covered figure of a mango'. Sixty metres would make it almost twice the height of the existing Dhamekha stupa. Even if the monk's estimate is exaggerated, it must have once been an impressive structure.

Beside the main temple, Mulagandhakuti, is part of the Ashokan railing which once sat on top of the Dharmarajika stupa. Made from highly polished Chunar sandstone, its function was to enclose and support the uppermost chattra (stylised parasol) of the stupa.

At the northern rim of the site are the walls of the last major monument built in Sarnath. The Dharmachakrajina monastery was built by the 'Queen of Banaras' around 1130 CE.

The most imposing and most important existing monument is the Dhamekha stupa, marking the site where the Buddha preached his second sermon, the Anattalakhama Sutra.

In this second sutra the Buddha outlined an essential aspect of his teaching. A clue to its substance lies in the name. Anatta means 'no-self'. In essence, 'the self' no matter how much we struggle to delineate or categorise, is fundamentally illusory and constantly changing. And that, our wish to cling to a permanent 'self', creates suffering or dis-ease. With his first two sermons the Buddha defined the three fundamentals that characterise all conditioned phenomena and which form the basis of Buddhist practice and understanding, to this day. Practice reveals that the 'self' is in fact anatta or 'no-self'. This understanding does not mean that 'you' do not exist, but what you sense as permanent is constantly changing, even minute by minute. Buddhist understanding reveals that impermanence pervades all things, material and immaterial; and that suffering (dis-ease) results from our attempts to make these fundamental realities solid and immutable.

A huge column of brick, the Dhamekh stupa stands more than thirty metres high. Much of the exterior is faced with elaborately decorated Gupta designs, with scrolls, foliation and geometric patterns. Statues of the teaching Buddha now in the museum were found here. From 1834, Cunningham spent three years excavating inside the stupa in the hope of finding relics. None were discovered, but he did determine that all the base-blocks of stone, which extend to a height of ten metres, were held together with iron clamps.

The main area of the site is filled with the brick foundations of small votive stupas and much larger monasteries.

TRAVEL AROUND THE BUDDHA HOMELAND

In the Buddha's time of course, there was no Nepal and no state of India. The region was governed by a collection of small princely states and the occasional proto-republic. Modern Bihar, where the Buddha spent much of his eighty years, now has more people than the entire sub-continent during his time. It is estimated there was a total of 50 million for India then, and 1.3 billion today, with the entire world population in Buddha's time around 500 million.

Road travel through India is always interesting as so much 'life' happens on the street. However, the regions that you travel on this tour are not especially scenic. Swathes of green paddy, interspersed with small hills, punctuate small towns of haphazard brick and concrete awash with the plastic detritus of modern existence. Every public place and roadside has a broad tidal strip of plastic junk, a tsunami of which threatens to ultimately submerge the nation.

Most people in the regions you travel are poor, even by Indian standards, and it shows. Their homes, dress and general standard of living are low. At all sites we visit you will find numerous beggars and ragged kids, thus adding poignancy to the teachings—whether Buddhist, Hindu, Jain or Muslim.

SASARAM: SHER SHAH'S TOMB

It takes two hours to drive from Varanasi along the historic Grand Trunk Road, to the small town of Sasaram. Here is the tomb site of one of India's legendary characters. Sher Shah (Lion King) was his given name. He had been born in Afghanistan to the 'Sur' clan of the Pathan tribe. A redoubtable warrior and skilled administrator, he ruled most of India for only five years.

ABOVE
**Dhamekha
Stupa, Sarnath.**

In 1540 he had defeated the forces of the second Mughal Emperor Humayun. A visionary and effective ruler, he introduced many reforms. His accidental death in 1545, from a gunpowder explosion, allowed the Mughals to reconquer India. Had Sher Shah lived longer, the whole history of northern India would have been different. There would not have been a Mughal revival, and no Taj Mahal. His tomb, an example of early Indo-Islamic architecture, sits in the middle of a small lake, near to the road.

Bodhgaya Town

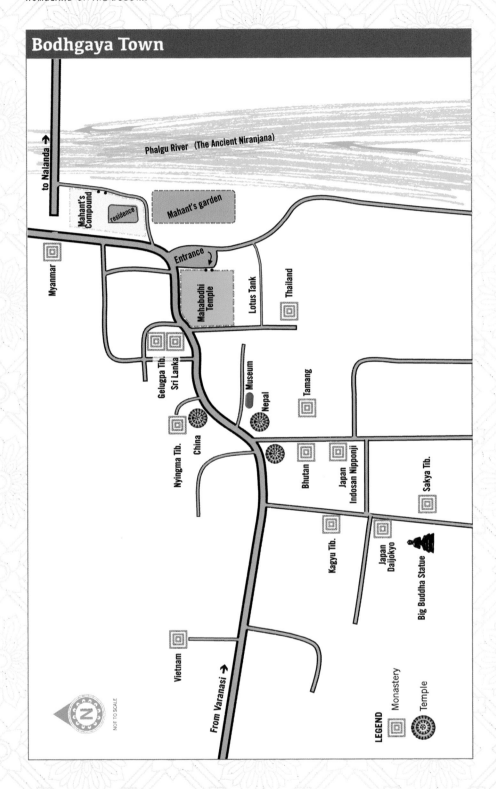

CHAPTER THREE

Bodhgaya

BODHGAYA is the place where the twenty-nine year old Gautama attained enlightenment. As such, it is the most important of all Buddhist places of pilgrimage and for many Buddhists, the very navel of the earth—'the only place sufficiently strong, to support the weight of the Buddha's attainments'. Some believe that, at the end of this kalpa (time period) it will be the last place on Earth to disappear, and the first to appear again when the world is restored. It is also the place where Gautama-Siddhartha was given a new name, the one by which he became universally recognised—The Buddha—'the one who has awakened'.

SUJATA'S GIFT

At the age of thirty-five, Gautama had come to an important realisation. If he was to achieve spiritual release, his practice would have to change. He had spent six years starving and abusing his body to a point that his very survival was precarious. Yet, despite these extreme efforts he had not achieved his sought-for liberation. Asceticism was for him a dead end.

On the banks of the Niranjana ('pleasant water') river near modern Bodhgaya, he had a fateful encounter with the milkmaid Sujata. Sujata saw the starving Gautama and was moved to offer him nourishment. To her, Gautama probably appeared no different from scores of other holy-seekers she had seen in the past, and she could not have anticipated that this one was to become exceptional. She simply saw a starving human and was moved to offer him a bowl of curds.

It was a pivotal point in Siddhartha's life. Rejection of Sujata's gift committed him to the blind path of self-denial. A path that he already knew was futile. If he took the meal, there was no turning back. He would have to abandon the way of asceticism and find a different route to liberation. His courageous decision to take Sujata's curds broke his fast and set in train the moderate 'middle-way' of the Buddha-to-be.

ABOVE
The Mahabodhi Temple, Bodhgaya.

37

Sujata offers the starving Gautama a bowl of curds, while his five companions look on with horror. (Indosan Nipponji Temple, Bodhgaya).

For his five companions, it was also a critical time. They saw Gautama's meal as weakness, an act to be despised, which inevitably detached Gautama from their fold. Expressing their displeasure, they left him to flounder in 'luxury'. From now on, he was alone.

THE GIFT OF GRASS

Shortly after, a grass cutter, called Svasti, befriended the ascetic. To make his meditation more comfortable, he gave Siddhartha a gift of kusa grass as a seat. Kusa, is the willowy plant about one metre high that grows readily in the sand around Bodhgaya, lining the banks of most rivers and streams. At the tip of the tallest stems is a graceful white frond, a botanical echo of the white yak-tail whisk, used as a symbol of Indian royalty.

Svasti was an 'untouchable', so both his friendship and his gift exceeded the boundaries of caste. Later he was to become one of the first disciples and thus reinforce the inclusive nature of early Buddhist practice. Some traditions have Svasti a teenager, some an old man. And one version says that he was a Brahmin rather than an untouchable. Take your pick.

THE ENLIGHTENMENT OF SIDDHARTHA

Whoever gifted the grass, Siddhartha carried it across the river, to the vicinity of Uruvela village, a place we now call Bodhgaya. Here Siddhartha found an appropriate tree under which to meditate and resolved to not shift until he had become enlightened.

Here on this seat my body may shrivel up,
my skin, my bones, my flesh may dissolve,
but my body will not move from this seat
until I have attained Enlightenment,
so difficult to obtain in the course of many kalpas

During this time Gautama was tempted to abandon his striving for supreme enlightenment. Tradition relates that Mara, the great tempter and illusionist, manifest his forces to divert the aspiring sitter. Hosts of frightening demons were followed by visions of his seductive daughters seeking to return the Gautama to a life of sensual pleasure. These were easily ignored or rejected. A penultimate, and perhaps more seductive offer, was to tempt Siddhartha with the possibility of becoming a cakravatin, a great ruler of all the temporal world. This also had no appeal. Finally, Mara scornfully suggested that Gautama had no support for his intention of supreme enlightenment. In response Gautama touched the fingers of his right hand to the ground, and in response the earth shook in affirmation. This episode is famously depicted in Buddhist iconography, as the bhumiparsa or 'earth-witness' gesture portrayed in myriads of statues and paintings. From that time Mara abandoned his attempts to seduce this future-Buddha.

ABOVE
The main
Buddha image,
Mahabodhi
temple. 10th
century CE.

The scriptures relate that Gautama sat unmoving for six days and nights until, on glimpsing the evening star, on the full moon night of April-May, underwent that fundamental change in awareness, which we call enlightenment.

NAMING OF THE BUDDHA

After his enlightenment experience Siddhartha was changed and this change was apparent to others. People of ancient Uruvela spoke Magadhi. In that language to 'awaken' is pronounced 'budh'. The locals saw Siddhartha as different. He was the 'Awakened One' so from that time he was called Buddha. Many names are used to refer to the Buddha, among them: Sakyamuni (Sage of the Sakyas); The Tathagata (the thus come one); The World Honoured One; and The Blessed One. However, it was as Gautama, the name of his clan, that he was most commonly known during his teaching life.

Subsequently Buddhism was known as 'The Path of Awareness which leads to perfect Awakening.' As a language, Magadhi became Pali, which as writing developed became the earliest written form of Buddhism.

The history of the Bodhgaya Temple

The very earliest shrine on this site was probably a platform beneath the Bodhi tree. Similar structures can be seen, celebrating the local gods, in every village and town throughout India, a style of practice common for thousands of years.

Ashoka visited the Bodhgaya site in the 3rd century BCE, erecting a column with an elephant capital. There is no absolute proof, but it is likely that he also constructed a temple. Evidence for an Ashokan temple is found on one of the Bharahut friezes erected a century after Ashoka, and during the earliest excavation in 1881, Alexander Cunningham found signs of a structure dating back to Mauryan times. Given Ashoka's penchant for celebrating sites associated with the Buddha, Cunningham's discovery is likely to have been built by the Emperor.

Around the 2nd century, during the Kushan period, a brick pyramidal temple was constructed. The museum in Patna has a two thousand year old snapshot of this in the form of a clay tablet, 'the Bodhgaya plaque'. This depicts a single spire in the form much as we see the Bodhgaya temple today. Later, around the 5th century, major reconstruction took place, possibly in response to earthquake damage.

The great Chinese pilgrim Xuanzang, paid Bodhgaya a visit in 637. He was then, twelve years into his seventeen year odyssey to find original Buddhist scriptures and return with them to his homeland.

He was impressed with the temple spire, rising 170 foot from a large platform, ornamented with gold and silver and capped with a 'gilded copper amalaka fruit.' The amalaka is a ribbed flattened disc resembling the Indian gooseberry fruit. As 'the first tree grown in the universe'—from tears of all the gods—it is sacred to Hindus, crowning the shikara, or spire, of most northern temples. As a 'sweet connection' between heaven and earth, it was a natural embellishment to Buddhist temples. In niches on either side of the temple chamber Xuanzang described a pair of statues '...made of white silver and ten feet high'.

With the later decline in Buddhism and centuries of neglect, there was inevitable deterioration. However, a sketch by the British artist William Daniell, ca. 1790 shows the temple structure pretty much intact. Restoration of the temple and site was undertaken by the British in the 1880s. At that time, four corner towers were added and the spire refaced and plastered.

THE PILGRIMS

For the Buddha, the village where he became enlightened was named Urevela because of the large amount of sand (vela) in the area. Later, it was called a variety of names—Sambodhi (All pervading Way-enlightenment), Vajrasana (Diamond seat) or Mahabodhi (Great Enlightenment) with the name Bodh Gaya being used from the 18th century.

From earliest times, pilgrims came to Bodh Gaya from all over India. The most notable of these was the Emperor Ashoka. His visit in 260 BCE added prestige and legitimacy to the site. He probably built the first Bodhgaya temple, a building which was to have several reincarnations, and he definitely sent cuttings from the Bodhi tree to Anuradhapura in Sri Lanka.

Pilgrims have always travelled to Bodhgaya from the lands to which Buddhism had spread. There are ancient records of monks from nearby

Sri Lankan
pilgrims approach
the Mahabodhi
Temple.

Myanmar, Vietnam, Sri Lanka and Thailand—to give these countries
their modern names—but many pilgrims in search of knowledge or
enlightenment, travelled even greater distances. In the 7th century there
is an account of one from Samarkand in Uzbekistan, and others from
Indonesia. Up until very recent times any such long distance travel was a
hazardous undertaking.

Around 402 the first Chinese monk known to have reached India, Faxian, fetched up at Bodhgaya. His epic overland journey through Central
Asia had taken three years. He found three monasteries with resident
monks where:

> *The families of the people around provide the congregation of these
> monks with abundant sufficiency of what they require, so that there
> is no lack or stint. The disciplinary rules are strictly observed by
> them. The laws regarding their demeanour in sitting, rising and
> entering when the others are assembled, are those that have been
> handed down since the Buddha was in the world, down to the pre-
> sent day.*

His more famous countryman Xuanzang visited Bodh Gaya at least
twice in the mid-600s. Both wrote accounts of their journey which
inspired contemporary pilgrims to travel. Later, their journals were of
immense assistance to western scholars seeking the location of buried
Buddhist sites in northern India and the deserts of central Asia.

Four hundred years after Xuanzang, the practice of Buddhism in India
had entered a terminal decline. One Tibetan, who arrived in 1234 CE

found only four monks in residence in the Bodhgaya temple. Fearful of a Muslim attack, they had bricked up the shrine containing the Buddha statue and posted a sign indicating that the place was in fact a Jain temple. Their deception may have been successful, as there is no evidence of significant Muslim damage to Bodhgaya.

By the late 1200s the Bodhgaya complex was largely abandoned. Only a trickle of pilgrims from nearby countries made visits so from that period there are only scanty records until the arrival of British explorers in 1811.

THE MAHABODHI MONASTERY

In the early 300s, Sri Lankan patronage enabled the construction of the Mahabodhi Monastery which grew to become a great centre of Theravadan scholarship, a university which thrived for a thousand years due to continuing help from Ceylon. Ultimately, it rivalled the universities of Nalanda and Vikramasila.

In 637, Xuanzang noted there were a thousand monks at this monastery, with hundreds of others in vihara belonging to different traditions. The monastery impressed Xuanzang with its size and opulence:

> *This edifice has six halls, with towers of observation of three stories; it is surrounded by a wall of defense thirty or forty feet high. The utmost skill of the artist has been employed; the ornamentation is in the richest colours. The statue of the Buddha is of gold and silver, decorated with gems and precious stones. The stupas are high and large in proportion; they contain relics of the Buddha.*

This Mahabodhi Monastery once stood outside the north gate of the temple precinct. Now, only foundations remain. These can be seen from inside the temple precinct on the outer khora (circumambulatory path). Cunningham's excavations confirmed the size of the monastery, but then the splendour had long departed.

THE MUSLIMS AND BODHGAYA

Muslim invaders had become established throughout north India by the early 1200s. It is widely stated that they were responsible for destruction of Bodhgaya's Buddhist monuments, but there is no evidence to support this. Although Bodhgaya was subject to at least two minor Muslim attacks the monastery continued to function as a centre of Buddhist practice and study at least until the end of the 1300s.

Continuing Buddhist occupation was commented on by several sources. In 1234 CE one pilgrim recorded 300 Sri Lankan monks at the Mahabodhi Monastery and towards the end of that century other visitors were helped by resident monks who were engaged in active practice. In the 1300s pilgrims from Sindh recorded their presence by scratching inscriptions and drawings on paving stones inside the Mahabodhi temple.

Monastic activity at Bodhgaya gradually ceased as interest in Buddhism waned and royal patronage dried up. The last record of any resident monk was in 1412. The site was abandoned to jungle and wild animals with all memory of the Buddha, and the significance of this holy place, forgotten to all within India.

THE BURMESE AND THE BRITISH

The temple had long been recognised by the Burmese as the site of 'the Bud's' enlightenment, and hence of great religious and historic importance. Several times during the 1800s delegations from Burma visited Bodhgaya, the most important being in 1877. This latter group, under the patronage of the Burmese king Mindon Min, had little understanding of archaeology. Their misdirected zeal in enthusiastically renovating the temple, swept away many of the ancient landmarks and damaged many statues, making later restoration more difficult. A plaque detailing their mission can be seen within the Mahant's (head priest's) compound. In 1878 the Burmese had to leave because of palace rebellion and the eventual death of their supporter King Mindon. Later, the British, under Alexander Cunningham assumed responsibility for restoring the temple.

Cunningham, as first Director General of the Archaeological Survey of India, had appointed Joseph Beglar, to oversee restoration. Beglar, officially a photographer, had experience of recording many archaeology sites. Controversially, he took it on himself to add four corner shikaras to the main temple. Fortuitously, his decision to do this was later supported by the discovery of a small ancient model which showed these features. The British intervention was timely and useful. Unfortunately many fine statues and other historical material were removed to distant museums, especially Calcutta.

Whilst repairing paving stones within the main temple chamber, Beglar discovered a Pala period altar built over an even earlier one. This second shrine contained a small collection of gold and silver objects and a gold coin from the 2nd century CE. To the excitement of the investigators, beneath the second altar there was a third shrine of Mauryan style, the time of Ashoka. It was of highly polished sandstone, bearing on its front, four pilasters that were identical to those on the Bharhut railing. Cunningham was delighted to claim that he had unearthed the remains of Ashoka's temple. That conclusion seems indisputable. Today, these structures lie invisible, within the modern temple chamber immediately below the main Buddha statue. Each shrine of the three, were built over existing structures. Reflecting their perceived importance at those times, older construction was not demolished and precious items were added. The oldest had a highly polished sandstone slab on a pedestal, identifying it as the most ancient Vajrasana—or Diamond Throne—site of the Buddha's enlightenment.

THE HINDUS—BODHGAYA AND ANAGARIKA DHARMAPALA

At some later time, probably in the 16th or 17th centuries the temple was adopted by a Hindu priest whose successors, the Mahants, increasingly saw the place as their own. Being ignorant of Buddhism, they worshipped the statues as Hindu gods.

Hindu possession of the temple was not challenged until 1891. A young Buddhist pilgrim from Sri Lanka, Anagarika Dharmapala, was shocked by the venal conduct of the incumbent Brahmin priests, their worship of Buddha statues as Lord Shiva and their banning of Buddhist worship.

The most beautiful statues of the teacher of Nirvana and the Law... are still uncared for and quietly allowed to perish by exposure. ...I came across statues plastered to the walls of an irrigating well... Stones carved with Buddha images are to be found used as weights to the levers for drawing water... I have seen ryots (farmers) in the villages surrounding the temple using admirably carved stones as steps to their huts. I have seen 3 feet high statues in an excellent state of preservation buried under rubbish.

Born into a wealthy Sri Lankan family, he expressed interest in the religious life from an early age. His adopted name, Anagarika Dharmapala, means 'Homeless guardian of the Dharma'. Educated and charismatic, Dharmapala embarked on an international campaign to restore Bodhgaya to Buddhist control. His efforts stimulated the fledgling Mahabodhi Society, to adopt this objective. In response, the Mahant of the time became intransigent. He saw both control, and access to lucrative pilgrim fees being lost. He claimed the whole site now belonged to the Hindus by right of occupation, especially as the Buddhists had abandoned it for centuries.

Later, when Dharmapala tried to install a Japanese statue of the Buddha in the main shrine there was a fracas between Hindu and Buddhist protagonists. Reluctantly, the local authorities and British rulers in Calcutta were forced to intervene to keep the peace. In 1949, after many years of legal wrangling and several court cases, the Mahabodhi Society achieved partial success, with formation of a committee of four Hindus and four Buddhists to oversee management of the temple. Unfortunately, the District Magistrate of Gaya was the appointed chairman, so there was inevitably a Hindu majority on the governing body.

The inherent tension between the two controlling groups exists to this day. Near-riots occurring in 1992, warranted the placement of Indian troops. The desire of the international Buddhist community to control their most sacred site is directly countered by the current Mahant who envisages his political, religious and financial benefits whittled away. A recent rise in Hindu nationalism supports his view, so a 'final solution' to control of Bodhgaya seems some way off.

Today's Bodhgaya

THE MAHABODHI TEMPLE ENVIRONS

Like any entrance to a holy site, the road to the Mahabodhi Temple is initially a distraction of food stalls; beggars; and touts offering charms; CDs of favourite Buddhist chants; cheap necklaces; and images of bone and plastic. There are garish 3 D pictures of the Tathagata, sutra books and rosaries along with floral offerings and incense sticks. And, for those who plan to spend a lifetime or two at Bodhgaya, there is a nifty selection of mosquito-netted meditation shelters—like tents for Hobbits.

Appropriately for a Buddhist site, you cannot enter without confronting the issues which started the young Prince on his quest for enlightenment. There's a clutch of gaunt mothers with ill-nourished kids; a less vocal group of the very-old who mostly sit in silent need; and the deformed who hop or hump their way beside you to the entrance-gate in the hope of a few rupees—'a gauntlet of entrepreneurial misery'. You are not likely to see any dead, but there are masses of monks in all colours of the Buddhist spectrum—the cool grey of the Vietnamese; sonorous maroon of the Tibetans; and the vivid saffron of Thais and Sri Lankans. And, given that in India, the benefits of darshan are available to all comers, there are numerous Hindu visitors and a sprinkle of Muslims.

On arrival at the temple gates, it is a surprise to find that the base of the shrine is a good eight metres lower, so that you look directly at the temple spire a fifth of its way to heaven.

You are standing on the embankment of the ancient Niranjana River, which as the modern Phalgu, flows a hundred metres behind you. The main object of veneration is the tree and the latest version of the adamantine seat which lies beneath. However, neither tree nor seat, are immediately obvious. To see them, you have first to circumambulate the temple, through scores of small votary stupas with pleasant patches of lawn and groups of chanting devotees.

A visit to Mahabodhi temple is rewarding, no matter what time of day. There is always a lot of activity as well as areas for quiet contemplation. National groups clad in distinctive robes or coloured caps circumambulate, chant or sit. Near dawn, and at night before the closing time of nine are times when national groups are particularly active. At night a searchlight illuminates the main spire which in turn provides sensitive illumination around the gardens. One special section is devoted to pilgrims who express their devotion making full prostrations. Some Tibetan monks provide a modern touch by using iPads for their sutra reading.

What's immediately obvious for today's pilgrim is the imposing pyramid of the Mahabodhi Temple, rising fifty metres from its base. Smaller replica-spires complete each corner, while the central chamber, below, houses an ancient statue of the Buddha. Although the spire of the temple

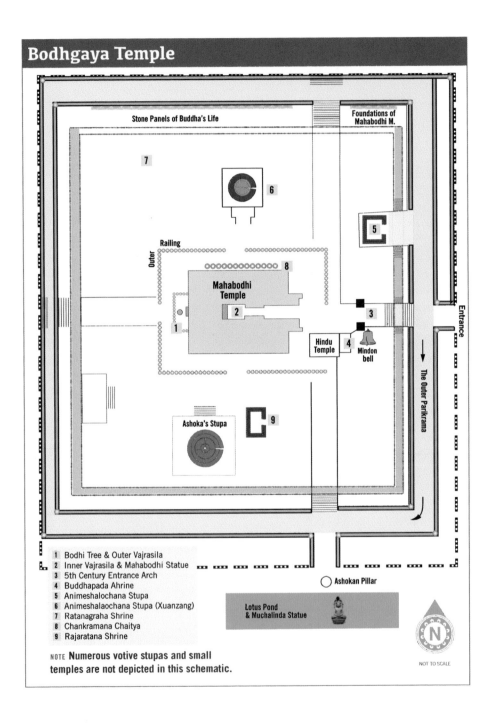

Bodhgaya Temple

Stone Panels of Buddha's Life

Foundations of Mahabodhi M.

7

6

5

Railing

Outer

8

Mahabodhi
Temple

2

1

3

Hindu
Temple

4

Mindon
bell

Entrance

The Outer Parikrama

Ashoka's Stupa

9

1 Bodhi Tree & Outer Vajrasila
2 Inner Vajrasila & Mahabodhi Statue
3 5th Century Entrance Arch
4 Buddhapada Ahrine
5 Animeshalochana Stupa
6 Animeshalaochana Stupa (Xuanzang)
7 Ratanagraha Shrine
8 Chankramana Chaitya
9 Rajaratana Shrine

○ Ashokan Pillar

Lotus Pond
& Muchalinda Statue

N

NOT TO SCALE

NOTE Numerous votive stupas and small
temples are not depicted in this schematic.

is dominant, it is useful to keep the historical concept of the site in mind. From a religious perspective, the tree is the most important shrine and the temple subordinate. Despite the visual incongruity, the temple is in effect 'under' the tree.

In 2013 Thai Buddhists contributed 300 kg of gold leaf, costing some 15 million dollars, to adorn the temple spire. Just how far this will cover the shikara, only time will tell. Such embellishment is in contrast to Buddhist sites managed by the Indian Department of Archaeology, where considerable effort is spent in preventing pilgrims from indulging in such activity.

PARIKRAMA PATHWAYS

It is Buddhist practice to walk around a temple, stupa or other holy site, keeping the object to your right. This activity signifies respect, and bestows merit. At Bodhgaya there are three paths of circumambulation (parikrama).

If you are unfamiliar with Bodhgaya walking the upper pathway is a good way to orientate yourself. It starts at the entrance gate at the same level. Immediately below this, at the level of the temple is the lower-outer path. The most popular path is immediately adjacent to the main temple. Here, at any time of the day the human face of Buddhist pilgrimage is colourfully manifest. Individuals or groups sit under the tree while changing devotees do their rounds of the temple.

BUDDHA SITES INSIDE THE TEMPLE AREA

In addition to the temple, the tree and the adamantine seat there are numerous holy sites within the complex.

BELOW

The 'Jewel Walk' or Chankramana, where the Buddha walked on the 2nd week after enlightenment.

Descending the entrance steps, towards the main temple you first encounter, on your left a large bronze bell donated by King Mindon in 1877. You then pass beneath a 5th century stone gateway. On its left pillar is an image of Jambala the god of wealth and protector of the northern direction. In one hand he holds a bag of gold coins signifying the glories of possible enlightenment and in the other a lemon. The lemon is a pun, as Jambala is a homophone for the Sanskrit name of the Asian lemon which in itself signifies wealth and fertility. As a liberal dispenser of wealth, Tantric Buddhists are comfortable with Jambala. They believe that the possession of his wealth results in spiritual liberation by allowing the recipient to reduce their personal efforts to achieve material prosperity. As a dispenser of spiritual and material wealth his worship was widely supported in Tantric Buddhism and he continues as a popular deity today. In the Hindu tradition he is known as Kubera. On the Bodhgaya pillar, he is depicted as comfortably obese, sitting in the relaxed lalitasana (ease posture) position.

Proceeding towards the temple, immediately on the left, is the small Buddhapada shrine. Before the 1st century CE there were no images of the Buddha in human form. Until then he was depicted symbolically—as a tree, an umbrella, a seat or as here, as footprints. Next is a collection of small Hindu shrines built at a time when there was no Buddhist activity at the site.

The entrance to the Mahabodhi Temple is immediately in front. In niches to each side are stone images of the Buddha which replace the silver ones seen by Xuanzang. You enter a barrel-vaulted chamber immediately beneath the spire. This is the garba-griha (womb-house), a feature of Hindu temples adopted by Buddhist architects. In Hindu temples this is the most sacred part of the temple, a place which can only be entered by priests. There are no similar constraints here. Attendants forbid photographs, but this injunction is cheerfully ignored by the pilgrims, who snap and flash a record of their enthusiastic visitation to Buddhism's most sacred site.

THE MAHABODHI STATUE

At the far end of the chamber is a tenth century image of the Buddha, taken from the Mahant's compound and placed here during Beglar's restoration. Carved from dark stone, it is now a dense golden hue. Late in the evening you may chance upon a group who have permission to enter the glass enclosure housing the statue. They repaint the Buddha with gold-soused paint, or replace his robe of golden silk. He sits in the bhumiparsha (earth witness) mode. This classic gesture, with the fingertips of his right hand touching the ground and his left in his lap, records the moment when the Buddha asked the earth to bear witness to his suitability to attain full enlightenment. In his lap is a begging bowl studded with diamonds.

The first image placed here became the most revered statue in Buddhism, copied to numerous other temples, including Nalanda, Vikramasila, Gyantse and China. Mentioned first in the 4th century, it was commented upon for almost a thousand years, with the last record during the 1400s. The statue in the temple today is one found in nearby ruins by Beglar. It is not the one originally described, as it dates from the 10th century.

The earliest representations of the Buddha were aniconic—trees, footprints, umbrella, stupas and the like. Around the 1st century of the current era the nature of Buddhist worship began to change, with the Buddha being depicted in human form. Legend has us believe that the Mahabodhi image, inside the main temple is his exact likeness but in truth, we really do not know the appearance of the Buddha.

Legend relates that, in ancient times, when a decision was made to enshrine a statue of the Buddha in the new temple, no suitable image could be found. An unknown sculptor offered to craft a statue providing he could be left undisturbed inside the temple for six months. Local citizens, impatient to see the results, opened the temple door four days before the appointed time, to disclose a statue of great beauty, and the sculptor gone. Later, Maitreya (the Buddha who is next to come) revealed that he was the artist.

THE BODHI TREE

The tree is impressively immense. As befits its antiquity, there are several iron crutches to support the limbs. Today's tree is a successor of that which sheltered the Buddha. It's a type of Indian fig tree, Ficus religiosa, known locally as a peepal.

BELOW
Pilgrims meditate at the Bodhi tree.

RIGHT
**Buddha statue
with abhaya
(reassurance)
gesture at the
temple entrance.
Gupta period 7th
century C.E.**

It is said that the original Bodhi tree under which the Buddha sat was destroyed by one of Ashoka's wives, jealous of the time her husband was devoting to Buddhism. Banyan trees are extremely robust so single-handed destruction would be difficult even by a determined queen, however there are numerous early accounts of the tree sustaining various types of damage. We do know that cuttings from the original tree were taken by Ashoka's daughter Sanghamitra, to the monastery of Anuradhapura in Sri Lanka, where it thrives to this day. Later, a replacement-cutting from this was brought back to Bodhgaya.

When Alexander Cunningham came here in 1881 he found a sapling growing from ancient remains. What you see today is that sapling grown large, a genuine descendent of the tree which sheltered the Buddha.

THE RAILING

During the earliest period the tree was enclosed with a wooden railing which, around the 2nd century BCE, was replaced with one of stone. When the temple was built an outer railing was added. Over the centuries the rails were changed as various rulers sought to establish their presence and in the 18th century many stone rails were purloined as building material for Hindu monuments. Some early examples, bearing inscriptions from donors as well as graffiti, survive in the museums of Bodhgaya and Kolkata.

There are two types of stone railing. The older, dated to around 150 BCE is made from sandstone. The younger set, made from granite, is from the Gupta period c300–600 CE. Both have carvings in low relief of scenes from the life of the Buddha, lotus motifs and other scenes.

THE OUTER DIAMOND SEAT—THE 'VAJRASILA'

Placed between the temple and the tree, on the eastern side is a large rectangular stone slab. It is made from highly polished Chunar sandstone. This may be a gift from Ashoka, as around the edge is a frieze of palm leaves and hamsa (geese). Because of their migratory habit, wild geese were an early Buddhist symbol of detachment. A similar frieze is around the capital of the Ashokan pillar at Sanchi.

If this is an imperial gift, it would originally have been located atop the early diamond throne, only to be shifted when the temple was constructed. Until a few years ago, the slab used to sit open to the sky. Now it is protected with a gold canopy and kept warm with a cover of golden silk. A surrounding double fence of stone and brass makes viewing the throne, as well as the base of the tree, almost impossible. Despite what the guides might say, this is not the original pitha, or seat, of the Buddha. It was intended by Ashoka as a platform where offerings to the tree could be placed. The young Gautama had sat on a seat of kusa grass which has long since been swept away.

PLACES RELATED TO THE POST-ENLIGHTENMENT WEEKS

After his enlightenment, the Buddha spent several weeks in contemplation of his new-found state. Having achieved a state of blissful enlightenment it was appropriate to savour the experience and to decide whether this sublime state should, or indeed could, be shared with others. Traditions vary as to how long, and to the exact nature of these periods, but most agree that he spent seven weeks in the immediate vicinity of the Bodhi tree.

• The first week was spent under the Bodhi tree.

• The second week, was spent standing in unblinking concentration gazing at the tree which had assisted his quest. This site is marked by the Animeshalochana Stupa (unwinking gaze stupa). This stone stupa is immediately to the right of the entrance at the same level. In design it mimics the main temple. Inside, one thousand tiny gold Buddhas sit behind glass. The main statue is a standing Avalokitesvara (Buddha of Compassion) with his right hand placed low, palm outwards—the boon-giving gesture. However, this building is probably mis-named as it faces away from the tree and is located high on the embankment, indicating that it is not ancient. Xuanzang said the Animeshalochana shrine was north of the existing temple outside the railing. In this location today, are old foundations which would look directly towards the tree. This place is a more likely site of the Buddha's second week of contemplation, a locality now enlivened by the prostrations of Tibetan monks.

• The third week was spent in walking meditation between the tree and stupa. At each step a lotus blossom sprang up to mark the 'Holy One's' passage. This episode is recorded by a recently constructed brick platform the Chankramana Chaitya (chaitya—'reminder' Skt.) or jewel walk. On its top are his footprints marked with eighteen lotus blossoms. This place is immediately beside the northern wall of the temple.

• The fourth week involved deeper meditation on what he had experienced. A time associated with the Ratanagraha Chaitya (jewel seizing shrine)—'Jeweled', because the Buddha was said to have emanated coloured rays during this period of meditation. On the north side of the compound, this small 9th century temple sits open to the sky, as only the original walls and doorway survive. It is surrounded by scores of mediation-boards for Tibetans engaged in full prostration meditation, while inside a small golden statue of the Buddha sits in stillness.

Pillar carving depicting the Bodhi tree with a surrounding wooden railing, ca. 7th century CE.

• The fifth week of meditation is marked by a pillar at the base of the entrance steps. This marks the location of the Ajapala Nigrodha tree; 'the Goatherd Banyan tree'. It is said that a goatherd planted the original tree to shelter the Buddha. It was under this banyan tree that the newly realised Buddha was once again visited by Mara. To prevent others becoming enlightened, 'the Great Tempter' did not wish the Buddha to preach. A much more satisfactory solution, from Mara's viewpoint, would be for the Buddha to immediately enter final nirvana, and die. Fortunately, the Buddha declined. Another story, located

here, tells that the Buddha instructed an enquiring Brahmin that '...
only by one's deeds did one become a Brahmin. Not by birth alone'.

• The sixth week of meditation was at Muchalinda lake. It was here, that
the serpent king of the same name rose up from the waters to spread
his hood and shelter the Buddha from a storm. Mara, having failed
in his attempt to dissuade the Buddha from becoming enlightened
had worked up a tempest in the hope, yet again, that the Buddha
would not preach to humanity. Beyond the site walls, on the south
is a large tank with a sign marking it as 'Muchalinda'. At its centre is
a newly erected statue of the great snake protecting the meditating
Buddha. In fact, this tank is an excavation site for the bricks used to
construct the Mahabodhi Temple. The sign wrongly identifies it as
Muchalinda lake, which is sited almost two kilometres further south.

• It was on his seventh week of meditation that the Buddha resolved
to preach and to thus save human beings from suffering, and it was
from here that he set off to the deer park of Sarnath to find his former
companions. Rajayatana is the place where in ancient times a silver
(rajat) tree stood. It was at this spot that two Burmese merchants,

Tapussa and Bhallika, offered the Buddha rice cakes and honey to break his fast. By accepting refuge in the Buddha and his teachings these two became the first of the Buddha's disciples. On requesting 'something sacred' as a memento, the Buddha gave them two hairs from his head. Burmese legend relates that on their return to Burma, these two hair-relics 'the Kesu Datu' were enshrined in the Shwe Dagon pagoda in Rangoon. In the late 1940s a replacement rajat tree was brought from Burma. It is the one you see today to the south of the main temple.

THE ASHOKAN PILLAR

An Ashokan pillar fragment stands just outside the southern gate. It is not known whether this is the original pillar which is depicted in two scenes from the Bharhut Stupa, as standing just outside the temple railing to the east. Neither of the two Chinese pilgrims mentioned an elephant-capital pillar, indicating that it had probably been removed by their time. The pillar seen today was brought from Gaya in 1956.

FULL PROSTRATION PRACTICE

One very obvious group are those who practice full prostration. Mostly, maroon-clad Tibetan monks or nuns, they make a standing bow towards the main temple and then lie full length on wooden sliding-benches before standing erect and repeating the process, usually for hours at a time. On their hands are pads which slide along the boards as they ease themselves to the ground. Most wear protective leather aprons along with pads to protect their knees. You might wonder how many prostrations they accomplish? In 1984, the American scholar, John Huntington met a Tibetan woman who was embarking on her second million. Unfortunately Huntington does not enumerate her years of practice. Those who prostrate are invariably cheerful and good natured. It is a practice that is simultaneously a meditation, merit enhancing and health-giving. As you might expect, none of them are overweight.

SCENES FROM THE BUDDHA'S LIFE

On the north side of the lower-outer parikrama are life-sized panels in red sandstone of the Buddha's life story. These are finely worked in low relief.

OFFERINGS OF WATER AND LAMPS

On stone platforms at several locations around the gardens, are water offerings to the Buddha. Scores of brass or silver bowls fill the whole space in mandala-like patterns, and some use paper 'Fine Coffee' cups. With luck, your visit may catch the time when the hundreds of butter lamps flicker into life.

VOTIVE STUPAS

Stupa means 'heap' in Sanskrit. In pre-historic times throughout India and Central Asia mounds of earth and stones were used to bury important people. When the Buddha was dying he requested that his remains be placed in stupas at crossroads as a reminder to passers-by of the enlightened state of living. From this time, stupas became places of religious devotion which signified the entire Buddhist path, and in fact, stupas are the oldest type of Buddhist monument. It was not necessary for a stupa to contain relics of a religious teacher. To construct a stupa, or other Buddhist building or statue was seen as an opportunity to acquire merit as well as to advertise the Buddhist way.

The grounds of the Bodhgaya Temple contain scores of votive stupas, built over many centuries. Those, most elaborately carved, with flat-topped domes date from Pala times. The ones with hemispherical domes are less decorated. These date to an earlier period.

THE MAHANT'S RESIDENCE

300m northwest of the main entrance is the walled compound of the Mahant. You are welcome to enter, although it may cost a few more rupees to view the sculptures which have been incorporated into the walls.

OUTSIDE THE TEMPLE PRECINCTS

The Great Buddha statue was financed by the Daijokyo sect of Japanese Buddhism. Seven years in construction it is made, appropriately, from the same Chunar sandstone used by Ashoka for his columns. Standing 25 metres high, the inside is hollow and conceals thousands of small bronze Buddha statues. Five of the Buddha's most important disciples stand either side of the Master. Each is named and although there is an attempt at individuality, they look like a family of identical brothers.

National temples

There are numerous Vihara (monasteries) established by national groups. They are open every day from 10am until 5pm, with a break at midday from twelve until 2pm. Each temple has its own flavour, with the following the most distinctive.

On the walls of the Bhutanese temple are three dimensional presentations of the Buddha's life depicted in soft pastels. The main altar has, for this part of India, uncommon images. On the left is Guru Rimpoche, the Indian guru who took Buddhism into Tibet. Centrally placed is Sakyamuni Buddha, and to the right is the multi-armed Buddha of Compassion Chenrezig, or Avaloketeshvara. The Buddha of Compassion, in today's world, is manifest in His Holiness the Dalai Lama.

Nearby is the Indosan Nipponji Japanese temple. Its single graceful sweep of roof contrasts with the multi-leafed pagoda-roof of the Bhutanese temple across the way. The interior has the austere feel that expresses Japanese taste. High on the interior walls are painted scenes from the life of the World Honoured One.

THE THAI TEMPLE

The sweeping tiled roofs of the Thai temple give good indication of its lavish interior. Here are excellent murals and golden Buddhas in ornate Thai style.

THE ARCHAEOLOGY MUSEUM

Daily 10.00–5.00, closed Friday and public holidays.

Although many items from Bodhgaya were stolen or transported to other museums, there are many important stone and bronze statues within the small museum. Most are from the Pala-Sena period (8th–12th centuries), with fine depictions of the Buddha and Tara.

The most notable relic is the stone railing, which used to surround the Bodhi tree. You can clearly see how its construction mimics wooden post and rail fences from earlier periods. Lotus flowers are commonly shown, along with scenes of the Buddha's life, but more common are secular events. One shows the donation of gold which covered the land to buy the Jetavana grove at Shravasti. Immediately beside this, three elephants pay homage to the Buddha—depicted as a tree.

Inside the central gallery, to the left, are three sandstone statues of Mathura style. The second, of a couple, is particularly naturalistic.

Near to Bodhgaya

ACROSS THE RIVER

Flowing past Bodhgaya, running north to south, is the Phalgu (merit giving) river. The Buddha knew it as the Niranjana. On its eastern shore, three kilometres from town are two locations which set the scene for the ultimate importance of Bodhgaya.

SUJATA'S STUPA

Sujata was a young milk-maid who was sufficiently moved to offer a meal of curds to a starving ascetic. She did not personally know the ragged heap of humanity who had arrived on the banks of her river but she knew that he needed nourishment. This was a moment of extraordinary change in Gautama's life. By taking Sujata's gift he was rejecting self-denial as a path to realisation. By implication, if he wished to continue his spiritual search, he had to find another way.

Here, on the banks of a muddy stream we celebrate that change in direction, and across the river, at Bodhgaya, its ultimate conclusion. Around the 5th century, a Gupta king recognised the significance of this event by constructing a brick stupa. Added to by other generations, there is now an impressive double terraced stupa, ten metres high. Downstream and across the river, is the Bodhi tree and spire of the Mahabodhi Temple, both site and celebration of Siddhartha's attainment.

Sujata's Stupa.

SUJATA'S THREE SHRINES

Nearby is a fascinating extension to the Sujata story. By walking 600 metres sw on a narrow trail through the rice fields you arrive at a monument that is possibly much older than the stupa. You walk towards the white shikara (spires) of a Hindu temple. Immediately behind this are a series of small shrines involved with Sujata's tale.

The first tableau is of three images. Centrally placed is the famished Siddhartha; to his right Sujata offers her bowl of curds; to his left is Sujata's maid; and lying comfortably below is Surabhi the life-giving cow of Hindu mythology. The images are obviously not old, but what sparks interest is the stone base on which the Buddha sits. Figures in the frieze are indistinct, but centrally placed are two deer worshipping the wheel of the dharma. This base is hundreds of years older than the statues above.

Behind the first shrine is a peepal tree festooned with flags. Tibetan flags; the red-orange-white patches of the Buddhist flag and the flags of Burma and Thailand. They are paying respects to the tree. Local tradition would have it that this tree is the exact place where Sujata found the emaciated Buddha and offered him sustenance. On a platform beneath the tree are ancient stone objects. At the centre is a 40 cm high plinth depicting the Buddha in bhumiparsha, (earth witness) position. To its right is a '1000 Buddha' column with scores of tiny Buddha images and on the left another with niches containing small depictions of 'the World Honoured One'. The ensemble is flanked by two waffle-cone-like objects. These are chattravali (umbrella) tops of old stupas. You can see them in situ at the main Bodhgaya Temple in the south garden area. This is art work of at least a thousand years antiquity. That and its legend make the site worthy of visit.

To complete the triple-sandwich of shrines is a small Myanmar shrine. Unfortunately, their iconography is well off base. A chubby-cheeked, well-nourished and post-enlightenment Burmese-Buddha sits in unwavering meditation as Sujata endeavours to attract his attention with her offering of curds.

THE TEMPLE OF THE GIFT OF GRASS

A few hundred metres upstream and right on the banks of the river, is the newest addition to Buddhist-Bodhgaya. The 'the Temple of the Gift of Grass' is today a modest shelter, more aspiration than art or devotion. Inside another plump Burmese-Buddha accepts his grass seat from an elderly Brahmin. If you could remove the brick wall enclosure, this statue would look through a sea of kusa grass fronds to the temple across the river that reverences his achievement. The Grass Temple is Buddhist kitsch, but fun.

DHUNGESHWARI CAVE AT PRAGBODHI (BEFORE AWAKENING)

A few kilometres from Bodhgaya are a group of wooded rocky hills. A good road takes you from town for forty minutes, to another section that provides a further twenty of pothole bouncing, to eventually deposit you at the foot of the mountain.

It's a 20 minute walk up a concrete trail to the small Tibetan temple and the two caves. A bunch of ill-nourished kids strive for rupees, along with a score of the seriously needy. The beggars on the Hill of Buddha, demonstrate better than elsewhere, the fate of human beings when deprived of basic medical or social care. If you don't like the uphill walk, a couple of locals will carry you up and down on a bamboo chair, or motorbike.

Gautama is said to have spent several hungry years here, before giving up on extreme austerities and walking to Urevela (Bodhgaya), to commence a different method of practice. There are two small caves, one with modern statue of the starving Prince and a larger cave with a statue of the realised Buddha. The small cave demands that you bow low to enter. Inside it is a few square metres of living space, where standing erect is a squeeze. You cannot become more intimate with an actual place where Siddhartha has once been.

GAYA

Twelve kilometres to the north of Bodhgaya is Gaya—the name means elephant. It is a city celebrated in the Hindu tradition but was once a town with Buddhist associations.

THE BUDDHA AND GAYA

The Buddha visited Gaya several times. On the summit of a hill now known as Brahmayoni, he delivered the famous 'Fire Sermon'. His audience were mostly Brahmin priests who used fire as an essential part of ritual. Using their favoured metaphor, the Buddha exhorts:

...All is burning monks. And what is the all that is burning monks?

The eye is burning... The ear is burning... The nose is burning... burning with the fire of greed, the fire of hatred, the fire of delusion.

He then goes on to illustrate how those flames can be quenched by following the Buddhist path.

DEVADATTA AND GAYA

Devadatta, the Buddha's jealous cousin was based here during the last phase of his life. If he heard the Fire Sermon, he certainly didn't follow his cousin's advice. Although the story of Devadatta has elements of exaggeration and legend, it probably reflects real episodes in the life of the Buddha. The intense rivalry which is said to have developed between the two cousins, is said to have dated from childhood. It culminated in a serious challenge to Gautama's leadership and several unsuccessful assassination attempts.

Towards the end of the Buddha's life Devadatta created a schism within the community of the Buddha's monks. He brought a splinter group here to Gaya. King Ajatasatru of nearby Rajgraha built them a monastery. Most of those monks returned to the Buddha's flock following intervention of two of the Buddha's most senior disciples, Shariputra and Maudgalyayana. Despite his attempts at killing his childhood companion, Devadatta eventually had a partial reconciliation with the Buddha but accounts vary as to the harmony, or otherwise, of his death.

When Xuanzang passed through Gaya he mentioned that the Emperor Ashoka had built a stupa at the top of one hill, but no trace of this remains today.

LORD VISHNU THE BUDDHA AND GAYA

In Gaya, the Hindu Vishnupad temple has a set of basalt footprints that are said to have been made by Lord Vishnu. Most scholars feel that the carving represents the footprints of the Buddha. Unfortunately for Buddhists, only Hindu believers can enter the temple so you can neither check the veracity of either claim, or pay homage.

Vishnu is the Hindu god who helps humanity in times of dire need. When competition between Buddhism and Hinduism heated up in the 9th century it seemed a logical move for Brahmin savants to merge the Buddha into the Hindu pantheon. Thus for followers of Vishnu, the historical Buddha is regarded as the 9th incarnation of Lord Vishnu and as such, is worshipped by them. Claiming his footprints seems a minor peccadillo by comparison.

For some modern Hindus, Buddhism was a reform movement similar to that mounted by Martin Luther in Christianity. In their view, once the Buddha had become an incarnation of Vishnu there was no need for Buddhism to exist as a separate religion. Others differ.

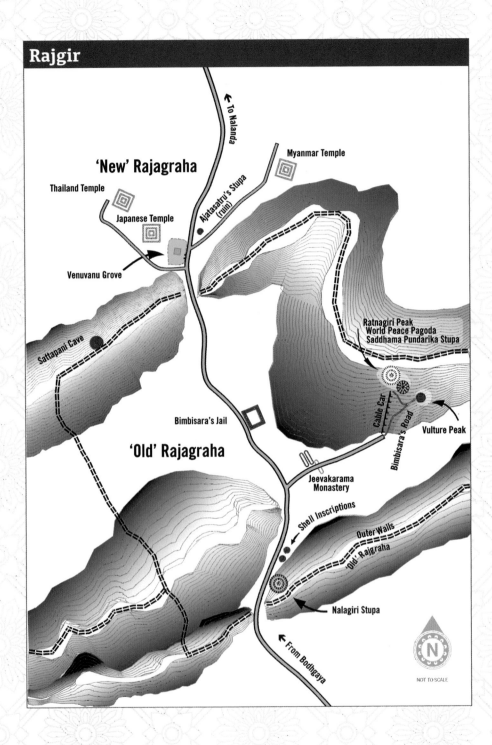

Rajgir

'New' Rajagraha

To Nalanda

Myanmar Temple

Thailand Temple

Ajatasatru's Stupa (ruin)

Japanese Temple

Venuvanu Grove

Sattapani Cave

Ratnagiri Peak
World Peace Pagoda
Saddhama Pundarika Stupa

Cable Car

Bimbisara's Jail

Bimbisara's Road

'Old' Rajagraha

Vulture Peak

Jeevakarama
Monastery

Shell Inscriptions

Outer Walls

'old' Rajgraha

Nalagiri Stupa

From Bodhgaya

N

NOT TO SCALE

CHAPTER FOUR

Rajgir

DURING the lifetime of the Buddha, Rajagraha was most powerful of all small states in the Ganges plain. Royal support for the Buddha in the early days of his nascent community meant that the Buddha spent several seasons here. And, it was from the cool heights of 'Vulture Peak' that many of his most important sermons were delivered. Rajagraha's long history and particular geography make it the one place where you can be sure that you literally walk on the same paths as the Buddha.

ANCIENT RAJAGRAHA

The ancient town of Rajagraha (palace of the king), capital of the kingdom of Magadha, has today become Rajgir. Situated at the junction of several trade routes, it was a wealthy town well protected by surrounding hills and protective walls. In the Buddha's time the city was divided into two, each protected by stone walls four metres high and almost the same across. The 'old city' in his time lay deeper within the hills, separated from the 'new city' by a narrow pass.

ABOVE
Indian Buddhist monks.

This new city had been built by the Buddha's friend King Bimbisara. Sited in a less geographically protected region, it reflects the increased wealth and stability of that time. The region had long been prosperous because of copper and iron mines but enhanced river trade along the Ganges, and grain surplus from fertile rice fields allowed the population to grow and the city's merchants to flourish. After the Buddha's death, Magadha was to absorb the other northern Janapada states, shift the capital to Pataliputra (Patna) and eventually become India's first empire, the Mauryan.

Since very ancient times Rajgir has been a place of both physical and spiritual pilgrimage. Physical—because of the hot-springs which still flow copiously in the region; and spiritual, because both the Buddha and Mahavira, the founder of Jainism, spent many years in the region. It would have been pleasant then, and it remains today a pretty wooded place.

THE BUDDHA AND RAJGIR

During his lifetime, the Buddha visited Rajagraha many times. It was here that he survived several assassination attempts and tussled with rulers who were at times supportive or in opposition. Many of his most important sermons, including the Prajnaparamita, or 'Perfection of Wisdom' sutra, were delivered here on Vulture Peak. More than most other sites, here at Rajgir you can literally walk in the footsteps of the Buddha.

EARLY UNPOPULARITY OF THE BUDDHA

It is relevant, especially in Rajgir, to understand that during his time of early ministry, the Buddha was not always a welcome visitor. His exemplary life, simplicity of his teachings and opposition to ritual and caste, led many to become followers—and these same qualities attracted opposition. Any charismatic spiritual teacher who 'spirits away' husband from household; sons from family; and labourers from the rice-field—might not be the most popular monk in town:

Why has he settled in our midst, this son of the Sakyas?—they asked. Were there not enough monks already, preaching to us about virtue? And they did not lure our young men away like this master. Why, even our children are leaving us. Because of this son of the Sakyas, how many women are widows! Because of this son of the Sakyas, how many families are childless! Evil will befall the kingdom, now that this monk has settled in our midst!

COMMUNITY SUPPORT

As the Buddha grew older, his backing from common people, from royalty and from the rich increased. In fact, it is inconceivable that Buddhist teachings would have become so widely disseminated without that groundswell of public belief and the very necessary support of the wealthy. The truths of Buddhism, may be reflected by, a few grains of rice, but for the Dharma to flourish it needed significant material support.

The Buddha and his community of monks and nuns were without possessions or occupation. Their very survival depended on the generosity of villagers. Long before the Buddha, the shramana way of life was an established tradition in the Ganges valley. For any stay-at-home villager, giving food to itinerant spiritual seekers was a relatively easy way of obtaining merit towards successful rebirth. However, such generosity must, at times, have stretched resources, especially when travelling groups could number in the hundreds. It is a reflection, on the region's prosperity; the degree of faith in the benefits of giving; and the popularity of the Buddha and his band of Sakyaputras, that the transaction was seen as mutually beneficial. The householder would give food or clothing and the Buddha or monks would impart spiritual teaching and guidance on how to live their life.

As the Buddha and his teachings became better known, rich people, kings and others of influence offered more substantial support in the form of land and buildings. The Buddha taught that wealth per se was not a problem. Difficulties arise in the desire for, and attachment to, riches.

Riches destroy the ignorant, yet not those who seek the further shore.

He saw that poverty was the cause of very real suffering, with secondary unwelcome effects, of crime, and the negative karma of social unrest. He taught that the accumulation of wealth in righteous ways was beneficial to all especially if it was utilised for the alleviation of suffering and poverty in others. As he said:

If you have little, give little; if you own a middling amount, give a middling amount; if you have much, give much.

THE BUDDHA AND THE DEVADATTA SCHISM

Gautama Buddha's lifelong difficulties with Devadatta read like a Hollywood script. Some authorities suggest that aspects of their relationship are inventions and indeed, some events certainly stretch credulity. What is without doubt however, is that Devadatta was Siddhartha's cousin; that they grew up together; that Devadatta became a respected monk and follower of the Buddha; and that towards the end of both their lives he challenged the Buddha's leadership.

At one level, their co-joined stories can be understood as a commentary on alpha-male conduct. The Buddha was both royal and privileged: a man, who was sufficiently confident in himself to change when necessary, and who ultimately manifested the pinnacle of religious aspiration. Despite being a respected member of the Sangha for many years, Devadatta is posited as the lesser of all these: a man who continued to harbour resentment about his relatively slighter fortune.

ABOVE
The outer walls of 'Old Rajgir'.

Their differences came to a head in Rajagraha when the Buddha was seventy two years old, in the 37th year of his teaching mission. For some time Devadatta had openly expressed desire to lead the Sangha. Twice he directly suggested to the Buddha that control of the Sangha be given to him. On each occasion the Buddha rejected the approach.

Who would lead the community of Sakyaputras after the Buddha's death was a concern to many monks. Gautama the Buddha, had put little stress on succession. He had effectively made Shariputra his deputy but it was not certain if this meant leadership by Shariputra after the Buddha's death. The Buddha saw self-reliant members of the Sangha becoming an enlightened lineage of teachers who were capable of transmitting his teachings without need for institutionalised verification. For many monks this was not enough, so it was not unreasonable for a senior like Devadatta to suggest change.

After the third request Gautama's response to Devadatta was astonishingly acerbic. The Buddha stated that he would not hand the Sangha to even his favourite monks Shariputra and Maudgalyana let alone to

...such a wastrel, a clot of spittle as you.

Whether the Buddha actually spoke these words, or whether they were added after the Buddha's death to further discredit Devadatta is not known. The net effect was that Devadatta resolved to overthrow the Buddha. The Buddha also publicly dissociated himself and the Sangha from Devadatta, saying:

Whatever Devadatta may do by body or speech neither the Blessed One nor the Dharma nor the Sangha should be held as having a part in it: only Devadatta himself is to be held responsible for it.

And he backed it up by getting a reluctant Shariputra, a friend of Devadatta, to publicly proclaim the Buddha's position in the streets of Rajagraha. With this announcement, the Buddha made clear that Devadatta was entirely responsible for his own actions and that his views were not those of the Buddha. Had there been newspapers at the time, it would have been a front page story as Gautama was well known, and the citizens were aware of the friendship between Devadatta and Prince Ajatashatru. There must have been considerable gossip about what it all meant.

DEVADATTA BEFRIENDS AJATASHATRU

Prior to his public discreditment, Devadatta had befriended Ajatashatru, son of Bimbisara. Some have it that Devadatta did this using his magical powers. In any case monk and prince became inceasingly close friends.

DEVADATTA CHALLENGES THE BUDDHA

Realising that he had nothing to lose, Devadatta decided to challenge the Buddha again with the hope that he would either be able to lead the Buddha's Sangha, or establish one of his own. Confronting The Teacher he said that the Buddha had become too soft and had strayed too far from the harder disciplines necessary for young monks. He demanded that that Buddha institute a set of rules that would require all monks to:

- Only live in the forest.
- For food, accept only alms and not accept invitations to dine at the homes of devotees.
- To wear only robes of rags.

- Live in the open forest and not in a monastery.
- To eat only vegetarian food.

Devadatta was playing a strategic game. He was no ascetic as he lived in luxurious style with the support of Ajatashatru. He expected the demands to be rejected by the Buddha allowing him to use that rejection to recruit other monks.

After discussion, the Buddha agreed that his monks could follow Devadatta's conditions but only if they made such decisions by choice. Such austerities may be useful for individual monks but they should not be compulsory, nor were they a requirement for achieving liberation.

ABOVE
**Thai monk,
Venuvanu Grove.**

DEVADATTA CREATES A SCHISM

Not content with the conciliatory stance of the Buddha, Devadatta resolved to form his own group. He was persuasive and must have been sufficiently charismatic to attract five hundred, mostly younger monks, to join him. This splinter group went to live in the hills near Gaya.

THE BUDDHA REUNITES THE SANGHA

For the Buddha, this was the most troublesome time of his ministry. For him, the Sangha was not a personality cult designed to support a teacher, but a group of like-minded monks who together could facilitate sharing of the Dharma. For young impressionable monks to be taken from his community by a false teacher was particularly disturbing.

He sent his two most senior monks Shariputra and Maudgalyana to Gaya with instructions to preach to the wayward monks. They were to offer the Dharma, and not to suggest that one or the other group was better. On their initial meeting with Devadatta, the renegade assumed that these two seniors had come to join his group. It seems unlikely, but the story goes, that so confident was he in this, that he encouraged Shariputra and Maudgalyana to offer a teaching to his group, while he fell asleep.

Shariputra and Maudgalyana preached the teachings of the Buddha. When the teaching was finished they made known that any monks who wished to return with them to the Buddha's Sangha at Rajagraha would be welcome. In the end, 'all the five hundred' went back to the Buddha. They had been given the chance to decide for themselves which teacher offered the genuine Dharma, and they had chosen Gautama Buddha.

AJATASHATRU OVERTHROWS BIMBISARA

Foiled in his direct attempt to take over the Buddha's Sangha, Devadatta devised another scheme. He encouraged Ajatashatru to overthrow his father anticipating that the loss of Bimbisara's patronage would lead to the Buddha's downfall.

Accounts vary, in regard to Ajatashatru's enthusiasm for a palace coup and just how this was achieved contains more than enough material in the differing versions for a string of operas. In any event, all sources concur, that Ajatashatru did overthrow his father Bimbisara; put him in jail; and, caused his death by starvation. He then set about building up the military might of Magadha, reforming the administration and establishing a well-equipped professional army.

Devadatta's First Attempt on the Buddha's Life—The Assassins

Devadatta realised that he had to kill the Buddha before he could become the dominant teacher. He embarked on a series of assassination attempts that border on the farcical.

First, he hired an assassin who, when he had killed the Buddha, would be himself killed by another party of two. They in turn would be killed by another group of four. And the process would be repeated with eight and finally sixteen assassins. It all turned sour when the very first killer was so impressed with his target that he refused to kill the Buddha and instead, became one of his followers. As you might predict, the process of conversion continued for the other killers and, from Devadatta's perspective, it was a disaster.

And the Second Attempt—The Rock

Realising that he had to kill the Buddha himself, Devadatta hurled a huge rock onto the Buddha when he was walking in the vicinity of Vulture Peak. This attempt seriously injured the Buddha's leg and does seem a credible episode as the Buddha needed the medical help of Jivakarama, the court physician, and was bedridden for several months. All human beings experience pain from injury, and they are subject to old age, sickness and death. Enlightened human beings, even The World Enlightened One, the Buddha, are no different. When Devadatta's rock hit his leg, the Buddha felt pain.

The Third Attempt—Nalagiri, The Wild Elephant

In the royal elephant stables was a notoriously difficult male elephant, Nalagiri, who had killed several people. Devadatta arranged for the mahouts to release the elephant when the Buddha was making his early morning begging round of Rajagraha.

Nalagiri was released, and trumpeted down the road with trunk upraised, intent on damaging the distant monk. The Buddha stood his ground as the animal approached, much to the consternation of his accompanying monks who urged him to flee. The Buddha told them not to be afraid as:

> *...it cannot happen, that anyone can take a Perfect One's life by violence. When Perfect Ones attain final nirvana, it is not through violence on the part of another.*

Nalagiri came to a halt in front of the Buddha, knelt in homage and raised his trunk in respect to Gautama. By manifesting loving kindness the Buddha had subdued the wild animal, just as his teachings can transform aspects of unruly nature in us all. The scene of Buddha with a submissive Nalagiri, had great popular appeal and has been depicted by Buddhist artists for centuries.

Devadatta's involvement in these assassination attempts was well known to the Buddha and his sangha, but the Buddha refused to encourage direct action against his cousin theorising that Devadatta's own actions would lead to his downfall.

WHO WAS DEVADATTA?

Many of Devadatta's reported actions seem barely credible. Some scholars suggest that the Devadattya schism was an attempt by a sincere monk to steer the Buddhist Sangha towards a self-denying forest practice similar to that of the Buddha's early years. However, this was not how the Buddha wished the Sangha to develop. He saw that for his teachings to flourish, the community had to increasingly become a settled monastic group. In the view of some, Devadatta's criminal acts were later additions to the canon to further discredit his influence. Whatever the truth of the matter, there is no denying that: the Devadatta tales, make the stories of Rajgir more exciting; they provide opportunities for Buddhist moral teaching; and have enlivened generations of Buddhist artists.

DISCIPLES FROM RAJGIR

Three of the Buddha's most loyal disciples, Kashyapa, Shariputra and Maudgalyana, were born near here. Shariputra and Maudgalyana were born in Nalanda on the same day, four years before the birth of the Buddha. They joined the Sangha as young men, lived their lives with the Buddha and died, six months before him, within a few weeks of each other. In 1851 the great British archaeologist Alexander Cunningham found their relics while excavating the '3rd Stupa' at Sanchi. Their remains lie together at Sanchi in a new museum. These two were said to be the right-hand and left-hand of the Buddha. So that, later when the Buddha was old, and feeling tired, it was only Shariputra, Maudgalyana and Ananda that he ever asked to expound the Dharma.

THE FIRST BUDDHIST COUNCIL

Shortly after the Buddha's death, the First Buddhist Council was called to formally agree the teachings. Five hundred of the most senior gathered at the Sattapani caves on Vaibhara hill between old and new Rajagraha. It was presided over by Kasyapa, the most senior monk. He excluded Ananda, the Buddha's beloved aide, because Ananda was not— in Kasyapa's view—sufficiently spiritually-clear. That very night Ananda attained full enlightenment and the next day, on being accepted into the conclave, recited word-perfect all the Buddha's discourses.

In all, there are more than 17,000 discourses attributed to the Buddha.

It is very likely that a group of senior monks and Ananda did convene to recall the direct teachings they had heard from the Buddha. And there is no doubt that these could have been remembered through the phenomenal memory and dedication of generations of Buddhist monks. However, there is copious evidence to suggest that numerous additions were made to the Buddhist literature for several centuries after the Buddha's death. Many of these teaching were by enlightened teachers of the Dharma. For contemporary Buddhists these latter additions are regarded as 'the words of the Buddha'.

At the time of the First Council there had been disharmony within the Sangha. Some monks desired a relaxation of the strict rules of conduct laid down by the Buddha. The First Council was successful in resolving the conflict by agreeing the rules of monastery behaviour.

THE CHINESE MONKS

Faxian found the Rajagraha ruins largely deserted, with only a few monks at Venuvanu. For Xuanzang, in the 7th century, the region was desolate. At the summit temple, he offered flowers in celebration of the years spent here by the Buddha. It is said that on Gridhakuta hill, Xuanzang bought a large Buddha image, one of the seven he took back to Chang'an and, in so doing, changed the artistic style of Tang dynasty China.

Today's Rajgir

THE APPROACH TO RAJGIR

Seventy kilometres north east of Bodhgaya, amidst a scattering of rocky hills, is Rajgir—'House of the King'. The road is initially flat, with occasional scruffy towns, relieved by long stretches of fresh-green paddy. Eventually, the steep hills that sheltered ancient Rajagraha appear. Forty kilometres of stone walls define its importance as capital of the early Magadha kingdom. Coming from Bodhgaya, you approach the hills of Rajgir from the south. Steep creamy red cliffs crowned with ancient stone walls lead via a narrow pass towards 'old' Rajgir.

THE NALAGIRI STUPA

A few hundred metres from the entrance pass is the stupa of Nalagiri, the enraged elephant. As an attempt to kill the Buddha, it was a disaster. Face to face with the Buddha, Nalagiri fell to his knees and raised his trunk in submission. From earliest times this was a popular story carved and painted by generations of artists. The large brick stupa offers no visual clues to support this tale.

THE CHARIOT GROOVES AND 'SHELL INSCRIPTIONS'

You are indeed, travelling an old road. To the right of the main highway, on a gradual slope of hard stone are the parallel ruts of ancient wagon wheels. The Mahabarata relates that Lord Krishna came several times to Rajagraha and local Hindu lore has the speed and power of Krishna's chariot 'burning' these furrows. More prosaically, the trail raises an existential question: how long would it take to scour such grooves with more earthly vehicles?

The depth of the wagon-ruts is a metaphor for Rajagraha's wealth and the huge amount of traffic which flowed along the Uttarapatha (North road) which in Buddhist times linked the Bangaladesh region with Taxila in modern Pakistan, and beyond into central Asia. Later, as The Grand Trunk road it became northern India's lifeline. Re-paved by Sher Shah Suri in the 1500s, it continues today in modern-day India as Highway #1, and is universally referred to today as 'GT road'.

Alongside the ruts are groups of curvaceous inscriptions, known as shankh-lipi, or shell-script, because of their fancied resemblance to a conch shell. Such inscriptions are found in many places throughout India and as far afield as Indonesia. The earliest date from around the time of Ashoka and are now thought to be an ornamental form of Brahmi, used mainly for names, rather like a flourishing signature when writing with pen.

BIMBISARA'S JAIL

A kilometre further on is where the king was imprisoned. These days, the rock walls which surround Bimbisara's jail would not restrain a goat. Around 490 BCE King Bimbisara was put here and reputedly, starved to death under instructions from his son Ajatashatru. From here you can clearly see, to the right of the white Peace Pagoda, Vulture Peak. Bimbisara had constructed a road up that hill so that, in better times, he could more easily attend upon the Buddha. It is said that the son generously gave his father a cell with a view towards the peak! What gives some credence to this being a jail was the discovery during British excavations in 1930, of iron manacles in one of the cells.

VENUVANA

King Bimbisara donated Venuvana, the 'Bamboo Grove' as a site for the Buddha's first monastery. In those times, and even today, travel was very difficult during the rainy season. During those three months the Buddha and his community undertook both a spiritual and physical retreat. The Bamboo Grove, was a favourite haunt during the monsoon retreat period—'neither too far from a village nor too near... conducive to privacy, and suitable for meditation'. As a permanent establishment, it was the first step towards making the Buddhist Sangha a property owning organisation.

At Venuvana a large open garden still survives. In the centre is a 100m square bathing pool used by the Buddha during his frequent stays at Rajgir. In 1971 a two metre stone statue of the Buddha, in 'earth-witness' mode, was salvaged from the depths of this pool. Dated to Pala times, it was probably placed here eight centuries ago when Buddhism was under threat. Now it sits overlooking its founder's bathing tank.

AJATASHATRU'S STUPA

Ajatashatru's Stupa is near to Venuvanu. Although one of the Maha-stupas containing the initial distribution of the Buddha's relics, little glory remains today and it is rarely visited. A couple of metres high and some thirty across, its rocks have been mined for other purposes.

THE JAPANESE TEMPLE

If your time permits, take a few minutes to visit the nearby modern Japanese temple. On its walls are a striking series of wood-block prints of the Buddha's chief disciples—large caricatures of his companions brought engagingly to life. These images, *Ten Great Disciples of the Buddha*, were carved by the noted Japanese artist Manakata Shiko in 1939.

TOWARDS VULTURE PEAK

A densely forested side valley provides access to the most important Buddhist sites of ancient Maghadha. It leads towards the ropeway accessing Ratnagiri (jewel peak).

JEEVAKARAMA MONASTERY

Venuvanu and Vulture Peak were the two main havens of the Buddha while residing in Rajagraha, they are about eight kilometres apart. Jeevaka was the physician to Bimbisara and a follower of the Buddha. Abandoned as a baby, he had been found 'jivati ' (alive) on top of a dust heap. Adopted by a Magadhan prince, he had medical training in Taxila for seven years before returning home to become the town's most noted surgeon and physician.

As the teacher aged, Jeevaka became concerned about the distances the Buddha had to travel. He donated his mango plantation as a place where the Holy One could stop and built Jeevakarama monastery. The Buddha often stayed at Jeevakarama. It was here, that the Buddha was brought when his leg was damaged during one of Devadatta's assassination attempts. The Buddha gave several important discourses at this place including one to his patron Jeevaka, outlining the responsibilities of a lay disciple.

The ruins, excavated in 1954, lie on either side of the road. They are of interest because they show three large halls with elliptical ends which could have accommodated hundreds, as each is roughly a hundred metres long and ten wide. Shortly after Jeevakarama the road crosses a bridge and mound, marking the moat and boundary wall of ancient old-Rajagriha.

THE WORLD PEACE PAGODA AND GRIDHRAKUTA PEAK – ACCESS

Walking up Bimbisara's road may seem like a good idea, but heat and distance can quickly dissipate enthusiasm. An aerial ropeway leads directly to Ratnagiri Peak dominated by the white dome of the World Peace Stupa. The easiest option is to take the ropeway to the pagoda, then walk down, and then a lesser distance up, to Vulture Peak. Finally, you can satisfy your instinct for pilgrimage, by walking down Bimbisara's road to the car park.

However, if there are crowds, access to the ropeway is slow, as it is a single seat system. In that case, you may decide to walk. It is a gradual upwards climb along Bimbisara's road to reach Vulture Peak in half an hour. Getting to the pagoda from Vulture Peak is forty minutes of uphill grind, as 'Pagoda' is more than a hundred metres higher than 'Vulture'.

RATNAGIRI PEAK—THE WORLD PEACE STUPA

At the top of Ratnagiri (jewel hill) is a large white Vishwa Shanti stupa 'World Peace Stupa', one of many similar ones built by the Japanese in Buddhist sites. Each of the four cardinal directions has a niche containing a golden Buddha statue in different positions. There are two paths of circumambulation defined by concrete railings that mimic those of Gupta times. Lots of Indian families come here for recreation. For them there is the excitement of the cable ride up the hill and a chance to be photographed in front of an exotic stupa. Few of these local tourists trudge over to Gridhrakuta. From the peace pagoda it is a twenty minute walk to Vulture Peak.

ABOVE
The Saddhama Pundarika (Lotus) Stupa.

THE SADDHAMA PUNDARIKA SUTRA STUPA

A few metres below the Peace Pagoda is a modern stone pagoda in Japanese style, standing at the edge of a large platform overlooking the valley, where hundreds could assemble. It is said that here the Buddha delivered the Saddhama Pundarika, or 'Lotus', Sutra. The original text has been lost, with most historians of the view that the Lotus Sutra was composed by several authors in the 1st or 2nd centuries CE in ancient Maghadhan language. The most respected early translation of the Lotus Sutra was made into Chinese by Kumarajiva, a renowned translator of the early 5th century. This translation was used throughout Tang dynasty China as an important text for the Chan sect of Buddhism, which in Japan became Zen.

In Buddhism a sutra is a teaching by the Buddha or one of his principal disciples. Traditionally a sutra begins with the phrase: *Thus I have heard...* a phrase which recalls Ananda's ability to recite all the Buddha's teachings from memory. Today, and since earliest times, the Lotus Sutra is particularly important to the Mahayana form of Buddhism, which prevails in China, Japan, Korea and Vietnam. In the Lotus Sutra the Buddha

ABOVE

Vulture Peak.

states that he is offering his final and highest teaching, which supersedes all others. As a matter of faith Mahayanists believe that the Lotus Sutra contains the Buddha's actual words which, in eloquent prose and verse express themes fundamental to the Mahayana schools.

- Although there are various paths to enlightenment, all are ultimately the 'Buddha vehicle'.
- That all beings have 'Buddha nature' and can become enlightened.
- That 'Buddha nature' pervades literally all things, animate and inanimate, throughout all space and time, which thus implies a cosmic unity of all existence.
- That the enlightened state is not dependent upon intellect but can be achieved by faith and devotion.

By stating the universality of Buddha nature, which in the sutra specifically includes women, and by making 'faith and devotion' legitimate avenues towards the enlightened state, the Lotus Sutra made possible a comprehensive lay Buddhist practice that was not dependent on the ascetic life of a monastic. This singular teaching delivered here at Grdhrakuta Peak greatly enhanced the spread of Buddhism within and beyond India.

TOWARDS VULTURE PEAK VIA BIMBISARA'S ROAD

It is satisfying to walk along the way built by King Bimbisara. It would have been a much rougher passage then. Now it is a paved path that winds gradually up the hill. You walk past elements that have survived from the time of the World Honoured One. They are identified by white painted signs of the IAD (Indian Archaeology Department). Unfortunately, the signs are barely decipherable.

Hiking Bimbisara's trail, you literally walk in the 'footsteps of the Buddha' seeing the same rocks and attended by ancestors of the lizards and birds which flitted across his trail. Xuanzang described it thus:

> *Bimbisara-rajah, for the purpose of hearing the law, raised a number of men to accompany him from the foot of the mountain to its summit. They levelled the valleys and spanned the precipices, and with the stones made a staircase about ten paces wide and 5 or 6 li long.*

The first historical site is Mardakukshi Monastery where the physician Jeevakarama treated the Buddha's injured leg after the stone-rolling assassination attempt by Devadatta. This was not a minor injury as the Buddha had to be carried by stretcher from the assassination point and then needed to convalesce for several months before recovering.

Next are the ruins of two stupas. The first, 'Dismounting from the chariot', is where King Bimbisara proceeded on foot. The other, 'Sending back the crowd' is the spot where the king separated himself from the common folk.

Alan Ginsberg, the American poet, put it like this:

> *...up the stone climb past where*
> *Bimbisara left his armies*
> *got down off his elephant*
> *and walked up to meet*
> *Napoleon Buddha pacing*
> *back and forth on the platform*
> *of red brick on the jut rock crag...*

> —ALAN GINSBERG: GRIDHAKUTA HILL, 1963

Further towards the summit, are two natural caves described as 'stone house'. Each shelter would have been used by the Buddha and his disciples. The interior of each now gleams from the application of gold leaf, a particular devotional habit of modern Thai pilgrims. In the stony forest around the summit are remains of ill-defined old brick structures.

GRIDHRAKUTA PEAK

At the top, is a paved terrace with low walls of a tiny shrine containing a statue of a meditating Buddha. The vulture-beak rock which gives name to the peak, is behind and is not readily obvious. This is a dramatic setting for Gautama Buddha to meditate, and to deliver some of his most significant teachings. It is easy to see why this place appealed. It is much cooler than the plain below; there are expansive views across the valley to the Rajgir hills and plains beyond; and there was space for the community to assemble and the Buddha to preach.

Nalanda

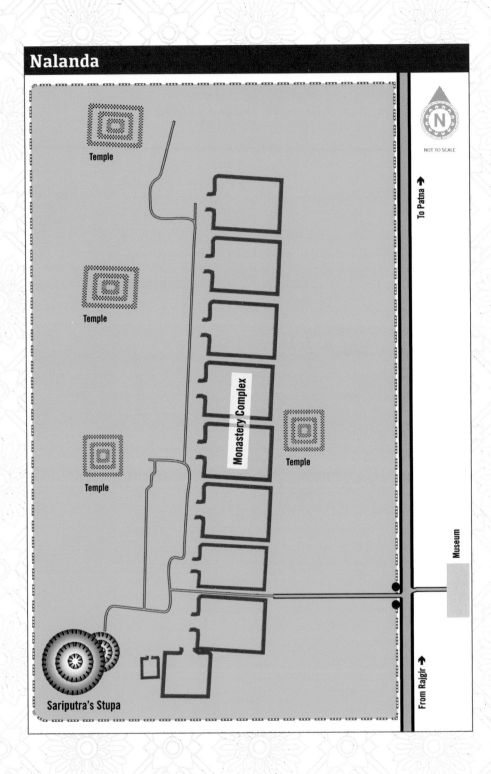

Temple

Temple

Temple

Monastery Complex

Temple

Sariputra's Stupa

N

NOT TO SCALE

To Patna →

From Rajgir →

Museum

CHAPTER FIVE

Nalanda

NALANDA is famous as the site of the world's first university. Long before it became a site of formal university education, the Buddha came here frequently. The region's early significance was enhanced when Ashoka erected a stupa to honour the Buddha's visitation and to enshrine the relics of the great monk Sariputra who was born here.

ABOVE
Walls of Nalanda University.

THE BUDDHA AND NALANDA

On the road between Rajgriha and Patna, Nalanda was a convenient stopping place. The Buddha preached several sermons here and had a famous encounter with a nonbeliever whose intention was to discredit the Buddha. The nonbeliever asked:

> *The bird which I hold in my hand—is it alive, or is it dead? If you make a mistake you will have a difficult problem.*

The Buddha famously responded by saying nothing. If he had said 'alive' the bird would have been crushed and presented to the Buddha as 'dead', and had he said 'dead' he would have been shown a live bird. One version of this story continues with the Buddha walking to the gateway, stepping over the threshold and asking his questioner:

> *Am I going in, or going out? If you make a mistake, great misfortune will befall you.*

The nonbeliever ran away without responding. He had learnt not to be trapped by words.

The remains of one of the Buddha's favoured companions Sariputra— 'foremost in knowledge' are buried in Nalanda's most imposing stupa. Sariputra's relics were also found in a stupa of Sanchi. There is no conflict in these two claims. Relics (saria) of notable monks were frequently divided after their death and distributed to the faithful. And, it was near Nalanda that the Buddha's successor Kasyapa joined the Sangha.

NALANDA UNIVERSITY

Nalanda boasted one of the earliest of all universities. The name means 'insatiable in giving', an ideal title for any successful educational institution. Nalanda was certainly successful. Xuanzang claimed that the name reflected Sakyamuni's habit of 'giving alms without intermission.'

Official accounts have it being established by the Gupta rulers of Pataliputra (Patna) in 427 CE. However, it is likely that it was a place of learning long before the 5th century as bricks from the 3rd century BCE lie beneath the imposing ruins, and there are records of early scholars.

Although Nalanda was devoted to Buddhist studies, it also trained students in fine arts, medicine, mathematics, astronomy, politics and the art of war. There were eight separate compounds, 10 temples, meditation halls, classrooms, lakes and parks. A nine-story library had three main buildings Ratnasagara, Ratnadadhi and Ratnaranjaka—'sea', 'ocean' and 'delighter' of jewels.

It was in these buildings that monks meticulously copied books and documents so that individual scholars could have their own collections. It had dormitories for students—perhaps a first for an educational institution; housed 10,000 students in the university's heyday; and provided accommodation for 2,000 professors. To cap it all, tuition was free for the students! Not surprisingly, Nalanda was the most global university of its time, attracting pupils and scholars from Korea, Japan, China, Tibet, Indonesia, Persia and Turkey. Much of our knowledge about Nalanda has been acquired from accounts of these foreign students and from donation inscriptions found on site.

It was prestigious to have studied at Nalanda. Aspiring students required a basic understanding of the scriptures and needed to pass a rigorous oral examination before being admitted. Many were turned away. There were no degrees or set course of study. Monks studied with individual masters, often for years at a time. Much emphasis was placed upon public debate where those with talent were distinguished and the less able were chastened.

Although the most important, Nalanda was only one of several educational establishments which flourished in Bihar during Pala times. It competed with, and collaborated with the other important institutions of Vikramshila and Odantapura by exchanging students, teachers and ideas. As a great university it flourished for five hundred years before slowly withering because of lessening royal patronage and diminishing Buddhist fervour. In 1197 Muslim invaders from Afghanistan torched the buildings to provide a final incendiary blow. The burning of the library—the Dharma Gunj—or 'Mountain of Truth' took several months and '...*smoke from the burning manuscripts hung for days like a dark pall over the low hills.*'

FAMOUS SCHOLARS OF NALANDA

As the principal seat of learning for seven hundred years many notable Buddhist scholars and teachers studied at Nalanda.

Nagarjuna, the great exponent of the Mahayana school, is said to have been here during the 2nd century CE, and for a period was head abbot. However this claim is disputed by modern historians, as the university is not thought to exist at that time.

Other notable scholars were Dharmakirti and Manjusrimitra, and Dharmapala, who took the teachings from Nalanda to Sumatra. In the seventh century Shantideva, studied at Nalanda. His most famous work Bodhicaryavatara —*The Guide to the Bodhisattva's Way of Life*—makes clear in simple verse how to live a life without conflict.

Xuangzang, who studied here for five years was held in high regard, being given the name Mokshadeva. Moksha is the Hindu term for 'liberation' or union with the gods and release from all rebirth, so his name implied considerable respect. Another Chinese scholar I-Tsing reached here in 673 CE, and stayed for ten years. Their two, very detailed accounts, vividly describe the active academic life of Nalanda.

Teachers important in the development of Tibetan Buddhism were Santarakshita and Padmasambhava, who is credited with first taking the Buddha's teachings to the 'Land of Snows'.

THE GUPTAS AND NALANDA

The Gupta period 320–550 CE was a time of great cultural and scientific flowering. During this time Sanskrit literature underwent its greatest development. The poet Kalidasa, whose poems and plays are said to have inspired Goethe, was one of the 'nine gems' of an early Gupta court. Under Gupta patronage, the Indian numeral system and use of 'zero' were developed; astronomers calculated that the earth was round and that moon and planets were bathed in reflected light; Indian metallurgy transformed weapons of war; and the Kama Sutra was written to long-lasting acclaim. When the Huns, from central Asia, invaded India towards the end of the sixth century the empire of the Gupta's collapsed.

THE PALAS AND NALANDA

Thereafter, India was ruled by a succession of smaller kingdoms until the rise of the Pala dynasty (750–1187 CE). Their empire, based in Bengal, was sufficiently rich and powerful to spread Indian culture and Buddhism throughout South-East Asia and the Himalaya. The great Buddhist monument of Borobudhur in Java, had its cultural origins here, as did the later monuments at Angkor in Cambodia.

From the middle of the 8th century, there was a four hundred year 'golden age' which manifested in outstanding art and architecture. The Palas—their name means 'protector'—were strong supporters of Buddhism. They established a network of universities including the great academy at Vikramshila, two hundred kilometres to the east, and reinvigorated the growth of Nalanda. It was during Pala rule that the Mahayana-Tantric form of Buddhism became dominant. One great Tantric master was Atisha. Having spent twelve years of study in Sumatra, he returned to India, and at the age of fifty-three set out from Vikramshila for Tholing in western Tibet. The consequences of his journey ultimately made Tibet the Buddhist nation we see today.

ABOVE
Meditating Buddha, Sariputra's Stupa. Gupta c. 5th century CE.

Today's Nalanda

Nalanda lies fifteen kilometres from Rajgir through rice paddy and shabby villages. There is little in the way of accommodation or restaurants, so it is best to make Nalanda a morning excursion and return to Rajgir for lunch or proceed directly from here to Patna. Because of traffic the drive onwards to Patna takes more than three hours.

The university site is what remains of ancient Nalanda. It is said that the university was once 'ten times bigger' but what you see is more than enough to impress. It is a place of brick, a massive quantity of brick—billions of bricks. Each successive dynasty, Gupta, Hashvardan and Palla, contributed their own monastery or enlarged existing structures, particularly the stupa of Sariputra. The nearest stone was Rajagriha, so brick was the favoured construction material, with only a few structures being embellished with columns or panels, of stone.

Gupta bricks are the most precise. Their edges are more sharp and the material more dense than those of the Pallas. And, inch for inch they are heavier. It would seem that the brick makers of Gupta times paid the same attention to their craft as their contemporaries who carved the sublime Gupta statues.

THE MONASTERIES

The high walls of eight almost identical monasteries stand in a straight line. Each separated from its companions by a brick paved walkway. You approach them from the rear, as they all face the west. They are impressively massive, more than two stories tall and fifty by eighty metres in area. What you see are the first two floors. Most had an additional storey of wood on top, which has long since gone. In each, are identical single rooms for students and teachers, with each monastery accommodating about sixty to eighty monks.

This was an international university, endowed by rulers both local and

BELOW

A courtyard, Nalanda University.

distant. One monastery was built around 854 CE by the King of Java and Sumatra. Guides claim that the ancient university stretched for ten kilometres and that ruins lie unexcavated beneath surrounding villages. To accommodate the thousands claimed by Xuanzang, what we see is not enough. There is no reason to doubt the Chinese monks account. So the Nalanda of a thousand years ago was probably much bigger than today.

The huge brick walls have little embellishment, apart from an occasional niche to accommodate a statue of the Tathagata. Most walls are impressively flat and vertical. And in the other plane, a thousand or more years after they were laid, each course lies horizontal, indicating that the foundations must have been substantial.

An interlinked series of drains carried off the monsoon rains, while drinking water was drawn from auspiciously sided octagonal wells—auspicious, because eight is the number of steps, in the path to enlightenment. One can only wonder at the glory of this campus, crammed with students and embellished with statues of the Buddha, furnishings and the colour of the market place.

LEFT
Votive stupas, Nalanda.

SARIPUTRA'S STUPA

Most obvious, is the vast stupa of Sariputra lying to the left of the line of monasteries. It swells up, hugely inflated from the original stupa built by Ashoka. The Emperor sought to reverence Sariputra, one of the Buddha's most important disciples with a stupa and one of his signature columns. The pillar of Ashoka has been lost and his stupa subsumed by subsequent additions. Every subsequent dynasty agreed with the imperial desire to reverence the monk, by adding layer upon layer of brick until it became the largest of all Nalanda monuments. The Guptas popped a subsidiary stupa against the main wall of brick. Some of the best Gupta images in Nalanda are housed in niches around the stupa walls. Unfortunately, they are not accessible to visitors due to security concerns.

NALANDA MUSEUM

Daily 10.30–4.30, closed Friday and public holidays.

The museum lies immediately across the road from the site. That's appropriate, as the university was a major centre for production of religious images, particularly during the Pala dynasty of the 9th and 10th centuries. During that time vast numbers of stone and bronze images of the Buddha and supporting deities were made at Nalanda and distributed widely to other centres. During those centuries the Tantric form of Buddhism had developed so the art of Nalanda depicts not only the Buddha and associated Bodhisattvas, but the later Tantric deities such as Padmapani, Prajnaparamita and Tara. The museum has fine examples of all these, along with Hindu deities, copper inscription plates, coins and pottery.

CHAPTER SIX

Patna

PATNA, at the junction of three large rivers, has three millennia of continuous habitation. Situated on rich alluvial soil and near mineral deposits, especially iron, it rapidly became important in ancient times. As Pataliputra it was capital of the Mauryan and Gupta empires, and later, a place of importance for the Pala dynasty, the Delhi Sultans and the British Raj. The name, Pataliputra has several derivations. Pattan means 'port' in Sanskrit. A more poetic version offers an origin from Patali—or 'trumpet flower' and putra which means 'son of'. In ancient times it is assumed there was a Queen Patali after whom the ancient town was named.

ABOVE
Pilgrim meditating, Bodhgaya.

FACING PAGE
Worship of the Bodhi tree (symbolising the Buddha) – Patna museum, Gupta ca. 4th century BCE.

During Buddha's life Magadha (Rajagriha) was the centre for bustling commerce and trade. King Ajatasatru recognised the need for a more strategic location and set about shifting the capital to protect his kingdom from the Licchavis, across the river. He called the new city Pataliputra. Today the city sprawls for twenty kilometres along the south bank of the Ganges, the largest city and capital of Bihar state.

BIHAR—HISTORICAL BACKGROUND

The name Bihar comes from the Sanskrit word Vihara—monastery. The monastic tradition started during the Buddha's time. During the rainy season, travel was impossible due to flooding, so the early Sangha spent three months of each year in one place. This became a time of contemplative retreat and occasion for many of the Buddha's most famous sermons. Those dwelling places developed into permanent vihara. As Buddhism became increasingly popular during the Gupta and Pala periods, many hundreds were built in the region—hence 'Bihar' the state. Monasticism was mostly a Buddhist practice, but the concept had sufficient appeal to be adopted by the Jains.

The Mauryans

In 326 BCE Alexander the Great abandoned his attempt to invade north India, retreated down the Indus and thence by land to Babylon, where at the age of thirty two, he died. Two hundred years before Alexander, the

Magadhans had shifted their capital from Rajagriha to the south bank of the Ganges. There they prospered, and with the death of Alexander a son of the Magadhan king was able to conquer all northern lands from the Indus to the mouths of the Ganges. Chandragupta Maurya, became the first Emperor of India and simultaneously founder of the Mauryan dynasty (321–185 BCE).

The Macedonians

In 305 BCE, Alexander's regional successor, Seleucus Nikator (the Conqueror), set about invading the lands beyond the Indus. The Mauryan army of six hundred thousand deterred his advance and a peace accord was negotiated which was very much to the advantage of the Indians. Much of modern Pakistan and Afghanistan was ceded to them and in return they gave Seleucus six hundred (said to be 'their oldest') elephants.

The Greek historian Megasthenes, arrived in Pataliputra as ambassador from the Seleucid court. He was astonished at the elaborate nature of the buildings and the lavish lifestyle of its inhabitants, describing a city of magnificent palaces, temples, a university, a library, gardens, and parks— 'the greatest in all India'. His four volume account gives the earliest record of 'Indica', where 'trees grew wool' (cotton) and 'reeds produced honey without bees' (sugar cane). With his extensive record of Indian customs, politics and religion he became 'the father' of Indian history. Much of what he wrote has been confirmed by recent excavations in Patna and elsewhere.

The Emperor Ashoka

It was Chandragupta's grandson who was to shine most bright. Ashoka (R 273–232 BCE) consolidated Mauryan rule and expanded the empire by military conquest. Ashoka, almost always referred to as 'The Great', holds a commanding position in world history.

An impeccable strategist and shrewd statesman he had a ruthless streak, coming to the throne by killing several brothers. There exists still, a well in Patna where he is said to have thrown their headless bodies. It is no surprise therefore that during the early part of his reign this callous quality earned him the nickname 'Chanda Ashoka'—heartless Ashoka.

As India's greatest emperor, a number of military conquests allowed him to reign over most of present-day India—'A frightening warrior and a heartless general'. His empire stretched from present-day Pakistan, Afghanistan in the west, to the present-day Bangladesh and the Indian state of Assam in the east, and as far south as northern Kerala and Andhra. He ran a very centralized administration with an efficient civil service. Taxes were fair, the empire was generally at peace and despite his strict nature he was popular.

The Kalingan war

In 265 BCE he was sixty-one years old and at the top of his game. The only region resisting his rule was Kalinga, (modern Orissa). They controlled the lucrative port trade in the Bay of Bengal and chose not to submit to the empire. Against Ashoka's vastly superior force, the Kalingans resisted, and they died. It is said that the rivers ran red with the blood of their 100,000 killed. A quarter of a million citizens were deported and many thousands of others died of disease and starvation. On witnessing the devastation of this conquest Ashoka was distraught, and in a famous monologue questioned the value of his actions:

What have I done?
If this is a victory, what is a defeat?
Is this justice or injustice?
Is it gallantry or a rout?
Is it valour to kill innocent children and women?
Did I do it to widen the empire and for prosperity,
Or to destroy the other's kingdom and splendour?

One has lost her husband,
Someone else a father,
Someone a child,
Someone an unborn infant...

What is this debris of corpses?
Are these marks of victory or defeat?
Are these vultures, crows, eagles the messengers of death or evil?

Ashoka the Buddhist

Thereafter, he enthusiastically embraced Buddhism. For the remainder of his life he promoted ahimsa (non-violence); adherence to the Dharma, or Buddhist teachings; tolerance of all sects and opinions; obedience to parents; respect for other religious teachers and priests; liberality towards friends; humane treatment of servants; and generosity towards all. A changed man indeed!

He travelled the empire propagating Buddhism; made it the state religion; built numerous monuments and monasteries; and sent missionaries to central and south-east Asia. Without his patronage it is doubtful if Buddhism would have spread so widely. Ashoka's support for Buddhism was pragmatic and ethical. His desire was to shift Buddhism from an academic religious philosophy towards a social force for good that was humanitarian, moral and popular. After his conversion to Buddhism, Ashoka built universities and monasteries. He banned hunting for sport and even set up animal hospitals. He brought new fields under cultivation and developed irrigation systems.

Throughout the empire he promulgated these teachings on carved rocks and stone pillars with magnificently carved capitals. It was India's first written language Prakit, recording the legacy of a wise and now benevolent ruler. With Ashoka as patron, Buddhism of the time exercised a tremendous influence on the lives of ordinary people. His support for missionary activity enabled wide dissemination of Buddhist belief throughout his empire and beyond.

Ashoka—the builder in stone

It was Ashoka who first made extensive use of stone for construction and sculpture. The quarries of Chunar yielded fine sandstone which was carved and polished to perfection. Ashoka's pillars, with their carved capitals, had no parallel within India. This Mauryan art flourished for only fifty years, leaving no lasting artistic influence when the dynasty collapsed.

During the reign of Ashoka, many of the wooden buildings in Pataliputra were replaced with stone structures. The royal palace alone is reported to have covered an area of four square miles. The magnificence and many pillars of the Pataliputra palace reminded Megasthenes of the great Persian palaces of Ecbatana and Susa.

Trade routes linked Pataliputra with the port on the Bengal coast, and from there to Sri Lanka, Malaysia, and the Far East. Ashoka built a system of roads which connected the Uttarapatha, the 'north road' from Pataliputra to Taxila in modern Pakistan. Today's Grand Trunk Road basically follows the route of this ancient Royal Highway.

Today's Patna

Modern Patna is a dishevelled city of four million. Despite its 2,500 years of occupation, it appears to have been assembled piece-meal from a dump yard, over the past few decades. The ancient city of the Mauryas, which so impressed Megasthenes around 390 BCE, and Faxian seven hundred years later, lies buried beneath the sands of the Ganges or has been dismembered by subsequent generations.

THE MODERN DISCOVERY OF PATALIPUTRA

Lawrence Waddell was a Glaswegian doctor who arrived in Calcutta in 1880 at the age of twenty-six. He spent six years as medical officer in Darjeeling, becoming both fascinated and shocked by Tibetan Buddhism. Despite his Calvanistic concerns, he found historical Buddhism intriguing. He strongly believed that the early Chinese explorers were accurate reporters and that Cunningham was wrong in his location of the birthplace of the Buddha. As a consequence, Waddell spent all his spare time trying to locate where the Buddha was born.

In the course of his investigations he was in Patna in 1892. Here he found remains of Ashokan palaces at Panch Pahari (the five brothers). These were five stupas described by Xuanzang. Just west of Panch Pahari, in Kumrahar, Waddell found fragments of sculptures and heard from local people that massive wooden beams were twenty feet below the surface. He had also heard, that in 1875 the Public Works Department had found similar buried beams one mile to the north. These beams match the description by Megasthenes two thousand years before.

Waddell wrote to the government of Bengal proposing that he be given permission to commence digging trial trenches. However his promotion as Professor of Chemistry and Pathology at the Calcutta Medical College prevented this. It was not until 1896 that excavation by Mr A.C. Mills uncovered stone carvings, wooden pillars and the Ashokan column described by Xuanzang. To further support Megasthenes description of a glorious Pataliputra, a 1914 excavation near the railway station exposed several hundred metres of colossal wooden walls which archaeologists assumed could extend for kilometres.

KUMRAHAR

Near the south-eastern rim of the city are the remains of Pataliputra's glorious past. Excavations at Kumrahar have revealed remnants of a massive eighty-pillared assembly hall. Faxian, came here in the 5th century and found the pillars *'shining bright as glass'*. He described a city of palace and halls so elegant that *'...no human hand of this world could accomplish'*. Faxian studied for three years in Pataliputra, copying texts and perfecting his Sanskrit.

It was here at Kumrahar, in 1914 that excavations revealed the famous 'Bodhgaya plaque', lying near to a bunch of Kushan period copper coins. This terracotta plaque is the earliest representation of the Mahabodhi temple at Bodhgaya is now on display in the Patna museum.

At Kumrahar there is a recumbent Ashokan pillar, minus its capital. Persian characters at its base indicate the close links that once existed between these distant lands. A small information centre has a model and photos of the excavation as aids to a greater past.

PATNA MUSEUM

Daily 10.30–4.30, closed Monday and public holidays.

Make sure to buy a ticket which allows entry to the 'Buddhist Relics Gallery'. You are welcomed to this rambling two-storey building by a statue of Lord Hardinge, Viceroy of India at the time it was constructed in 1915. Inside is a superb collection of stone and bronze images from the Mauryan and Pala dynasties. Displays are poorly lit and not well described but one upstairs gallery has plans for a stylish new museum, which, if funding eventuates, will more adequately display the collection.

ABOVE
Standing Buddha, Patna Museum – Pala c. 10th century CE.

87

RIGHT
Ceramic plaque of the Bodhgaya temple, Patna Museum. c. 340 CE.

THE BODHGAYA PLAQUE

Upstairs, in the Patalipatra gallery, is one of the museum's great treasures. A 15 centimetre clay tablet from around 340 CE, it is the earliest known depiction of the Bodhgaya temple. Compared to the building you saw in Bodhgaya, it seems a smaller version, lacking the four corner towers. It has the river running closely nearby with a collection of resident crocodiles.

The plaque shows a Bodhgaya-shrine similar to what Faxian saw at the beginning of the 5th century. On the right of the entrance is a prominent Ashokan pillar, with elephant capital. This pillar was not mentioned by the Chinese monk, indicating that the plaque was made before his visit. Sometime after that, and before the 7th century, the early shrine was either demolished to make way for a more grand and up-to-date temple or, more likely, it was overthrown by an earthquake. A larger structure, than what is shown on the plaque, was seen by Xuanzang in 637. It is that larger structure that you see today in Bodhgaya, with the addition of the corner towers.

Some authorities argue that the plaque is not Bodhgaya because it does not depict the tree; and because the Buddha figure shown at the base of the temple is not in 'earth witness' position but abhaya-mudra, or 'reas-

LEFT
Worship of the
'Vajrasana', the
meditation seat
of Buddha's
enlightenment,
with the Bodhi
tree above. Patna
Museum, Gupta c.
4th century BCE.

surance' gesture. However, the 'earth witness'—bhumipassa-mudra, did
not make its appearance in Bihar statues until about the 6th century, and
the earliest dated statue found at Bodhgaya by Cunningham shows the
abhaya-mudra. This would suggest that the plaque's statue depicts the
Buddha with a time-appropriate hand position.

It is also known that at Bodhgaya from an early date, a railing, subsidiary
shrines and elephant-capital pillar all existed. These are depicted on the
plaque. The argument that the plaque does not illustrate the tree can be
explained as a matter of perspective. Even today the tree can be difficult

RIGHT
Relics of the Buddha and model of the Shravasti Stupa – Patna Museum.

to see, depending on your location. And, given the tree's chequered existence, the plaque may have been made at a time when the tree was small.

All this suggests strongly that the plaque really does depict an early temple at Bodhgaya: a temple, sufficiently important to make the plaque a 'pilgrim's souvenir', one of the earliest known. Such plaques were made at various Buddhist sacred sites and sold to pilgrims as souvenirs of their journey. Their modern equivalents are usually more gaudy.

THE BUDDHA RELICS

There is a special gallery (extra charge) to see the Buddha relics found in the Shravasti Stupa in 1958. When the Buddha died in ca 350 BCE his relics were distributed to eight places. At each site a stupa was erected and these became known as the Mahastupas—or great stupas. Shravasti was one of that original eight. Two hundred years later the emperor Ashoka opened all but one of the Mahastupas, took 9/10ths of the relics and enshrined them within many other stupas throughout his kingdom.

It is not recorded how the Licchavi people of Shravasti felt about the emperor's high handed action. In an imperial stroke he had deprived them of nine tenths of their revered relics of The World Honoured One. You can imagine that they might decide to make sure they did not lose the other portion. Which is probably why they re-buried them, within their stupa, deeply and tightly in a fragile casket of turned stone, barely six centimetres high.

In the modern, well lit, relics gallery a photo of the 1958 excavation shows the tiny reliquary deeply buried, in earth and without the protection of a larger coffer. The Licchavis certainly concealed well.

Two hundred and fifty years after their efforts, the stupa was enlarged with bricks and another layer was provided later. Both of these additions to the stupa were opened by 'grave robbers', presumably without success.

It remained for the formal excavation in 1958 to find the sarira that you see in the Patna museum today. Of all the Buddha relics reverenced throughout the Buddhist world, these may be the most 'genuine'

STATUES

On entering the ground floor sculpture gallery, you arrive, face to bosom, with another museum treasure—The Chauri Bearer, dated to the times of Ashoka, roughly 300 BCE. She is life sized, carved from the same Chunar sandstone used for the emperor's columns, and with the same immaculate polish. Casually tossed over her right shoulder is a chauri, a white yak's tail fly whisk, traditional symbol of Indian royalty and power. At one time she would have stood guarding an imperial palace, now her compass is much less royal. She is not the lesser for that. This is a remarkable image of Ashokan style.

BELOW
The Chauri Bearer. Gupta c. 3rd century BCE.

Further into the same gallery, flanking the entrance to the next, are two justly acclaimed Buddhist images. Maitreya—the Buddha Who is Next to Come and Avaloketeshvara—the Buddha of Compassion, are masterworks of the 11th century Pala dynasty. They are carved from dark, highly polished stone. Each sits casually, with one leg folded half facing each other across the passage way with their right hand raised in the gesture of fearlessness.

GOLGHAR

Golghar, 'the round house', granary resembles a giant upside down turnip. It was built in response to the devastating famine of 1770. This disaster, a result of flawed policies of the East India Company caused the deaths of ten million people, a third of the population. Despite good intentions, it was never used.

BUDDHA GHAT

A few hundred metres from Golghar is Buddha Ghat, named during the Holy One's last visit. It was from here that he set off, at the age of eighty, on his final journey towards Vaishali and his eventual death at Kushinagar.

'Bodhi ghat' is not easy to find, and is only for the seriously competitive Buddhist pilgrim. A concrete pillared pavilion shelters a set of concrete steps that once lead to the Ganges, which is now more than four kilometres distant. The locals are intrigued by your presence. They do know the name, but not the significance of why you might be here to reverence a departed human sage.

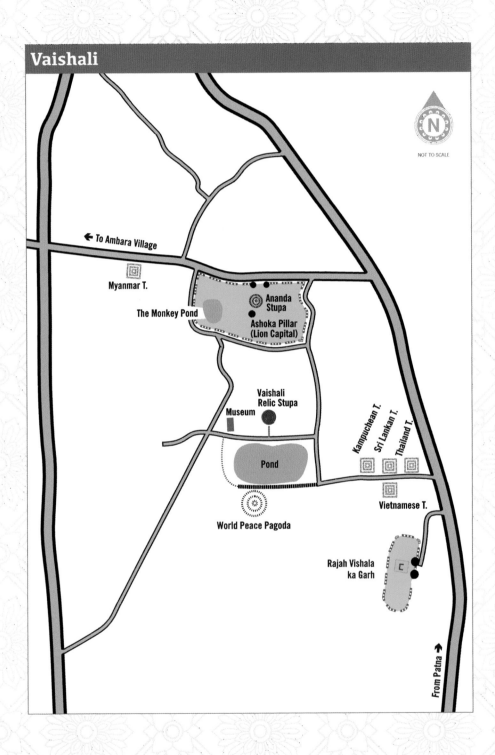

Vaishali

N

NOT TO SCALE

← To Ambara Village

Myanmar T.

The Monkey Pond

Ananda Stupa

Ashoka Pillar (Lion Capital)

Vaishali Relic Stupa

Museum

Pond

Kampuchean T.

Sri Lankan T.

Thailand T.

Vietnamese T.

World Peace Pagoda

Rajah Vishala ka Garh

From Patna →

CHAPTER SEVEN

Vaishali

·····

IT was in Vaishali that Gautama Buddha preached many important sermons, including the Vimalakirti Sutra and, the Sermon of the lamps. It was at Vaishali that he admitted women to the Sangha and where he is said to have received the gift of honey from the monkey. He came here from Rajgriha on his final visit and at that time predicted he would die within three months.

Vaishali was founded by the mythical King Vishala. He was a descendent of Manu, the First Man whose reign was many thousands of years before present times. Later, his kingdom became a republic, which during the Buddhist era was to prove a serious rival to the Kingdom on Magadha. Ultimately they were defeated by Magadha and were later absorbed into the Mauryan dynasty.

MAHAVIRA AND JAINISM AT VAISHALI

Mahavira, the 24th, and last, of the Jain tirthankaras (ford-builders), was born at Vaishali in 527 BCE, a slightly older contemporary of the Buddha. The paths of these two teachers, criss-crossed this region of India, but there is no record of them ever meeting.

Jainism and Buddhism differ from Hinduism in rejecting priestly ritual and distinctions of caste. However, unlike the Buddha's Middle Way, Jainism considers extreme asceticism to be the road to salvation—the accepted way for a Jain monk to end his life is to starve himself to death.

Jains accept many dietary and behavioural restrictions in order to avoid harming the multitude of souls that they believe are present in everything: animals, insects, plants and even inanimate material. A non-proselytizing religion, it never spread beyond the boundaries of India. Today, they are about 5% of the population. Because mercantile occupations offer the least chance of direct harm to plants and animals, Jain laymen tend to make their living as traders, merchants, and shopkeepers. Their

ABOVE

Ashokan Pillar with its lion capital and surrounding votive stupas, Vaishali.

93

significance within the modern Indian economy is much greater than numbers would suggest.

TEACHINGS ON KARMA

Both Jainism (the name means 'conqueror') and Buddhism originated as reactions to the ritualised Brahmanism, at that time the dominant practice of early Hinduism. All three religions share a fundamental belief in karma. For the Jains, it was believed that a person's situation in this present life is the result of good or bad deeds accumulated in previous lives. And Brahmins believed that certain ritual actions were inherently good.

The Buddha taught vigorously against these views. He agreed that karma, or action by an individual, had consequences which could result in a good effect, a bad effect or a neutral one. However, for the Buddha, karmic effects, good or bad, were dependent not only on the action, but also on the intention of the person performing that action. For Buddhists this teaching does not justify outrageous actions committed with 'good intent' as individuals are expected to use wisdom and compassion to assess a given situation.

Contrary to much contemporary and indeed modern belief, the Buddha did not hold that current misfortune was the result of 'bad karma from previous lives'. He taught that such a claim was essentially unknowable, but he was adamant, that negative unskilful actions performed now will inevitably bring future suffering:

If one speaks with an impure mind, suffering follows even as the cartwheel follows the hoof of the ox drawing the cart...

BELOW
The Ananda Stupa at Vaishali.

HINDUISM AT VAISHALI

Aeons before the Jains and Buddhists, Vaishali was sacred to the Hindus. As part of the Hindu creation myth, it was at Vaishali that the gods and demons conferred before stirring the cosmic ocean of milk, to bring forth the world as we know it.

THE BUDDHA AND VAISHALI

The Buddha visited Vaishali several times and it was here that he preached several important sutras. Unlike Magadha, it was not an absolute monarchy, but a form of republic where a small selection of leaders got to choose their leader on a regular basis.

The Vaishali republicans had long sustained an uneasy relationship with the kings of Magadha. Before the Buddha's final visit, King Ajatasatru of Magadha had consulted with him about impending hostilities between the two states. The Buddha's counsel of conciliation was ineffective. Within a few months of the Buddha's death, Vaishali was overrun and thereafter the republic was part of an ascendant Magadha.

THE ADMISSION OF WOMEN

At a time in which the status of women was regarded as an inferior one to that of men, the Buddha preached a different doctrine. Buddhism is unique among Indian religions in that Buddha explicitly stated that a woman was as capable of nirvana (enlightenment) as a man. The prevailing opinion of the time gave little status to women, with unmarried women in particular being regarded as particularly inferior. The Brahmanical view of the time was that women should do nothing independently and be forever subject to her father, husband and even her sons following the death of her spouse.

Despite his preaching and his views, Gautama resisted admitting women to the society of monks. A pragmatist, he felt that their admission would create too many problems. The Buddha was concerned that society would turn against his teachings if he were seen to be luring away their wives and daughters. This could be interpreted as a threat to the norm of male dominance. That this was a practical concern is obvious in the verse of a subsequent nun, called Mutta:

> I'm free. Ecstatically free
> I'm free from three crooked things:
> The mortar,
> The pestle
> And my hunchback husband.
> All that drags me back is cut—cut!

However, the unjust nature of exclusion was questioned by the Tathagata's step-mother Prajapati. She was the sister of Maya, the Buddha's birth-mother and was jointly married to the Buddha's father. After Maya's early death, Prajapati had suckled the infant-Buddha and was effectively his emotional mother. After his enlightenment, she had been a devoted follower of the Buddha for several years and frequently petitioned him for admission and was rejected. Later, she arrived at Vaishali with five hundred followers '...their feet swollen, tired and tearful...'. They were met by Ananda who twice requested the Buddha to allow their admission to the Sangha, but each time he was unsuccessful. On the third occasion Ananda convinced Gautama to change his mind. So it was, that at Vaishali women were admitted into the Sangha. As one modern authority says:

> ...in view of the available evidence, it may be concurred that the position of women in Buddhist India was more enviable and more honourable that it had been in pre-Buddhist days. Daughters and widows were no longer regarded with such undisguised despair and on the contrary, both they and wives commanded more respect and ranked as individuals. They enjoyed more independence and a wider liberty to guide and follow their own lives.

AMRAPALI THE COURTESAN

Amrapali was the most beautiful and most renowned of Vaishali's courtesans. In spite of her profession, she had great status in the town, being in effect 'first lady'. Her standing and indeed, notoriety, was in part due to her charms, and also to her relationship with King Bimbisara of Magadha. There are several stories.

One relates that at the age of sixteen, she fell in love with Bimbisara, at that time a young prince. They had a son called Jivaka. The story relates that mother and son were rejected by Licchavi society, and that this led her to become a courtesan. Because of her beauty and charm, fame and wealth followed.

Another story has the lovers more mature. A period when, Amrapali was the premier courtesan of Vaishali and Bimbisara was the King of Magadha. Hearing of Amrapali's great beauty, Bimbisara had sneaked into Vaishali in disguise for a week of dalliance. Unfortunately, this was a time when both nations were at war. When the King's impudence was discovered, the enraged citizens of Vaishali renewed their assault on the Maghadhans.

In the Buddha's time, strictures of caste determined who were to be your friends and associates, or your dining companions. The Buddha's teaching and conduct was in striking contrast to the social mores of the day. In his daily life, and within his community, he did not discriminate on the basis of a person's caste, occupation or gender.

His acceptance of all members of society is well illustrated by his relationship with Amrapali. They met many times. She became a significant supporter and ultimately a nun and respected member of his followers. During one early visit of the Buddha, she hastened out of the city to invite him for a meal. The Buddha immediately accepted her invitation, to the chagrin of the Licchavi princes who offered Amrapali a hundred thousand gold coins to give up her right to host the Buddha. Amrapali refused, dined with the Buddha and gave him a gift of her mango grove— Amrapali vana. A monastery was built in her garden, and it was here that the newly appointed female members of the Sangha were housed.

Soon thereafter, she renounced her position as courtesan and accepted the Buddhist faith. During her time as a nun she composed a famous poem, one of the earliest known by an Indian woman, detailing the reality of her ageing body. Its eighteen verses conclude:

> Such was this body,
> now: decrepit, the home of pains,
> many pains.
> An old house with its plaster
> fallen off,
> not false is the utterance of the
> speaker of truth.

She remained a nun until her death. When the Buddha heard Amrapali had died, he went to the cremation ground. He delayed the start of the fire by delivering a lengthy sermon, thus forcing the Sangha and nobles of Vaishali to see her beauty decompose and enabling Amrapali to use her body one last time, as a teaching on impermanence.

THE GIFT OF THE MONKEY

Less historically verified, but generally accepted as occurring at Vaishali, is the legend of the gift of the monkey. The story relates that a monkey observed an elephant attending the Buddha. Wishing to do something similar, he offers a stick of honey on a plantain leaf to the Buddha. Noticing that the Buddha does not eat, the monkey observes the presence of insect eggs on the honey. Removing these, he re-offers the honey which the Buddha readily eats. The monkey is so delighted he leaps around in a tree, loses his grip and falls to his death only to be re-born in heaven. The moral being, that good deeds rendered to others, especially towards the Sangha, may be rewarded by a better re-birth.

THE VIMALAKIRTI SUTRA

Vaishali is also the place where the Buddha preached many important sermons, amongst them the Vimalakirti Nirdesa Sutra—The Teaching of Vimalakirti. Vimalakirti was a wealthy disciple of the Buddha, a lay practitioner said to be as enlightened and clear as the Buddha. In the Sutra he feigns illness. When the Buddha hears of this, he asks each disciple in turn to visit Vimalakirti to ask about his health. Successively, the disciples refuse on the grounds of prior encounters with Vimalakirti when he had bested them in dharma encounters. Eventually Manjusri, the bodhisattva of wisdom agrees to visit. The sutra relates their encounter in Vimalakirti's hut. Some eighty thousand buddhas and bodhisattvas crowd in to watch. Tradition relates that the tiny house of Vimalakirti, where this encounter took place was in the mango grove of Amrapali. Unfortunately, no trace remains.

Essentially, the sutra is about non-duality. The sutra shows the illusory nature of what appears to be difference. It demonstrates that, the apparent differences between men and women, sacred and secular, samsara and nirvana are ultimately illusory. And, that the realities of this life are in complete accord with the spiritual, and are indeed one. And that nirvana is not a state aspired to after death, but a deep understanding that nirvana is the awareness of being awake to this life right now. And indeed that life and death, practice and enlightenment are fundamentally one thing.

Much of the sutra's appeal is its humour, especially where Shariputra takes the part of the 'fall guy', constantly asking dumb questions only to be corrected. The most famous encounter occurs when Vimalakirti is asked by Manjusri: '...what is a bodhisattva's entry into the Dharma gate of non-duality?' only to have Vimalakirti respond with silence. Saying nothing, may not seem like an answer to the profound question—how does a spiritual seeker get to 'know' reality? By staying silent, Vimalakirti eloquently demonstrates that language is not adequate to provide an understanding of non-dual reality, you have to experience this for yourself.

THE VAISHALI MAHASTUPA

When the Buddha died, some of his relics were given to the Licchavi's of Vaishali. They built a stupa which is now reduced to a mound of low bricks. Its location is exactly as described by Xuanzang. Excavation of this stupa in 1958 confirmed that it had originally been made of rammed earth which had been enlarged with bricks 250 years later and on four subsequent occasions. The 1958 exploration revealed the relic casket, now displayed in the Patna museum.

THE 'LAMPS' SERMON

During the last rainy season of the Buddha's life he stayed in the Vaishali area for three months. At the nearby village of Belua he became ill and was asked by Ananda what the community should do in the event of the Buddha's death. In response he delivered his famous '...be lamps unto yourselves' sermon:

> Therefore, O Ananda, be lamps unto yourselves. Rely on yourselves, and do not rely on external help. Hold fast to the truth as a lamp. Seek salvation alone in the truth. Look not for assistance to anyone besides yourselves...

The 'lamps sermon', does not mean that teachers and teaching are without value, just as Vimalakirti's silence does not mean that words and discussion are superfluous. But is does require that practitioners of the Buddha Way trust their judgement in assessing the value and truth of what is being offered to them.

Buddhism is unique amongst the great religions by not creating an infallible rule book. The Buddha, by rejecting religious authority; by not designating an heir apparent; and by encouraging his disciples to find enlightenment within their own self, opened the way for subsequent schism and dispute. That is true, but such an approach also encouraged a way of living that was vigorously self-reliant and not dependent on ritual or dogma. Buddhist practice is underpinned at a very fundamental level by each practitioner's personal experience of reality revealed during meditation, together with the guidance of realised teachers. This shared experience creates a profoundly unified Buddhist community such that the differences of sect, clothing and ritual are in essence, superficial.

THE BUDDHA'S DEPARTURE FROM VAISHALI

Eventually it was time for him to leave Vaishali. He was eighty years old and tiring. After assembling the community he delivered a sermon encouraging them to be steadfast in their practice and at the conclusion announced his impending death:

> ...the final extinction of the Tathagata will take place before long. I now exhort you, saying: All component things must grow old and be dissolved again. Seek ye for that which is permanent, and work out your salvation with diligence.

ANANDA AND VAISHALI

There is a story about the death of Ananda, who is said to have lived for one hundred and twenty years. When he knew he was dying, he set out from Rajgraha for Vaishali. On the bank of the Ganges he found on one side, the Magadhans of Rajgriha and on the opposite bank, the Vrijjans of Vaishali, each there to celebrate him, and to collect 'their share' of his remains. To avoid conflict, 'His worn out body suddenly divided into two equal parts and the body was left like a folded vesture on the two sides of the river.' Each community took their share of the holy monk's remains. Those belonging to Vaishali are buried in the stupa of Ashoka.

THE SECOND BUDDHIST COUNCIL

A hundred years after the final visit by the Buddha, Vaishali was the site of the Second Buddhist Council. The primary purpose of the meeting was to hammer out the rules of monkish conduct. They were success-ful in this, and also in a decision to dispatch missionaries to different parts of the world to spread the Dharma. Buddhist unity had started to fracture before this time. Despite their efforts, the council were unable to settle the differences which, in time, led to the development of Ma-hayana (Great Vehicle) Buddhism and its separation from the Theravada (Way of the Elders) group.

EARLY PILGRIMAGE TO VAISHALI—THE BUDDHA'S BEGGING BOWL

For several hundred years after the Buddha's death Vaishali was an important place of pilgrimage. Its fame depended on the various shrines commemorating events of the Buddha's life and the city's most famous relic, the Buddha's begging bowl. One of the few personal possessions of Buddhist monks, then and now was a begging bowl. The Buddha was no exception. His bowl was probably made from bronze or copper. On his final walk to Kushinagar the Buddha laid down this bowl to discourage the citizens of Vaishali from accompanying him. This exchange took place at Kesariya.

This original bowl was taken back to Vaishali for veneration. In the centuries following the Buddha's death the early container was replaced with a large polished rock bowl, almost a metre high and of larger diameter. By the time of the Kushan ruler Kanishka, in the 2nd century CE, this large stone bowl weighing many kilograms, was acknowledged as 'the' Buddha's begging bow. It was an object of reverence within a Vaishali temple

ABOVE
The Buddha's bowl, Kabul museum.
Donna Mulhearn, Kabul 2011.

and was probably used to receive donations. Despite being a great supporter of Buddhism, the Kushan ruler King Kanishka invaded Vaishali and took the bowl to his capital of Purushpur—present day Peshawar in Pakistan. Two centuries later, around 402 CE the stone bowl was seen by Faxian who commented on its miraculous properties, in that:

> When poor people throw into it a few flowers, it becomes immediately full, while some very rich people, wishing to make offering of many flowers, might not stop till they had thrown in hundreds, thousands, and myriads of bushels, and yet would not be able to fill it.

And, Faxian noted that a different royal thief was less successful in securing the relic for himself:

> ...he made a large elephant be grandly caparisoned, and placed the bowl upon it. But the elephant knelt down on the ground, and was unable, to go forward. Again he caused a four-wheeled wagon to be prepared in which the bowl was put to be conveyed away. Eight elephant were then yoked to it, and dragged it with their united strength, but neither were they able to go forward. The King knew that the time for an association between himself and the bowl had not yet arrived, and was sad and deeply ashamed of himself. Forthwith he built a stupa at the place and a monastery, and left a guard to watch (the bowl), making all sorts of contributions.

With time, and a different invader, the bowl became a Muslim relic and was inscribed with six rows of verse from the Koran. Until a few decades ago it was used in the Jama Mosque in Kandahar as a storage bowl, for washing hands and feet before prayer. It now graces the entrance of the Kabul museum in Afghanistan. Carved from speckled black marble, its Buddhist origins are attested by a graceful lotus base. The Koranic inscription undoubtedly saved it from obliteration during the destruction of more obvious Buddhist items by the Taliban.

Today's Vaishali

It is seventy kilometres from Patna to Vaishali, sacred to both Jains and Buddhists. You drive north across 'the largest single river bridge in the world'. A touch short of 6 km in length the Gandhi Setu spans the main Ganges river, to link the northern and southern regions of Bihar.

RAJAH VISHALA KE GARH—THE FORT OF KING VISHALA

Coming from Nalanda, the first archaeological site encountered is one attributed to the mythical founder of the city, King Vishala. A low mound stretches for several hundred metres. Only a small section has been excavated of this presumed fort of Vaishali's founder.

Old books describe a huge assembly hall, built around the 3rd century CE. It was said to be capable of seating an auspicious number of delegates—7,707. But in fact, the ruins you see today are those of accommodation or administration. The hall remains buried, somewhere in the surrounding area.

However, at this site the Buddha delivered his famous Vimalakiriti Sutra and it was here that his favoured disciple Shariputra became enlightened.

THE STUPA OF THE RELIC

In 637 CE, when Xuangzang passed through Vaishali he found few practicing monks. He reported where and what the Buddha taught at Vaishali and it was he who described the significance of the relic temple:

> *...After the nirvana of the Buddha, a former king of this country obtained a portion of the relics of his body, and to honour them as highly as possible, raised this stupa.*

At one time the relic stupa must have been large and impressive. Nowadays, it is at ground level, protected from the elements with a corrugated iron umbrella. Inside this stupa the Licchavis placed their share of Buddha's remains, which were divided by Ashoka two hundred years, later. The Licchavis were so successful in concealing their remaining relic that it was not discovered until the excavations of 1958. That soapstone casket, now in the Patna museum may be the most 'genuine' of all relics of the Buddha.

RIGHT
Sheltering dome, the Stupa of the Relic, Vaishali.

ARCHAEOLOGY MUSEUM

Daily 10.00–5.00, closed Friday and public holidays.

Immediately adjacent to the Relic Stupa, is the museum. Most of the display is of small terracotta objects. Other notable objects are few, but rewarding.

Facing the entrance is a black-stone statue of a crowned Buddha in earth-witness position. From the Pala period, it has an inscription of the donor: *Uchaba the writer, son of Manikya.*

One stone upright from a railing has a representation of the purchase of the Jetavana grove at Shravasti five hundred kilometres to the west. This delightfully depicts the square gold coin's required to 'cover the ground' arriving by bullock cart.

THE PILLAR SITE

Where Ashoka placed one of his most impressive columns is one of the prettiest locations, of all the eight places of pilgrimage. It is sited here by the Emperor as a reminder that the Buddha was often in this region. There is visual harmony between the superb Ashokan column; the large imperial stupa which it overlooks; the clutch of surrounding small stupas; and the tank of the monkeys, dug by them to serve the Buddha.

On top of the Vaishali Pillar is a life-sized recumbent lion, symbol of royalty. The lion faces north in the direction of the Buddha's final journey. The highly polished sandstone carving is stylistically similar to that at Sarnath but less dramatic. There is some debate as to whether this is an 'Ashokan' pillar. The pedestal for the lion-base is square, instead of round, and the lion is not well rendered, but it is an appropriate symbolic statement for what would seem to fit the emperor's intent, and for this author it is Ashokan.

LEFT
**Remains of the
Stupa of the
Relic, Vaishali**

Of the twenty known Ashokan pillars, only those at Vaishali and Sarnath have their capitals intact. All Ashokan pillars found in different parts of the country have been made from Chunar sandstone, brought from a quarry beyond Varanasi, at least 350 km upstream from here. It beggars belief how this 18 metre single block was brought to this place more than two millennia ago. It does not bear the usual Ashokan inscription in graceful Brahmi. Instead, near the base is an inscription in the as yet untranslated 'shell' script. High on the column are many graffiti from early English travellers.

THE ANANDA STUPA

The lion capital faces a large brick stupa built by Ashoka to rehouse the relics of Ananda, the Buddha's cousin and a favourite disciple.

THE WORLD PEACE PAGODA

There is something comforting about the series of World Peace Pagodas built by the Japanese. It's like putting on a familiar garment from another time. Their offering at Vaishali is much the same as others, but impressively large. A small portion of the Buddha's relics found at the nearby Stupa of the Relic, are enshrined here.

AMRAPALIVANA

Amrapalivana, the mango-grove of Amrapali, was at her home village of Ambara seven kilometres to the west of the pillar site. Today, there is little to see. Of Amrapali's gift of a mango grove, there's a tank overlooked by an old pipal tree decked with Buddhist flags. To reassure you that you are in the right place, there is a sign from the Bihar Department of Archaeology pointing you towards a school, where her house is said to have stood. And, there's the ageless story of how a courtesan was transformed.

CHAPTER EIGHT

Kesariya & Pava (Fazilnagar)

THESE two places lie along the route between Vaishali and Kushinagar, the final route taken by the Buddha. The distance is about two hundred kilometres. At least a ten day walk for an ailing eighty year old. When the Buddha set out, it was early May, the pre-monsoon time, when survival on the plains of India is a struggle for all living things, including Buddhas. The countryside at that time, is dessicated and dusty, with temperatures in the high 30s celsius. It could not have been an easy final journey.

THE KESARIYA STUPA

When the Buddha left Vaishali for the last time he was accompanied by many citizens begging him not to leave. At Kesariya (Kessputta) the Buddha put down his begging bowl in an attempt to divert them but the crowd pressed on. It was not until he created an illusion of a river in flood that they were deterred. This begging bowl of the Buddha, was first enshrined at Kesariya before being taken to Vaishali. Ashoka built a stupa to commemorate this event. Subsequent dynasties, added extra layers of bricks like a growing onion. Its final enlargement was with the Guptas, probably in the 5th century. A huge terraced structure ultimately resulted.

ABOVE
Taiwanese monks at Kesariya.

FACING PAGE, UPPER
The Kesariya Stupa.

FACING PAGE, LOWER
Taiwanese monks pray at Kesariya Stupa.

Today's Kesariya

The drive from Vaishali is through an immensity of fertile, rich, productive fields. Rice and sugar cane stretch to the horizon. Despite this agricultural largesse, the workers who service these fields are poor. Their homes are mostly hovels of bamboo, with thatch roofs and dirt floors. Maybe a third, are made from haphazard brick. They are clean in a house-proud sort of way, and on public view, is the family's wealth, a few goats or a tethered buffalo, and many children. These are fields where the First Noble Truth, that suffering exists, is patently obvious.

The Kesariya stupa.

At Kesariya, a vast stupa now stands in open farmland, miles from any major centre of population, then or now. At '104 feet' tall it is higher by a foot than the great Borobudhur complex in Indonesia. Both were made in the shape of a mandala, or cosmic diagram. Most levels have numerous niches to house Buddha images. These are unusual in construction, being made from a composite of brick dust and lime, reinforced with iron rods. Unfortunately, they lack the usual Gupta grace. The stupa's impressive size and significance was commented on by the Chinese pilgrims, Faxian in 450 CE and Xuanzang two hundred years later.

ANCIENT PAVA

Ancient Pava is now the Muslim town of Fazilnagar, a hundred kilometres from Kesariya and about fifteen kilometres east of Kushinagar. Pava was the second capital of the Mallas, rulers of the Kushinagar region. Pava is also the town where the great Jain saint, Mahavira attained enlightenment and it is the town where the Buddha took his last meal.

THE BUDDHA'S LAST MEAL

For the walking Buddha, several days beyond Kesariya brought him to the village of Pava. Here he was invited to a meal by Cunda, usually described as a blacksmith. Cunda was probably a wealthy man, as metal was a much more rare commodity during those times.

Immediately after taking the meal the Buddha took violently ill but insisted on carrying on to Kushinagar. Before leaving, the Buddha sought to reduce any guilt felt by Cunda. He stressed to Ananda that whatever happened Cunda should not be criticised for providing food which was tainted.

Today's ancient Pava (modern day Fazilnagar)

A hundred metres down a rough lane, is a little-cared-for brick pile, the Cunda Stupa, erected over the site of his house. The original stupa was built shortly after the Buddha's death and was added to by the Guptas. It must have been impressive once.

Few modern pilgrims come to Fazilnagar. The guides say it is because they choose not to acknowledge 'the man who killed the Buddha'. This seems a harsh judgement on Cunda, who was being hospitable by offering a meal. It would be interesting to track down Cunda's descendants. Most trades in India are hereditary. So it is not totally unrealistic that one might find Cunda's relatives, even allowing for their probable change in religion and one and a half millennia of separation.

TOWARDS KUSHINAGAR

Fifteen kilometres further on is the small town of Kushinagar, where the Buddha died. It was the full moon night in the month of Veshakha (May). The generally accepted year is 483 BCE but some modern scholars feel that 404 BCE is more correct. At that time of the year, the whole of India awaits the monsoon. The countryside is cracked and baked from months of punishing sun. Plants and people wilt, and even the birds are silenced. On that day, feeling very unwell, fatigued and old, the Buddha must surely have welcomed his final resting place.

BELOW
Indian monks at Kesariya.

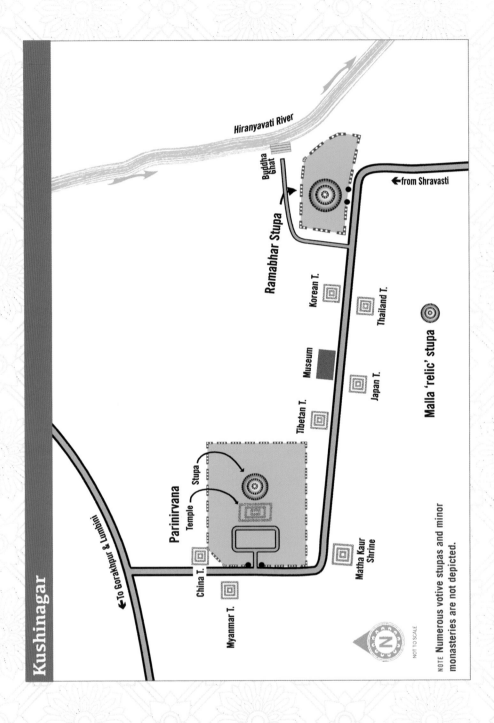

Kushinagar

Hiranyavati River

Buddha Ghat

Ramabhar Stupa

←from Shravasti

Korean T.

Thailand T.

Museum

Japan T.

Malla 'relic' stupa

Tibetan T.

Parinirvana

Stupa

Temple

To Gorakhpur & Lumbini

China T.

Matha Kaur Shrine

Myanmar T.

N

NOT TO SCALE

NOTE **Numerous votive stupas and minor monasteries are not depicted.**

CHAPTER NINE

Kushinagar

KUSHINAGAR was the place where the Buddha died. He died as a man, like any other. But, as the Buddha, his passing had extra significance. His passing is described as Parinirvana, (completed nirvana), a state which is beyond life and death.

At Gautama's time, belief in the certainty of reincarnation was universal throughout the sub-continent. Everyone knew in their deepest marrow, that to be reborn was an inevitable accompaniment to living. They lived and died hoping that rebirth would make things better. For modern humans, who grew up

ABOVE
**The Parinirvana
Stupa (left)
and temple,
Kushinagar.**

with the 'one life' model of the Judeo-Christian and Islamic traditions, it is not easy to appreciate the oppressive nature of living with perpetual rebirth. Yet it was a belief that deeply permeated the world of the Buddha, such that Gautama told his followers that in previous lives they had left behind *'a pile of bones bigger than a mountain'* and *'shed more tears than the waters of the four great oceans'.*

This endless cycle was anticipated with dread rather than optimism. Few could be certain that they had performed sufficient good works to assure a favourable rebirth. What if their return was as a low-status human; into one of the hellish realms; or as an animal? Being human is the most fortunate state, no matter how materially lowly. In the human form there is always the possibility to enhance one's merit by good works, and thus raise the stakes in your future rebirth. As an animal, spiritual advancement is well-nigh impossible and might take a myriad of lifetimes.

Today, if privileged, we are not likely to experience extreme hunger or the indignities of disease without medical relief. Yet, such were the circumstance of most humans who have ever lived, and it was a reality during Gautama's time. Thus the prospect of many lifetimes of uncertainty and the accompanying realities of war, of disease and of pain was not a future to anticipate with enthusiasm.

However, for many at the time, it was probably 're-death' that caused the greatest dread. The process of dying in humans is rarely easy, and much more so in pre-medical times. An endless succession of death, and death, and death, would daunt even the most phlegmatic. Seeking a spiritual release from such horror was a natural development.

It was widely believed that exceptional individuals could go beyond the cycle of rebirth to a state of cessation. The Parinirvana of the Buddha was the expression of this longing for the ultimate goal. Just how contemporary Buddhists interpret nirvana, as well as the Parinirvana of the Buddha, depends on the school to which they belong and to their degree of individual realisation. Appropriately, there is no single defining interpretation. Ultimately, you have to work it out for yourself.

THE PARINIRVANA–'DEATH' OF THE BUDDHA

It is fifteen kilometres from Pava, site of his last meal, and Kushinagar. The Buddha was exhausted and thirsty. After crossing the Hiranyavati river he rested and asked Ananda to bring water from the stream. Two times Ananda resisted, saying that the water had been made dirty and undrinkable, by passing wagons. After the third request, Ananda went to the river to find it miraculously cleared. At this place the Matha Kaur statue was erected to commemorate the event.

In the Buddha's time Kushinagar was not an important place. For Gautama's constant companion of twenty five years, Ananda, it lacked the gravitas which he felt should be associated with the death of the Buddha. To him it was a rundown provincial nowhere. Not a proper place for any death, let alone that of 'The World Honoured One'. Kushinagar was in Ananda's view:

'...a wattle and daub town, a town in the middle of the jungle, a branch township!'

But the Buddha would, or could, go no further. He lay down in a grove of sala trees belonging to the Mallas. He laid on his right side, with one leg resting on the other and asked the assembled monks if they had any doubts as to the truth of his teaching. None responded. His last words before dying were:

'Decay is inherent in all component things, but the truth will remain forever. Work out your salvation with diligence!'

The next day, Ananda went to Kushinagar and told the Mallas to deal with the body in the way they deemed proper for 'a king of kings'. Elaborate homage was paid to the dead Buddha. Various delays meant that the cremation did not take place for seven days. When they heard of the Buddha's death, followers came from all directions to attend the cremation. Eventually things were ready at the site of the Ramabhar Stupa, about one kilometre east of the Parinirvana temple, but the fire would not light because Mahakasyapa had not yet arrived. When he came, the pyre spontaneously ignited.

1ST DISPERSAL OF THE BUDDHA RELICS

Upon hearing that the Buddha had died and had been cremated, eight groups claimed the relics so they could build a stupa over them. A war-like situation developed, with little willingness to compromise, until a Brahmin called Drona, reminded the contestants of the Buddha's doctrine of non-violence. He arranged for the relics to be divided into eight parts which were distributed to:

- The Mallas of Kushinagar–today, a known stupa, at Kushinagar.
- The Magadhans of Rajagriha–a known stupa, at Rajgir.
- The Licchavis of Vaishali–a known stupa, at Vaishali.
- The Sakyas of Kapilavastu–a known stupa, at Kapilavastu.
- The Bulis of Allakappa.
- The Koliyas of Ramagrama–a known stupa, at Ramagrama.
- The Brahmans of Vethadipa.
- The Mallas of Pava.

There were insufficient relics for:

- The Moriyas of Pipphalavana, who took residual ashes,
- or for the peace-maker Drona himself, who took the urn.

Today, we know the location of five of the original-relic stupas. These are The Mahastupas. There are three 'lost' Mahastupas as well as the two 'lost' secondary stupas which held the ashes and the urn.

BELOW
Votive stupas, Kushinagar.

ASHOKA'S DISPERSAL OF THE RELICS

After his conversion to Buddhism, Ashoka sought to divide the Buddha's relics. While redistribution of the relics was ostensibly an act of faith for Ashoka, it was also a smart political move. Redistribution helped consolidate his empire by establishing the boundaries of his ideal Buddhist kingdom protected by the relics of the Buddha.

Relics from seven of the eight Mahastupas were collected by the emperor for division into 84,000 portions. Eighty-four thousand was believed to be the number of atoms in the human body, hence one stupa for each atom of the Buddha. One should not take the figure of 84,000 literally, but there is good evidence that a major re-distribution of relics did take place under Ashoka's supervision. Thus the faithful could simultaneously visit sites of the great events in the Buddha's life and acquire merit by taking darshan, by being in the presence of his actual remains.

Obviously, survival of these re-distributed relics would depend on the degree of devotion of each local community, its resources, and just how strong the Ashokan administration was in each region. It is not surprising therefore that only a few of the Ashokan-distribution stupas have survived to the present day. The most famous Ashokan Stupa is at Sanchi, near Bhopal in Madhya Pradesh.

This act by Ashoka, as well as his own pilgrimage and the marking of Buddhist places, helped consolidate the notion of pilgrimage in the early Buddhist community thus providing much of the early devotional basis for lay Buddhism, a stimulus which continues to this day.

THE PARINIRVANA STATUE

During the time of the Guptas a devout Buddhist installed a 'reclining' Buddha statue here. It is one of the earliest large-size Buddha images still surviving and the undoubted prototype for later images of the 'reclining' Buddha. This discovery helped confirm Kushinagar as the place of the Buddha's Parinirvana.

XUANZANG AT KUSHINAGAR

When Xuanzang came to Kushinagar in 637 it was a region of forest, filled with wild oxen, elephant and savage bandits. Inside a brick temple was the statue of the dying Buddha and nearby the large stupa raised by Ashoka to contain the Buddha's relics as well as a Mauryan pillar. That pillar has not been found. Xuanzang found the area devoid of Buddhist practice, and shortly after his visit the site was abandoned and largely forgotten.

MODERN EXCAVATION

In 1861 Cunningham's attention was drawn to the area by local people who reverenced a large black statue, which they referred to as Matha Kuar—the dead prince. Cunningham suggested that Kushinagar was the place where the Buddha died, the site of The Great Decease. It remained for his assistant A.C.L. Carlleyle, fifteen years later to confirm Cunningham's intuition.

Carlleyle was attracted by a ten metre mound of broken bricks covered in dense thorny jungle, which he hoped concealed the reclining Buddha statue described by Xuanzang. After sinking a shaft in the centre of the mound, and digging three metres he came upon the upper part of the thigh of the huge stone statue. The location of Kushinagar was confirmed. Carlleyle completed the excavation, repaired the statue and built around it a new brick temple.

Today's Kushinagar

The Mahaparinirvana temple enclosing the reclining image is a 1956 replacement based on the famous Visvakarma Temple in Cave 10 at Ellora. Its style is probably very unlike the brick structure constructed in the 5th century to protect the statue. Immediately behind is the cylindrical main stupa along with several smaller remnants of stupas and monasteries.

It is so small, so that sixty or eighty pilgrims are a squeeze. It is often crowded, particularly early in the morning or approaching the full moon. At these times there is some competition to be inside, especially if the covering robes on the statue are to be changed. It is rewarding to visit several times. With luck, you may have a more intimate and even solitary experience, of the Buddha's death place.

The 'Reclining Buddha' six metre statue lies facing the temple entrance with his right hand supporting his head. In style it is closely related to 5th century Mathura school and is made of the same red sandstone characteristic of that region. It is now covered with gold leaf and draped in silk robes. At times the robes are removed so it is possible to see the original form of the statue, although its stone core is concealed by layers of gold. At its base is a lamenting figure at each front-corner. In the centre of the base, facing towards the statue, is a kneeling figure which is thought to represent the donor, Haribala. Just below this image is an

BELOW
The Parinirvana Stupa and Temple.

**The Ramabhar
stupa.**

inscription recording his gift and
the name of the reigning Gupta
monarch, Kumaragupta, who
ruled from 413 to 455 CE.

The Mahaparinirvana Stupa, is
behind the temple, is said to be the
exact site where the Buddha died.
Like many others it comprises an
'onion' of stupas which lie one
within the other. When excavated
by Carlleyle in 1876 he estimated
that the stupa had once stood
more than forty metres tall. This
is within the ball park for Xuan-
zang's comment that it was sixty metres in height. An excavation in 1910
revealed Gupta silver coins from the 5th century; a small Buddha statue
dated to the beginning of the current era; and a copper plate with the
inscription that it had been donated by the same Haribala who gifted the
nirvana statue. This is the same man who had enlarged the stupa during
the 5th century.

THE RAMABHAR STUPA

At the southern entrance to Kushinagar near the Hiranyavati river is a
stupa marking the site of the Buddha's cremation. The large brick stupa
we see is where the Sakyas of Kushinagar housed their share of the Holy-
One's relics. Like most of the major Buddhist sites, it stands in a large
expanse of lawn and garden.

BUDDHA GHAT

A lane to the north of the Ramabhar Stupa takes you to a modern
construction, Buddha Ghat. A series of concrete steps descend to the
Hiranyavati river. In the 'dry' when the Buddha died, this river might
have been only two or three metres across.

Hindu tradition was to burn bodies by the riverside. The Buddha did not
oppose that tradition, when he was alive. When he died, his body would
have been carried with great ceremony to the bank of this stream to be
burnt. Give or take a few hundred metres, this place is where the body of
The Tathagata—The Buddha—became the ash of all humanity.

KUSHINAGAR MUSEUM

*Daily 10.30–4.30, closed Monday and public holidays,
and 'Sunday following the second Saturday'*

Try to get it right, as the museum is worth a brief visit. It contains items
excavated from the region. The most noteworthy is Gandharan stucco
statue of Lord Buddha in meditation pose.

MATHA KUAR SHRINE

It was here that the dying Buddha had water from the Hiranyavati river. The black stone statue seen by Cunningham was three metres high and broken in two pieces. It depicted the Buddha in earth-witness position.

Nowadays, the repaired Buddha projects from his surrounding stele protected by a pair of leongrif (lion-horse). He sits on a double lotus throne with his hand in the bhumipasara mudra. Now, he and the throne are a shimmer of gold from thousands of gold foil applications—this glitter clashes. Once, this statue was the dark grey of the surrounding stele, unembellished, not a gold-embellished Buddha, but simply Buddha. An inscription on the base suggests it is from the 11th century, but some authorities offer a much earlier date.

ABOVE
The Matha Kuar statue.

THE PLANNED MAITREYA STATUE

Nearby it is planned to construct a statue of Maitreya. The project was originally intended for Bodhgaya, but because of local controversy, the site has been shifted to Kushinagar. Whether construction will go ahead is currently uncertain.

At 150m in height and an anticipated $200 million in construction costs, this statue of Maitreya, 'the Future Buddha' says a great deal about the links between religion and money. Seated on a throne, the height of a seventeen storey building; with internal elevators gardens and restaurants; one might see it as a Buddhist Disneyland. The construction engineers claim that it will:

> ...operate for 1,000 years without major renewal works, while enhancing the lives of those using the project and the lives of those living in the region.

Uttar Pradesh is one of India's most deprived states. Whether the statue will add to the welfare of its people is a guess and one has to question what impact it will have on the lives of the locals, let alone the image of Buddhism.

> Construction of the statue is not the goal —it is the method for achieving the goal. The goal is to benefit as many people as possible for as long as possible.

–LAMA ZOPA RIMPOCHE, SPIRITUAL DIRECTOR
OF THE MAITREYA PROJECT.

CHAPTER TEN

Gorakhpur

FROM Kushinagar, it takes less than an hour to drive to Gorakhpur. Another twenty kilometres brings you to Maghar, home to one of the most revered of all Sufi poets. Al-Kabir, who lived in the early 15th century, lived his life in accord with Buddhist principles, and expressed his enlightened state with lyrical poetry. He was not a Buddhist. In fact, it is unlikely that he ever heard that word or had any inkling of that religion's significance in the region, but his message of peace and harmony would have resonated with Gautama, just as it continues to appeal today, with spiritual seekers of any shade. Kabir's universal story, makes a day excursion from Kushingar to Maghar and Gorakhpur rewarding.

Gorakhpur history

Lying along the banks of the Rapti river, the city is now a regional centre for agriculture and industry. It has a rich religious heritage. Both the Buddha and his contemporary, the Jain sage and founder of that religion, Mahavira, visited Gorakhpur. In their time, the town was part of the kingdom of Kosala, the capital of which, Shravasti, lies more than two hundred kilometres to the north-west. For a thousand years after the death of the Buddha, this whole region was a major locus of Buddhist monastic practice. Gleanings from Buddhist and Jain temples are in the city museum.

During Mughal and British rule it was an administrative centre, and for the British, a recruitment depot for Gurkha soldiers from nearby Nepal. During the 'Mutiny' in 1857, there was widespread opposition to British rule that led to vigorous suppression and subsequent lack of trust between ruler and ruled. Nowadays, the region has a justified reputation for political and religious volatility, at heart driven by ancient issues. Hinduism is the dominant spiritual force today, with Muslims comprising 15% of the population.

ABOVE
Entrance to the mazaar of Kabir, Maghar.

FACING PAGE, UPPER
The mazaar (Muslim tomb) of Kabir, Maghar.

FACING PAGE, LOWER
Silver plaque on the base of Kabir's Hindu shrine, Maghar.

ABOVE
Hindu Samadhi (shrine) of Kabir, Maghar.

The invasion from central Asia by Muslims and a more vigorous form of Hinduism contributed to Buddhist decline throughout north India. In the 11th century, the accomplishments of a Hindu saint, Gorakshanath, changed the city's name. It was he who articulated the skills of Hatha Yoga (Discipline of Force), which emphasises mastery of the body as a way of attaining spiritual release.

Today, his temple in the city attracts practitioners from around the globe. Another important cultural feature of modern Gorakhpur is the Gita Press, a publishing giant of contemporary Hindu literature.

MAGHAR – THE MUSLIM TOMB (MAZAAR) & HINDU SHRINE (SAMADHI) OF KABIR

It is rare for a saint to be celebrated by religions as different as Islam and Hinduism. The 14th century Sufi poet Kabir, was one such. Revered and loved by both communities, they competed to bury him, and eventually arrived at a satisfactory solution.

KABIR'S EARLY LIFE

Abandoned by his mother, the infant Kabir was taken into a poor Muslim weaving family of Varanasi. His birth date of 1398, has some uncertainty. Although his adoptive parents were Muslim his father's family had recently converted from Hinduism. The child was raised within Islam, and given the name Kabir, (great) the 37th name of God in Islam.

This name was opposed by Muslim teachers of the time, as they felt it was suggestive of heresy. The young Kabir was raised as a Muslim, but his father's mixed religious sensibility, the reality of living in the holiest city of Hinduism and the implied irreverence of his name contributed to his life-long unease with religious orthodoxy. When as a youth he took instruction from the Hindu sage Swami Ramanand, it excited a Hindu storm of protest. They said:

> *Muslims are becoming disciples of a Hindu sage and thus degrading the religion and bringing on the Kali Yuga (the age of Darkness).*

BELOW
Modern painting of Kabir within his Hindu Samadhi, Maghar.

He had no formal education, and is usually described as illiterate. Intelligent and outspoken, from a young age, he regularly partook in religious debates, whether Hindu or Muslim. A master of the smart retort and pithy expression he was regarded as 'difficult' by authorities of both religions, who could not have been pleased with such verses as:

> *His death in Benares*
> *Won't save the assassin*
> *From certain hell,*
> *Any more than a dip*
> *In the Ganges will send*
> *Frogs—or you—to paradise.*
> *My home, says Kabir,*
> *Is where there's no day, no night,*
> *And no holy book in sight*
> *To squat on our lives.*

His facility with language enabled him to deflect official criticisms and to garner public support because of the beauty of his poetry and his unconventional lifestyle. It is estimated that Kabir wrote approximately two thousand songs and fifteen hundred couplets. Many address situations of everyday life in an earthy, vernacular manner. Like many saints, his life has been wrapped in a cloak of legend, of miracles and of stories. It is best to approach an understanding of Kabir through his own words:

> *Hiding in this cage*
> *of visible matter*
> *is the invisible life-bird*
> *pay attention to her*
> *she is singing your song*

By continuing to challenge both Hindu and Muslim hypocrisy and dogma, he alternately enraged and delighted the two communities. He mocked the way each group sought to isolate and claim the ultimate God to themselves, saying: *'...the fact is, that Ishwar (the Supreme Lord) and Allah are present in the hearts of all living beings'.*

Are you looking for me?
Are you looking for me? I am in the next seat.
My shoulder is against yours.
You will not find me in the stupas,
not in Indian shrine rooms,
nor synagogues,
nor in cathedrals:
not in masses, nor kirtans,
not in legs winding around your own neck,
nor in eating nothing but vegetables,
When you really look for me,
you will see me instantly—
you will find me in the tiniest house of time.
Kabir says: Student, tell me, what is God?
He is the breath inside the breath.

NOTE: (kirtan—Skt: to repeat: call & response chanting)

On one famous encounter, he enraged the Sultan of Delhi, Sikander Lodhi, by refusing to bow to the ruler. That meeting, actually seems to have happened, but what follows has the air of legend. Lodhi had the rebellious Kabir bound in chains and tossed into the Ganges. Kabir, used his yogic powers to remove the chains and return to shore. He was then bound and burnt on a fire, but again Kabir was able to magically extinguish the flames. Finally an exasperated Lodhi chained Kabir in front of an enraged elephant, only to have the elephant bow in homage to the saint. Lodhi acknowledge Kabir's abilities but banished him from Varanasi for a time.

Trained as a weaver, he continued to earn his living in this trade. Some accounts have him married with two children, others say he remained single. He is said to have travelled widely throughout India. His inclusive non-judgemental teaching influenced Guru Nanak, the founder of Sikhism.

Nearing the end of a long life, some say one hundred and twenty years, he journeyed towards Maghar. There were two reasons for the journey. He had been asked to come and relieve a serious drought which was troubling the region. And, he was exasperated by a legend that all who died in Maghar would be reborn as an ass. He had taught against superstition all his life, and saw his death as a way to dissolve such nonsense.

When it became known that Kabir was to leave Varanasi for the last time, thousands came to pay homage and to dissuade him. His departure, it was said, *'...will leave Kashi a desolate desert'.* Thousands are said to have accompanied him on his last journey. At Gorakhpur, he met with the local saint Gorakshanath for a meal. As host, Gorakshanath provided water for the gathering by thrusting his thumb into the ground to release a gushing spring. This did nothing to solve the drought, so Kabir ushered up a serious storm which resolved the agricultural problem. What remained to be challenged, was the matter of the ass.

THE DEATH OF KABIR

Journeying on to Maghar, the saint knew he was dying. At his request, a leaf hut was constructed, with a bed of flowers arranged, for him to lie in. The story tells, that having closed himself inside the hut, his followers outside arraigned themselves for war. Each side wished to possess Kabir's body after his death. Hindus claiming Kabir as their Guru, felt he should be cremated according to Hindu custom. Muslim supporters, insisted the saint was one of theirs, and thus should be accorded proper Muslim burial. Suddenly, thunder rolled from within the hut, and the sky filled with light. The opposing sides were transfixed. Laying down their arms and they entered the hut to find no sign of a body and only flowers beneath the bed sheet.

The flowers were divided. The Hindus cremated their portion, building a samadhi (Hindu shrine) on the site. A mazaar (Muslim tomb) was constructed over the place where the Muslim portion was buried. Both buildings stand side by side, celebrating the first time ever that a saint had been interred by two major rival religions.

Throughout his life Kabir had preached the futility of religious dogma and the insanity of communal aggression. That his death was initially a stimulus for aggression is potent measure of the dark heart of religious tension. That this tension was ultimately resolved with harmony and reason, gives cause for hope. To this day, Hindus and Muslims come to Maghar to offer their respect to a great soul.

ABOVE
Kabir offers reassurance in his meditation chamber, Maghar.

Having Crossed the River
There's no road to tread,
No traveller ahead,
Neither a beginning, nor an end.
There's no water, no boat, no boatman, no cord;
No earth is there, no sky, no time, no bank, no ford.
You have forgotten the Self within,
Your search in the void will be in vain;
In a moment the life will ebb
And in this body you won't remain.
Be ever conscious of this, O friend,
You've to immerse within your Self;
Kabir says, salvation you won't then need,
For what you are, you would be indeed.

Today's Maghar – the tombs of Kabir

It is convenient to visit Maghar first, before returning to Gorakhpur for lunch and a visit to the museum. A kilometre off the highway, along a narrow trail, are the two tombs celebrating the life of Kabir. Whatever your native tongue or religious avocation, the reception will be warm and friendly—appropriate for a saint, so eloquent in his celebration of humankind. The countryside location, numerous trees and absence of crowds form an appropriate resting place for such a man.

To the right of the entrance, on a small terrace, is the white dome of the

Hindu Samadhi with a pillared entrance. Through the inner green door is a small room. A silver-framed painting of the saint gazes steadily at you. Between you is a table-sized plinth draped with a white cover. The cover, mounded from below, to simulate the absent body at the time of his death, is strewn with flower offerings. A few metres to the left, on a slightly lower terrace is the Muslim mazaar. As a sign of respect, one has to bend almost double to enter this tomb, where a raised, coffin-sized mound, cloaked in green silk, covers the burial site.

Behind the twin tombs is a cool underground chamber where Kabir is said to have meditated for years. This claim, along with the historical suggestion that he died soon after arrival at Maghar, is only inconsistent for those desirous of certainty.

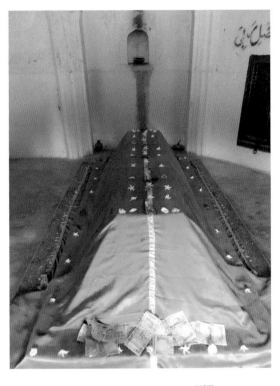

ABOVE
Rupee offerings on Kabir's Muslim burial mound, Maghar.

Today's Gorakhpur

You will not be bothered by crowds at the Government Buddha Museum. Like so many museums of India it suffers from a poverty of signage, lighting and patronage, but it is definitely worthy of a visit. For more than a millennium, there was intensive Buddhist and Jain religious activity in the region of greater-Gorakhpur. From the start of the Common Era, devotees of both religions sculpted and painted their version of religious reality. On display are examples of what they achieved. Visit if time permits.

In the central city, is Goraknath Temple. The current building, of white marble, replaces others which have stood here since the time of the saint Gorakshanath. Three white marble shikara rise above his shrine. The Nath sect which he founded does not follow conventional caste rules, so non-Brahmins may serve as priests. In recent years the sect has been a focus of political activity, attracting widespread support and many converts back to Hinduism. There are always numerous devotees, especially on the holy days of Tuesday and Saturday.

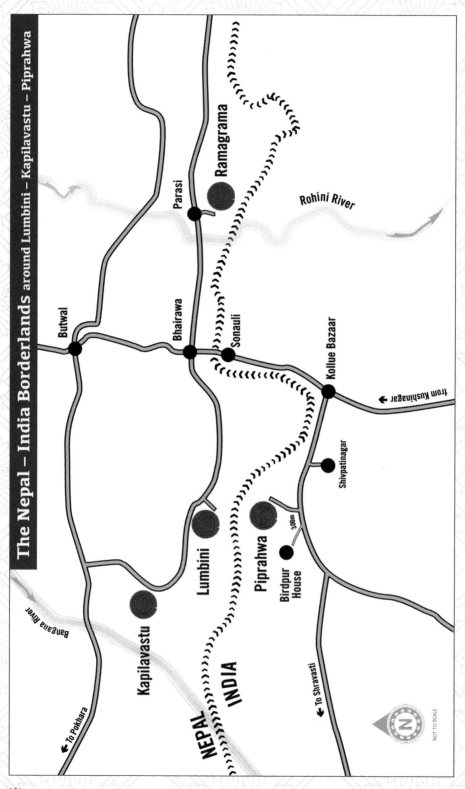

The Nepal – India Borderlands around Lumbini – Kapilavastu – Piprahwa

Ramagrama

Parasi

Rohini River

Butwal

Bhairawa

Sonauli

Kollue Bazaar

from Kushinagar

Shivpatinagar

Lumbini

Piprahwa

300m

Birdpur House

Kapilavastu

Banganga River

To Prokhara

NEPAL

INDIA

To Shravasti

NOT TO SCALE

CHAPTER ELEVEN

Being First
The Buddhist Archaeologists

FOR one and a half thousand years, the religion of the Buddha had thrived in the land of its birth and beyond. By the end of the first millennium, Buddhist belief and practice was widespread throughout the sub-continent, south-east Asia, and the vast swath of north-west lands from Pakistan through to central Asia. Throughout that time, daily support from villagers enabled communities of monks and nuns to thrive and with the patronage of merchants and rulers, for them to build monasteries and monuments.

ABOVE
Thai nuns with flower offerings behind the outer railing, Bodhgaya. (Gupta ca 300 CE).

However, from the start of the second millennium, support for Buddhism waned within India. A more engaging form of Hinduism had greater appeal for the populace; royal patronage declined in parallel with the rise of Hindu kingdoms; and the arrival of Moslem invaders dealt a final death blow.

The great Buddhist universities and monasteries fell into disuse and the monuments were abandoned to the jungle, their significance forgotten. By the mid-1200s the way of life established by Gautama was forgotten. His story and even his name were unknown in the land of his birth.

THE 'DISCOVERY' OF BUDDHISM

Officials of the British East India Company slowly teased out the history of early India, but it was not until the early 1800s that the name of Buddha and the significance of his religion became associated with India. And it was another hundred years before the location of Buddhist sites within India and Nepal were defined.

The first use of the word 'Buddhism' in print came from an essay *On the Religion and Literature of the Burmese* by Dr. Francis Buchanan. A surgeon and botanist, Buchanan had been on a 1797 diplomatic mission to, the then, Kingdom of Ava in Burma. Buchanan was later posted to Kathmandu. Here he noticed similarities in the statues of the Kathmandu Valley with those he had seen in Burma. Similar reports were collected from British officials in Ceylon.

It was from Nepal that Buchanan first surmised that Buddhism might have originated on the Indian sub-continent. By 1811, Buchanan was back in India. On a visit to Bodhgaya, he noted statues similar to those he had seen in Burma and Nepal. And it was here, that he learnt of delegations from the Kingdom of Ava, who had come to Bodhgaya because it was a holy site for the founder of their religion. The importance of the Bihar region for the origin of Buddhism was thus confirmed.

British scholars of the Asiatic Society and the Archaeological Survey of India, especially James Prinsep, Brian Hodgson and Alexander Cunningham gradually teased out details of Buddhism as a separate religious tradition. They also established that the 'Priyadasi' mentioned on numerous edict columns throughout northern India was the Emperor Ashoka. Slowly, the Buddha emerged from the realm of myth to become a historical figure.

COMPETITORS IN THE SEARCH FOR BUDDHIST SITES

By the late 1890s it was well established that the Buddha had lived his life in the plains of India and Nepal. What excited the early British explorers, was the exact location for events of the Buddha's life. Being the first to report such a place was the major motivation, as it carried both professional and public acclaim. This desire, when coupled with less than honest reporting, and sometimes frank dishonesty, led to false claims and counterclaims. Disputes were not infrequently conducted in public, with bruised egos and fluctuating reputations the order of the day.

Urgency drove their exploration. This was motivated mostly by professional jealousy, but also by the realisation that progressive clearing of jungle was destroying ancient sites before they had been investigated. A further frustration was the politically restricted access to the southern region of Nepal, the Terai.

The Terai, a name derived originally from Persian meaning marshy land, referred to the fifty kilometre strip of low lying land where the foothills of the Himalaya joined the plains of the Ganges. For the most part it was dense swampy jungle, difficult to traverse even by elephant. An uncomfortable place at the best of times, made more hazardous by seasonal malaria and numerous wild animals. Increasingly, the Terai was thought to be the likely location of the Buddha's early life. Getting permission from the Rana government of Nepal to excavate in the Terai was a major prize, not easily arranged. It was a heady playing field. Some players conducted themselves with honour, and others in a much less worthy fashion.

Leading the latter group was the German Dr. Anton Alois Führer. His outright lies and descriptions of non-existant ruins brought temporary fame and sowed considerable confusion amongst his contemporaries, until his professional unmasking.

Less publically challenged for dishonesty, was Dr. Laurence Austine

Waddell, a year younger than his German rival. Trained as a doctor at the University of Glasgow, Waddell had come to India at the age of twenty-six to work for the Indian Medical Service. His interest in Buddhism had been stimulated by an expedition to Burma and seven years amidst the Tibetan culture of Darjeeling. He had a jealous unforgiving nature, perhaps reflecting his Calvanist upbringing. His deceptions were sneaky and mean spirited. Ultimately, these adverse traits were so troublesome, that the authorities banned him from sanctioned exploration.

Dr. William Hoey and Dr. Vincent Smith were career officers of the ICS, the Indian Civil Service. As members of this elite corps, 'the heaven born', they had greater flexibility to follow their interests in early history than Waddell, who was subject to the demands of his medical and military employers in the IMS, the Indian Medical Service. Their high status; the fact that both graduated top of their entrance exams; and both were professionally trained academics, allowed Hoey and Smith to rarely manifest bad-form in the race to find the Buddha's homeland.

ABOVE
Vincent Smith in 1919 age 71.
The Board of Trinity College, Dublin.

The least publically celebrated, but in many ways the most exemplary, was a little educated Brahmin, Purna Chandra Mukherji. A man who lacked formal training in archaeology, Mukherji, had the lowly occupational status of 'Babu' or clerk, and in race-conscious British-India, he was Indian to boot. What Mukherji did possess, were the hands of a skilled draftsman; doggedness in the face of obstruction; and the wit to take advantage of good fortune when it chanced his way.

BELOW
Dr. William Hoey (1880's) aged approximately 36.
Courtesy Hoey Family.

EXCAVATION IN THE TILAURAKOT REGION

The Rana family in Kathmandu had disempowered the Nepalese king and were effectively the rulers of the country from 1856 until 1951, when a form of democracy was established. As hereditary Prime Ministers, the Ranas kept Nepal isolated from the outside world. Justifiably, they feared invasion by the British and strictly controlled any access to their dominion by foreigners.

During the late 19th century the location of places significant to the Buddha were still being identified. Increasingly, Nepal's Terai region in the south of the country became the focus of interest. Fearful of invasion, but not wanting to miss a chance to claim the Buddha as a Nepalese ancestor, the Ranas gradually allowed a limited number of scholars access to the Terai. This restriction was to cause problems for the quality of early excavation around Tilaurakot and Lumbini.

DR. ANTON FÜHRER

Dr. Anton Führer was the first foreign person allowed to investigate the Terai in the search of Buddhist sites. Führer, a German national, was at the time 'Archaeological Surveyor to the Government of North

West Provinces and Oudh', universally referred to as NWP&O. Based in Lucknow, the British administrative centre of the 'Awadh–Oudh', he was well placed to enter the Nepalese Terai, a hundred kilometres to the north.

Führer and Nigliva

His first visit in 1895, was to investigate reports of Ashokan columns in the Tilaurakot region. He was directed to Nigliva, where there was a column, known locally as 'Bhimsen's smoking pipe'. Bhimsen Thapa had been Prime Minister of Nepal in the early 19th century. Bhimsen had the misfortune to clash unsuccessfully with British East India Company forces. At the Treaty of Sugauli in 1814, Nepal lost a third of

ABOVE
Dr. Führer in later life.
From *Ins Verbotene Land* 2010, Dr. Wolf Donner.

its territory and were forced to accept a British Resident in Kathmandu. The sterling qualities of Nepalese troops led to their subsequent recruitment into the British Army to form the famous Gurkha regiments.

Führer found 'Bhimsen's pipe' to be an Ashokan column broken in two. It carried several inscriptions the most important recording a visit by emperor Ashoka to worship at the birthplace of Konakamana Buddha. Führer's language skills, enabled him to recognise the importance of his find, which was a justifiable triumph.

From the Chinese accounts, Führer would have deduced that ancient Kapilavastu was nearby, but he did not have time or permission to investigate. Instead, he invented imaginary ruins around Nigliva, conflating his official report with outright lies. Quite falsely he claimed that near to the Nigliva column was a:

> *...hemispherical dome being about 101 feet in diametre, and its present height still about 30 feet... surrounded by ruined monasteries, fallen columns and broken sculptures.*

Both stupa and ruins did not in fact exist. Führer's desire to be first, and his degree of self-deception, was sufficient to report that he had discov-

LEFT
Seated, in 1896, beside the Ashokan pillar at Lumbini are: Vincent Smith, General Rana, William Hoey and Duncan Ricketts.
Dr. Charles Allen.

ered the ruins of Siddhartha's Kapilavastu. Back in India, this account was taken at face value. Because Führer's claims could not be easily verified, it took some years for this fabrication to emerge.

Führer and Lumbini

The next year 1896, Dr. Führer was unexpectedly asked to assist with investigations being conducted by General Khadga Shumsher Rana, fifty kilometres south-east of Nigliva. Ten years previously, Khadga had masterminded a Kathmandu palace coup which brought his Shumsher clan to prominence as the political rulers of Nepal. Subsequent family intrigue had side-tracked him to the governorship of Palpa, in the Terai. He was never allowed to return to Kathmandu. An intelligent resourceful man, he welcomed the opportunity to dabble in archaeology. The General's attention had been drawn to a large tree-covered mound with a pillar projecting from near the summit. Anticipating an inscription, the General had summoned Führer to help with translation.

Before he could address the column, Führer made a very useful discovery. At the top of the mound was a recently constructed brick temple containing an almost life-sized statue which had been removed from the ruins below. Ascribed by the local people as a Hindu deity Führer immediately recognised it as:

> *Mahamaya in a standing position, bringing forth the infant Buddha from her right side...*

He had found the statue of Maya Devi, the Buddha's mother which is now placed in the temple of her own name at Lumbini.

The Ashokan pillar projecting from the slope was of more significant interest. Khadga Rana had been made aware of a column, first reported in 1893 by an English farmer, whose estate was just to the south on the

Indian side of the border. Duncan Ricketts had sneaked across the border, taken a rubbing of the inscription on the pillar and shown it to Vincent Smith. Smith was an ICS (Indian Civil Service) officer, and acknowledged expert of early Prakit scripts. The inscriptions seen by Smith were grafitti from the upper, exposed, part of the column. Smith justifiably dismissed the writing as 'medieval scribblings'. It was a judgement which he later regretted bitterly. Smith had missed the opportunity of a lifetime. Had he paid more attention to the circumstances of Ricketts tracing he might have been first to identify the exact location of the Buddha's birthplace.

General Rana had brought with him soldiers to excavate the pillar. Rana and Dr. Führer watched as the soldiers excavated the base of the standing pillar. About a metre below ground level, lines of Brahmi script of a type typical to Ashokan columns were revealed. Vincent Smith later described it as:

...four and a half lines of beautifully incised and well-preserved characters, averaging about 30 millimetres, or a little over an inch in height.

Führer was well versed in this script and it is inconceivable that he could not have immediately provided a translation. It says something about the devious nature of the man that he did not immediately express delight, as the first two, easily translated, lines said:

Beloved of the gods. King Piyadasi (Ashoka) when twenty years consecrated came to worship saying here the Buddha was born Sakyamuni.

Instead, Führer said nothing to the general or to the other European present, Duncan Ricketts, who had ridden from his estate across the border in India, to join the fun. Two copies of the inscription were taken by the General and given to Dr. Führer, who sent them off to his professor in Vienna, Georg Buhler, for expert translation.

The inscription on the Lumbini pillar confirmed the Buddha's birthplace. Führer must have immediately grasped that Kapilavastu must exist to the north-west of the Lumbini site, a location quite different from his imaginary claims of a year earlier.

His few hours at Lumbini on the 1st of December 1896 cannot have been easy for the doctor. He had remained silent about the true nature of the inscription. And, he had suddenly been provided with a clue to the likely location for Kapilavastu. He must have hoped that by proceeding directly to that spot from Lumbini, and by using General Rana's soldiers, he would be able to find sufficient evidence to smooth over his lies of the previous year. Unfortunately, these hopes were dashed by General Rana insisting that all further investigations in Nepal be stopped so that Rana's attention, and the labour of his troops, could be directed towards the famine which was troubling the Nepalese Terai.

On returning to India, Dr. Führer immediately sent a telegram to the Pioneer newspaper baldly announcing that he had discovered the site of the Buddha's birth at Lumbini and that he had also discovered Kapilavastu. This was heady stuff, which rapidly attracted national and international attention. That Führer neglected to point out that the Lumbini pillar had been: commented on by Ricketts; brought to his notice by General Rana; and excavated by the General's troops, was not a smart move on his part. These omissions elicited protest and frustration from the others involved at Lumbini, but the important nature of Führer's claims, meant that such gripes were regarded as 'sour grapes' from jealous rivals. There was concern amongst some scholars about Dr. Führer's trustworthiness, but public awareness the doctor's deceptions and his ultimate downfall was a couple of years away.

Führer and Sagarwa

January 1898 found Führer at Sagarwa. He initially thought he had found the elusive remains of Kapilavastu. However, the presence of the lake, a group of votive stupas and another large stupa were in general agreement with what had been said by Faxian and Xuanzang. These findings, together with the absence of extensive settlement enabled him to correctly conclude that Sagarwa was the site of the Sakya massacre.

Führer excavated eighteen small votive stupas. Each contained a metal reliquary, along with bricks decorated with stylish military emblems. Führer was later to claim in detail, that each relic case was inscribed '...*in pre-Ashoka characters...*' with a name of a Sakyan warrior. The presence of the stupas, the inscribed bricks and the seventeen relic cases was true, but his statements regarding the inscriptions, proved to be an elaborate lie.

The large stupa at the western end of the lake, had already been inadequately explored by General Khadga Sumsher Rana. Führer's group dug more deeply to reveal an earthenware casket containing fragments of bone along with small pieces of gold, silver and a few gems. All of which were sketched by Führer's draftsman. The relic casket was covered by a copper lid which the worker's drawing, showed without an inscription. Later, in his report of this excavation, Führer claimed that he had found the stupa of King Suddhodana's successor, Mahanama. According to Führer, the copper cover was inscribed: *Relics of the Sakya Mahanama*. There was in fact, no inscription on the cover. Dr. Führer's claim was not true.

Dr. Führer's downfall

His reputation as an archaeologist started to more seriously unfold a few months later. It came to the notice of officials in his department that for some years the doctor had been sending 'genuine relics' of the Buddha to a Burmese monk U Ma. Ma was miffed that a large tooth proved to be that of a horse and was not satisfied with Führer's explanation that as the Buddha '...*was 18 cubits in height, as your sacred writings state...*' he would have been endowed with suitably large dentition.

About the same time Führer's report *Antiquities of Buddha Sakya-muni's Birth-Place in the Nepalese Terai* was published. Instead of the critical acclaim hoped by most authors, his Antiquities excited official enquiry. As a senior, Vincent Smith was asked to investigate the veracity of Führer's Buddhist activities, his apparent forgeries, and the quality of work in other areas. By September 1898, Smith's concerns, expanded to become damning evidence of widespread fraud and when confronted, Dr. Führer immediately resigned.

Hoping to keep the scandal under wraps, the government had removed *Antiquities* from circulation but by that time interested and offended parties had already made their feelings known in letters to the editor. Führer's downfall was public.

What subsequently happened to Dr. Führer, is intriguing. An incongruous feature in Antiquities was the inclusion of many sections that can be described as Buddhist tracts. Some thought this indicated Führer had taken refuge in the Dharma. It must have been a very stressful time for the doctor, so his unusual behaviour may have been part of a psychological breakdown, or perhaps a rekindling of earlier spiritual roots?

As a young adult he was 'Father Führer', an ordained Roman Catholic priest, who arrived in Bombay in 1878 to serve the church at St Xavier's College. He had already studied Sanskrit in Germany and continued this interest in Bombay under Professor Georg Buhler at the University of Bombay. Führer left Bombay in 1884 for Germany where he abandoned the priesthood and married. Little is known of Frau Führer, who lived throughout the ups and downs of her husband's career.

The possibility that Dr. Führer had adopted Buddhism was stimulated by a report in the February 1902 Ceylon Standard, which said: 'Much interest has been excited in Buddhist and other circles at the prospect of Dr. Führer coming to Ceylon to join the Buddhist priesthood.' In fact, there is no evidence that Dr. Führer went to Ceylon and indeed, by 1901 he settled in Switzerland, becoming pastor of a Christian Catholic community at Binningen, near Basel. He died in Binningen in 1930, at the age of 77.

The death of Professor Buhler
Over several years, as Dr. Führer's claims had become public, the professor wrote glowingly of his former student's many triumphs. Gradually however, as the claims proved dubious or untrue, Professor Buhler's professional dismay at the deception was significant. Dr. Führer's disgrace was the likely tipping factor in, Buhler's widely believed, suicide by drowning in Lake Constance, on the German-Swiss border. His death was in April 1898, six months before the final unmasking and resignation of Dr. Führer.

DR. WADDELL

At the age of twenty-six, in 1880, Laurence Austine Waddell had joined the IMS (Indian Medical Service) in Calcutta. An interest in Buddhism was stimulated by subsequent service on an expedition to Burma and six years in Darjeeling, where he taught himself Tibetan and worked on the publication of several books. One of these, *The Buddhism of Tibet or Lamaism*, and a similar volume on Sikkim, made Waddell an acknowledged authority on matters Tibetan. Like other would-be archaeologists of the time his interest in the early history of Buddhist India was guided by publication in English of the reports by Faxian and Xuanzang.

By the early 90's Waddell was spending all his spare time striving to be first to identify the remaining Buddhist sites of Kushinagar, Ramagrama and Kapilavastu. Right at the top of this list was the location of Kapilavastu, the young Siddhartha's home town.

Self-effacement was never a problem for Waddell. He saw himself as inherently more competent than the others searching for the early Buddhist sites, and was frustrated that his IMS job did not give him freedom to choose where to work. In 1893, ill health forced him to take two years sick leave in the United Kingdom. This must have been particularly galling, as it was a crucial period in Buddhist exploration.

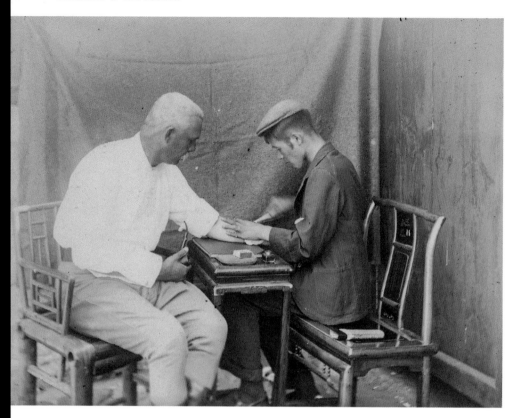

Waddell and Führer

Returning to India in 1895, Waddell was aware of Dr. Führer's discovery in Nepal of the Nigliva pillar with its Ashokan inscription. Although he requested Dr. Führer and the officials in Lucknow for a copy of the inscription, it was not forthcoming. Both Führer and Waddell saw themselves as arch rivals and deliberately did not share information. When Waddell eventually got a copy of the translated Nigliva inscription, he immediately realised that this was a clue to the location of both Kapilavastu and Lumbini.

Frustrated by the lack of official response Waddell wrote a letter to the Calcutta 'Englishman' pointing out just where, in relation to Nigliva, Lumbini and Kapilavastu were to be found. He was correct about Nigliva being an important marker, but his directions and distances to the long lost sites were completely wrong. However, his letter did stimulate public and government interest. The Government of Bengal offered to fund six weeks of exploration but, as Major Waddell was refused leave by the Calcutta Medical College, the task was given to Dr. Führer. Waddell was furious that his rival had been chosen. His wrath would have been compounded, if he'd been aware that Führer's claims about finding a huge stupa near Nigliva and other vast ruins nearby, were lies.

A year later, in December 1896, Dr. Führer was back in the news, with his claims to have personally discovered Lumbini. These assertions vastly overstated Führer's contribution to events at Lumbini. Nursing a very bruised ego, Dr. Waddell pointed out that he had been first to point out the location of Lumbini, and it was to him that credit for the discovery of the Buddha's birthplace should be directed. Waddell's claim was flimsy and wondrously inflammatory. With the intention of scoring points, rather than imparting clarity, Dr. Waddell ignored that his Englishman letter had given directions that were very specific and fundamentally wrong.

The editors of the time must have been delighted. Newspapers and learned journals were full of claim and counter claim as the two aspirants sparred. Everybody was well aware of the animosity between Waddell and Führer. What adds spice to the tale, is that few, except Dr. Führer, were aware that his claim to be instrumental in the discovery, excavation and publication of the Lumbini pillar were massive exaggerations.

By the end of 1898, the lies and deliberate falsifications of Dr. Führer had been revealed. His resignation must surely have left Dr. Waddell feeling confident that his own natural superiority would shortly triumph. Unfortunately for the Scottish doctor, another competent and honest rival was to hand.

Dr. Waddell and Babu Mukherji

In the early 1890s Waddell had carried out preliminary excavation at Patna. As far as Waddell was concerned, ancient Pataliputra was his to explore, as of right. When in 1897 Babu Mukherji used his initiative to excavate the remains of Mauryan columns at Patna, Dr. Waddell was offended. He set the tone for their future relationship by dismissing the Mukherji report as a: '...*wholesale perversion of truth...*'

With the location of Lumbini now established, both Waddell and Mukherji realised that discovery of Kapilavastu was imminent—the key being permission to work on the Nepalese side of the border. Vincent Smith at Gorakhpur, did not support Waddell's complaints against Mukherji. In a telling riposte to Waddell, Smith appointed the Indian Babu as the government archaeologist to replace the now-disgraced Dr. Führer in the Nepalese Terai.

Waddell immediately objected to Mukherji's appointment, demanding that he be the one to head the Nepal operation. An unsatisfactory compromise was reached between the Government of Bengal, representing Dr. Waddell, and that of the NWP&O, representing Mukherji. It was agreed that both would work in Nepal together, with Babu Mukherji working '...*in conjunction with and under the direction of Doctor Waddell.*' Given the personalities, it was an arrangement that suited neither party. The events which followed resemble a French bedroom farce, minus the humour. The two actors moved on and off stage as each sought to outwit the other. It was dramatic and bitter.

Waddell continued to complain to Gorakhpur about the activities of Mukherji in Patna. Unaware of this, Mukherji, acting on instructions from Smith to find the city of Kapilavastu, proceeded immediately to Taulihawa to start excavation. This area, he correctly surmised, would contain the ruins of the Buddha's home city. On arrival at camp, he was handed a telegram by Waddell ordering him to return immediately to India.

Back in Gorakhpur, Mukherji once again successfully defended his actions in Patna. He was sent back to Nepal with his appointment confirmed and was admonished to be careful not to offend Major Waddell. In a separate instruction, Waddell was enjoined to be scrupulous about working on good terms with the Babu. The Gorakhpur authorities could only hope their two charges would behave. Only one did.

During Mukherji's absence, Waddell also returned to Gorakhpur. His investigations at Nigliva had uncovered further evidence of Führer's deceit. Führer had reported a huge stupa and numerous nearby ruins. None of which existed. Waddell was eager to heap more discredit upon Führer who he continued to see as his main rival. Seeking official validation of his views he set off to Gorakhpur to help put a final nail in the German doctor's reputation. Driven by righteousness, his visit was to prove a serious tactical error. Waddell had been touring Nigliva and Lumbini with William Hoey, the Collector at Gorakhpur. The two confirmed that Führer had lied about imagined discoveries at Nigliva and that the German's claims to have discovered both Kapilavastu and Lumbini, and to have excavated the pillar inscription, were completely untrue. Having unmasked the untruths of his principal rival, Waddell must have set off back to Tilaurakot with a righteous glow. His triumph was shortlived.

At Tilaurakot, with Waddell fortuitously absent, Mukherji was able to uncover the extensive walls, a surrounding moat and the palace remains of old Kapilavastu. By the time Waddell returned to offer 'direction' to his Indian rival, the game was effectively over. Mukherji had uncovered and mapped the site and had also detailed eight reasons why Tilaurakot was in fact, ancient Kapilavastu.

To any impartial observer it was obvious that Mukherji had discovered the real location of Kapilavastu. Waddell, being neither impartial nor reasonable, persisted with his attacks on Mukherji and, incredible as it might seem, he made false claims about the importance of his own involvement. Returning to Calcutta, Waddell wrote a report claiming that he had found Kapilavastu. His report gave no credit to Mukherji's discovery and documentation of the site, and went on to urge that Mukherji be withdrawn as the Babu was '...*causing the Nepalese government needless trouble in excavating sites to no useful purpose...*'

Within a few months, their conflicting claims enlivened the newspapers, to the renewed delight of editors and readers. The dispute was only partially stilled with the publication of Mukherji's official report in 1901. Predictably, Waddell continued to complain about both Mukherji and Führer, insisting that his character and reputation had been sullied. Wearily, one suspects, Vincent Smith was detailed to once again, to investigate Waddell's complaints. Smith was not deceived by Waddells' bluster. He recommended that it was *'...not desirable to entrust him with the duty of further exploration.'*

It would be nice to relate that Babu Purna Chandra Mukherji went on to a lifetime of acclaim, but unfortunately that was not his fate. His excavations of Sagrahwa, Kapilavastu, Lumbini and Piprahwa, and his impeccable maps were acknowledged as highly competent. However, his lack of professional qualifications caused the new Director General of Archaeology, John Marshall, to employ him as pandit, or learned man, and not as archaeologist. Within a couple of years the learned pandit was dead, probably from fever in 1903. That the

ABOVE
**Bodhgaya
temple, dawn.**

circumstances of his death are uncertain says something about how he was regarded by the British.

Lieutenant Colonel Waddell never worked again as an archaeologist in India. He served in China, the North West frontier and the British invasion of Tibet, before retiring to Scotland in 1905. Teaching himself Sumerian, he spent the last years of his life arguing the primacy of the Sumerians. He saw them as the original Aryan culture, source of the Indus, Egyptian and the other 'old world' civilisations. His numerous publications were controversial and elicited little scholarly backing. He died aged 85 in September 1938.

Lumbini

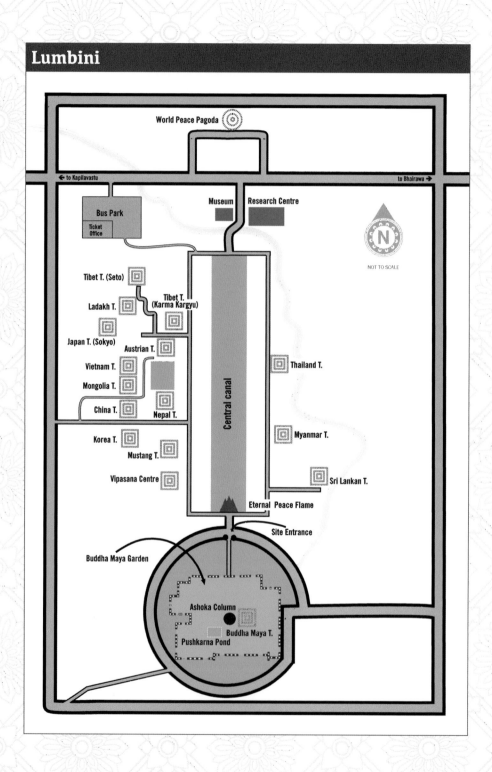

World Peace Pagoda

← to Kapilavastu   to Bhairawa →

Bus Park
Ticket Office

Museum   Research Centre

N
NOT TO SCALE

Tibet T. (Seto)
Tibet T. (Karma Kargyu)
Ladakh T.
Japan T. (Sokyo)
Austrian T.
Vietnam T.
Mongolia T.
China T.
Nepal T.

Thailand T.

Central canal

Myanmar T.

Korea T.
Mustang T.
Vipasana Centre

Sri Lankan T.

Eternal Peace Flame

Site Entrance

Buddha Maya Garden

Ashoka Column

Buddha Maya T.
Pushkarna Pond

CHAPTER TWELVE

Lumbini

THERE is no argument about the site of the Buddha's birth at Lumbini in the flat Terai region of modern Nepal. The discovery here of an Ashokan column declaring exactly that, makes the claim indisputable. It was an important place of pilgrimage for centuries, but with the decline of Buddhism the religious significance was forgotten and the monuments were overwhelmed by jungle, until their modern discovery at the end of the 19th century.

THE BUDDHA AND LUMBINI

Mayadevi, the future-Buddha's mother was from the Koliya clan, a people who lived to the east of Sakyas, across the Rohini river. Their main town Devadaha, was about fifty kilometres distant from Kapilavastu. The ruins of Devadaha are probably near the modern town of Butwal, but have not yet been identified.

When time came for her delivery, Mayadevi set out for her family home. It was said to be tradition amongst the Sakya for the first-born to be delivered at the mother's parental home. The tradition may not have been all that strong as neither Prajapati, Maya's sister, nor Yashodhara, the Buddha's wife, did this for their first delivery. Whatever the tradition,

ABOVE
**The Buddha-
Maya Temple.**

Mayadevi was travelling towards Devadaha when time came for her give birth. Then as now, babies arrive when they will. At a place we now call Lumbini, she was overcome with labour pains. She first bathed in a pool. Then, standing with one hand grasping the branch of a sal tree, she gave birth to the infant Siddhartha.

Some accounts hold that the infant was miraculously delivered through her right side. The god Indra was there to receive the baby, who was born fully conscious and with full faculties. In the legend, the infant stepped to the ground and took seven steps in each of the four directions. With each step, a lotus sprang up to mark his progress. The infant proclaimed:

- To the east—'I shall reach the highest Nirvana.'
- To the south—'I shall be the first of all beings.'
- To the west—'This will be my last birth.'
- And to the north—'I shall cross the ocean of existence.'

[NOTE: there are several versions of these statements.]

Following the birth, Maya returned to Kapilavastu with the infant Siddhartha. Within a week she was dead from causes that we can only guess. In the pre-scientific era, childbirth was much more hazardous than today, even commonplace. From that time, he was suckled and cared for by Mayadevi's sister, Prajapati, another wife of Suddhodana. Just how much the early death of his mother influenced the young Siddhartha can only be guessed. Prajapati cared for him as her own child, and there were strong emotional ties between the two. Later it was Prajapati who convinced the reluctant Buddha to admit women into the Sangha.

When Siddhartha had grown beyond childhood it is likely that he passed through Lumbini in the course of his normal life. In his life as a teacher, Lumbini was not important. It remained an insignficant small town on the road between Kapilavastu and Devadaha.

ASHOKA AND LUMBINI

It was Ashoka, who 'gave us' Lumbini. In 249 BCE, as part of his tour of major sites of the Buddha, he visited here one hundred and fifty years after the Buddha's death. He recorded the event with one of his pillars. The Lumbini one is inscribed:

King Piyadasi (Ashoka) beloved of the Gods, in the twentieth year of his reign, came himself and worshipped—saying 'Here Buddha Sakyamuni was born'.
He caused this stone pillar to be erected.
And, because the Worshipful One was born here, tax for the village of Lumbini was reduced to one eighth part.

Ashoka placed a horse-capital on top of the Lumbini pillar. It was still there eight hundred years later during the visit of Xuanzang in 637 CE, but the column had been split by lightning, with the horse-capital lying at its base. Subsequently this capital has been lost. That one hundred and fifty years after the death of the Buddha, Ashoka could be confident about the location of the sage's birth, suggests that the significance of Rummindei (ancient Lumbini), was well known at his time. With the decline of Buddhism and especially after the Muslim invasions, pilgrimage and practice largely ceased.

ASHOKA'S PILLARS

The stone artisans of the emperor were skilful. Throughout northern India, there are forty known Ashokan columns, and it's likely there were once many more. All of them are highly polished sandstone from the Chunar quarry upstream of Varanasi. They were heavy, and are usually described as monoliths. However, a 1998 scholar found that at least three of Ashoka's pillars, including the Vaishali one, were composed of several cylindrical blocks.

If monolithic, each finished column, weighs around 35 tonnes. An extra ten tonnes can be added for the capital and supporting bracket. It is not known for certain, but because of the risks of transporting the finished article, it is suggested that each column and capital received its final shaping on the site where they were erected. All were erected during a twenty five year period, towards the end of Ashoka's reign, from 257–232 BCE.

In the twenty years following his coronation, Ashoka erected three columns in the Kapilavastu region—at Lumbini, Niglihawa and Gotihawa. The first two appear to be monoliths, while the Gotihawa one is too fragmented to be certain. Given the religious significance of these sites, it is a fair assumption that the Emperor would have commanded his stone masons to provide the best and biggest. Two thousand years later, the quality of the final product is stunning. Today's artisans, would find it difficult to achieve a similar refinement of polish and design. We have to hope that the Emperor's craftsmen were well paid and appreciated.

The Chunar quarries which provided Ashoka's columns are still in use to-day. In them are the remains of some columns the Emperor did not use. Today, transporting a 40 tonne cylinder of rock is no easy task, and much less so in the 3rd century BCE. From Chunar to Kapilavastu is more than 400 kilometres in a straight across-country line, and more than double that if you first take a boat downstream to Patna and then travel by land by the Uttarpatha—the northern road. It must have taken months to transport these stones from the quarry, even with the assistance boats and a score of imperial elephant.

KING RIPU MALLA AND LUMBINI

In the year 1312 CE, Lumbini was visited by King Ripu Malla from western Nepal. At that time Lumbini was probably part of his dominion. We know of Ripu's visit as he carved several lines of graffiti at the top of Ashoka's column. His visit is significant. It confirms that, at least until 1312 CE, Lumbini continued to be known as the birthplace of the Buddha and was a place of Buddhist pilgrimage. Fifty-six other smaller inscriptions on the pillar confirm the universal human instinct to make their mark.

After Ripu Malla's visit Lumbini and Kapilavastu became overgrown with jungle only to be rediscovered by German and Nepalese archaeologists in the late 1890s.

THE CHINESE PILGRIMS AND LUMBINI

BELOW
Marigolds decorate a votive stupa.

As you would expect, both Faxian and Xuanzang visited here. Unlike their visits to 'Kapilavastu', both men visited the same place, now known as Lumbini, Nepal. In his usual style, Faxian offers little description, commenting only on the presence of the tree under which the future-Buddha was born and the bathing tank used by Maya Devi after the birth of Siddhartha. For Xuanzang, this pool was 'bright and clear as a mirror'. He observed the presence of several stupas as well as the Ashokan pillar which even then was split. Xuanzang did not mention the pillar-inscription, which almost a thousand years after the emperor, may well have been buried.

MODERN EXCAVATION

Professional archaeologists are critical of Keshar Shumsher Rana's excavations in the 1930's. His efforts were not professional. A charitable assessment would describe his approach as a 'clean and clear' operation. Old photographs show a large tree-covered stupa with Ashoka's column projecting from the debris. General Rana flattened this structure to almost ground level, so the clues as to what lay here have become confused by his efforts.

Today's Lumbini

The Nepalese government were generous in gifting large areas of land around the archaeological site to preserve the monuments and create a peaceful environment. The Lumbini Development Trust is the body responsible for overall management of the Lumbini park.

A large portion of the park is a wildlife reserve of grassland, forest and wetland. During your travels you are like to see small antelope and the much larger nilgai, or 'Blue Bull' as well as Sarus Cranes, the tallest of the world's flying birds. Their height, elegant grey plumage and red throats make them distinctive additions to the Lumbini landscape. Bonding for life, pairs of Sarus cranes never separate, and are thus a symbol of fidelity and love. Eating their eggs, or killing a bird is guaranteed to bring misfortune. It is said that Devadatta's longstanding feud with the young Siddhartha was due him shooting one of these lovely birds.

One section of the park, around the ancient monuments, is now a World Heritage site. The rules require that visitors leave and enter by a single gate; be ticketed only at one spot; and travel around only by cycle rickshaw or on foot. The Garden is huge: six kilometres long and two wide. Thus, you need both time and stamina to visit. To visit the main site, the Maya Devi Temple, takes at least three hours, leaving not much time to

BELOW
The 'Eternal Flame' and Central Canal with the World Peace Pagoda in the distance, Lumbini.

The 'Great Lotus' Stupa and Karma Kargyu Tibetan Temple, Lumbini.

visit some of the national temples. If you want to visit the national temples, a sensible programme is to spend a full day in Lumbini and another full day in the sites around Kapilavastu.

THE CENTRAL CANAL

One and a half kilometres in length, and lying in a north-south axis, the canal is a major orienting feature. At the southern end is the Eternal Peace Flame, brought here in 1986 from the UN headquarters in New York, to symbolise the Buddha's universal message of peace. At the opposite end the white spire of the Japanese Peace Pagoda is just visible. Near to the ticket area, is an architecturally striking museum, containing fragments from various excavations, along with photos of other important Buddhist sites. Visit the museum if time allows.

On either side of the waterway are numerous national monasteries: Theravadan to the east and those of Mahayana sects on the west. Farthest south are the ancient monuments, lying within The Sacred Garden— themselves surrounded, and protected from flooding, by a circular pond a kilometre in diameter.

THE SACRED GARDEN

The major historical monuments are grouped near to Ashoka's Pillar in the Sacred Garden. From the rickshaw drop-off point, you walk several hundred metres to the temple area. A brick causeway leads across a recently constructed moat to the Sacred Garden, site of the Buddha's birth. There are spacious lawns, trees draped in Tibetan flags and the remains of surprisingly few stupas or monasteries.

The Temple of the Birth or Maya Devi Temple, is a large white modern structure, surmounted by a facsimile stupa, which in turn is topped by gold umbrellas resembling the Swyambunath Stupa in Kathmandu. Built over the foundations of previous temples by the Nepal Institute of Engineering, its insensitive appearance reflects its parentage.

THE MARKER STONE

Inside the temple an elevated, square, wooden walkway follows the walls. This offers a much more angular parikramama than the circular one which probably once lay below. Off-centre, a pier of bricks, pierces the ceiling, to define the old stupa. Immediately below this is a brick lined space containing the 'marker stone' exposed during the 1992 excavation. This is claimed to be the stone placed by Ashoka to identify the exact spot where the infant Siddhartha took his first step. Covered with a plate of bullet-proof glass, the sandstone slab lies at the bottom of a 'well' of more recent brick. Fragments of charcoal found here are said to come from the root of a Sal tree, the type of tree said to be held by Maya as she gave birth.

ABOVE
Foundations of ancient monasteries, Lumbini.

THE EARLIEST WOODEN STRUCTURE

In 2011 and 2012 a joint Nepalese/University of Durham team, excavating inside the Mayadevi temple, found evidence of a wooden structure predating the brick temple of Ashoka by several hundred years. They suggest that a wooden fence, which enclosed a sacred tree, was the earliest religious edifice at Lumbini and was used to orientate subsequent construction. The radio-carbon dating of this construction and the presence of ritual religious activity for centuries prior to Ashoka, suggests an 'early' rather than a 'late' date for the Buddha's birth. However, like much early-Buddhist archaeology, these findings are disputed.

THE NATIVITY SCULPTURE

Above the marker, is the strikingly modern looking sculpture of the birth scene. Carved in the round from a two metre slab of Mathura red sandstone, it dates from the Gupta period. At some later date it split along the frontal plane creating a flattened view of the participants. Maya stands grasping the branch of a sal tree with her right hand and her left, casually resting on her hip. Prajapati supports Maya's waist and to her right are the tall-crowned Vedic gods Brahma and Indra. Brahma stands, hands outstretched waiting to receive the infant. The sculpture depicts the moment immediately after the birth. Born from Maya's right side, the infant Siddhartha stands below, awaiting his first, lotus-enhanced steps.

PUSHKARA—THE SACRED POND

The shape of the original bathing pond, which Maya used before giving birth is not known. It now resembles, thanks to Kesher Rana, a brick lined swimming pool, with ghats descending to the water on each side. In 1993 when the pond was drained, and a metre of mud removed from its bottom, two artesian wells were found in the base. This suggests that Lumbini was once a traveller's resting place, and, by implication, a suitable spot for the pregnant Maya to take respite.

ASHOKA'S PILLAR

Beside the temple is Ashoka's column surrounded by a protective railing to prevent devotees plastering it with gold leaf or anointing it with offerings of butter and oil. The various inscriptions are readily apparent. Ashoka's is at railing-height.

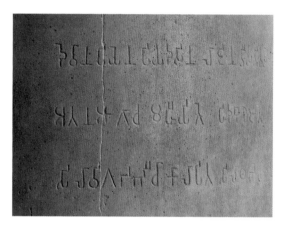

ABOVE
Brahmi script on the Lumbini Ashokan Pillar – 249 BCE.

Ripu Malla's inscription recording his 1312 visit is near the top of the column. There are three lines. The first is the well-known mantra to the Buddha of Compassion *Om mani padme hum.* The second line records Ripu Malla's name; and the third is probably the name of his accompanying son, Sangrama Malla. Before the 1896 excavation of General Shumsher Rana, this was the only inscription that lay exposed. A rubbing of this was sent by Duncan Ricketts to William Smith in Lucknow. Smith failed to appreciate that Ripu Malla's 'scribblings' on an Ashokan pillar might indicate that this was a place of importance, worthy of further consideration.

Steel bands encircle the pillar to secure the vertical crack which extends most of the length. Squashed between the pillar and surrounding guard rail, is the lotus base of the capital. It has lost the high polish typical of Ashoka's finest artisans. No sign has been found of the horse-capital which once topped the column.

NATIONAL TEMPLES AND STUPAS

In recent years, Buddhist nations have built temples to celebrate their involvement with Buddhism. Even the most charitable are likely to agree that there has been a nationalistic element in this display. The Asian nations have all built in the style of their country. Most have accommodation for monks, their own nationals, and sometimes foreigners. The most interesting are mentioned below. If you are unfamiliar with the various 'flavours' of Buddhism, a few hours spent touring these temples will impart a sense of their artistic differences.

The Great Lotus Stupa—'The German temple'

The Kargyu school of Tibetan Buddhism is celebrated in this complex. Around the main stupa are pleasant gardens with sculptures depicting events in the life of the Buddha. Inside the walls are covered with excellent paintings of mandalas, Buddhas and Bodhisattvas of the Tibetan canon.

Swayambhu Mahavihara—A Nepalese temple

The Nepalese offering resembles the dome of Swyambu Temple

which stands above the Kathmandu Valley. In a large pillared hall within the dome is a six metre seated Buddha in bhumiparsha (earth-witness) position, a masterwork of the Nepalese coppersmiths.

The Chinese temple

It is appropriate to be greeted at the entrance of the Chinese temple by a fat Laughing Buddha, symbol of prosperity. Inside, tree lined courtyards are flanked by walkways roofed in tiles of dull gold-yellow, in a style typical of the Qing dynasty. The Buddhism practiced here is Chan, a term derived from the Sanskrit word dhyana, which means meditation. In the 10th century Chan was taken to Japan, where it became Zen. With an emphasis on meditation, the Zen form of Buddhism is mostly practiced in Japan, Korea, Vietnam and, increasingly in the West.

The Korean temple

Three tiers of sweeping concrete roof and undecorated walls of grey give an unfinished appearance. It may change, but the Buddha Hall, with 20 metre walls of bare concrete sparsely decorated with three textile banners has a spare, gritty appeal.

The Myanmar Golden Monastery

The contribution from Myanmar, is a smaller version of the Shwe Dagon Golden Pagoda in Yangon. Statues of major events in the Buddha's life occupy the cardinal points, and within the pagoda base is a relic of the Buddha.

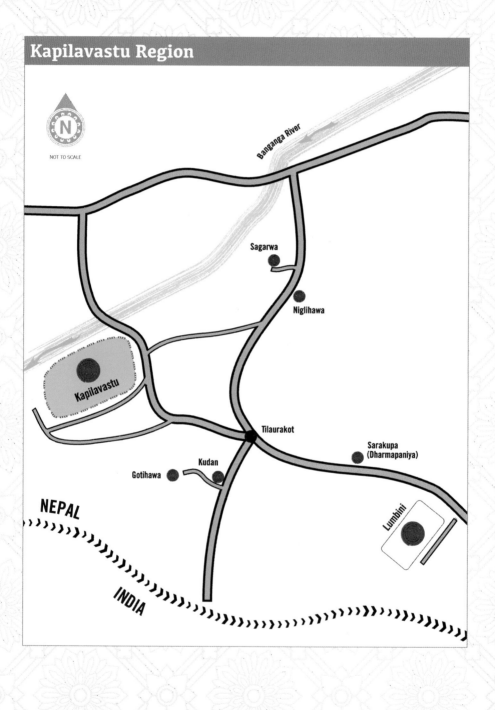

Kapilavastu Region

CHAPTER THIRTEEN

Tilaurakot
Nepalese-Kapilavastu

Only in the mid-19th century were the origins of Buddhism unravelled. Gradually it became apparent that the historical Buddha had been born and had lived his early life, somewhere on the plains of India or Nepal. Tales about his life and stories of other legendary Buddhas of the area, make the region an important pilgrimage destination.

Textural references provided many details of the Buddha's birth and subsequent life. Missing, was archaeological evidence to back the written claims. In the latter part of the 19th century, early archaeologists competed to become the first to uncover the exact locations of the Buddha's life. There were many examples of scholarship which were not self-serving and without bias. And there were other early explorers, driven by the universal poisons of greed anger and ignorance, whose conduct was deplorable. These conflicted personalities were especially evident in the search for the historical Lumbini and Kapilavastu. Their striving, adds extra spice to visiting the region.

ABOVE
**Ruins of the
'Royal Palace',
Kapilavastu.**

Kapilavastu was known to be the home to the youthful future-Buddha. Many stories and related monuments commemorate his youthful twenty-nine years around the district, and later visits after becoming enlightened. Fortuitously, the region was also home to several legendary Buddhas who were believed to have visited earth in times of great human need. In modern times, the discovery of sites related to these legendary Buddhas helped with the location of places relevant to Gautama Buddha.

Kapilavastu

By the 8th century BCE, the town of Kapilavastu was one of the most prosperous kingdoms north of the Ganges. It was ruled by the Sakya family, whose name derives from the Sanskrit for 'able' or 'worthy'. Their clan-name Gautama, comes from an ancestor sage, Kapila Gautama. The Sakyas were of the warrior caste, a group noted for their adherence to custom. The ancient literature abounds with stories of Sakyan pride in the purity of their heritage. Sakyan nobles believed in their racial superiority because they were directly descended from the Sun God. That pride was to cause problems and lead eventually to the destruction of the clan during the Buddha's lifetime.

When the future Buddha was growing up, Kapilavastu was a small republic. It was of sufficient power to have extensive walls, a moat and numerous buildings with a city population of possibly ten thousand. Nowadays the land has been cleared, but in Siddhartha's time it would have been heavily forested, with numerous dangerous animals. In 406, when Faxian came he fretted about wild elephant and lions which *'...render it impossible to travel negligently.'*

His *Record of the Buddhist Kingdoms*, found the region bleak: *'There was neither king nor people. All was mound and desolation. Of inhabitants, there were only some monks and a score or two of families of the common people.'*

Two hundred years later, Xuanzang found it no better. In more modern times, this Terai region of Nepal-India was notorious for malaria. Because of this, there were few inhabitants. Only in the last one hundred and fifty years has the dense jungle been cleared for fertile rice paddy.

BIRTH OF THE PRINCE

Around 484 BCE, the future Buddha was born into a noble family of the Sakya . Most traditions say he was royal, a 'prince of the Sakya ' and offer a birth date more than a hundred years earlier, around 600 BCE. Dating the Buddha's life excites vigorous argument. Fortunately, there is general agreement about his privileged upbringing and the broad sweep of his life, although the details may be embellished by myth.

His mother, Mayadevi, whose name in Sanskrit means 'Queen of Illusion' was wife of Suddhodana, King of the Sakyas. Their home was Kapilavastu. On becoming pregnant she dreamt that a white elephant with six tusks entered her womb. This dream was interpreted as the birth of a future prince who would either be a cakravartin (universal monarch) or a Buddha—a great spiritual leader. Suddhodana did not wish a spiritual life for his son, so resolved to raise him, in every way, as an earthly and worldly, prince.

As time for her delivery drew near, tradition required that Mayadevi return to her family home of Devadaha to give birth. She had been a princess of the Koliya clan who traditionally intermarried with the Sakyas. At a small village, now called Lumbini, she was overcome with labour pains and there she gave birth.

All Buddhist accounts agree that about seven days after the birth, Mayadevi died so the young prince was raised by Maya's younger sister, Prajapati (Leader of Many), who was another wife of King Suddodana. The child grew up an advantaged youngster. His language was probably ancient Magadhi, a derivative from Sanskrit. He was called Siddhartha, 'he who achieves his aim' but was also known as Gautama 'remover of darkness' and later as Sakyamuni 'sage of the Sakyas'.

CHILDHOOD AND YOUTH OF SIDDHARTHA

We can only infer the details of how the prince grew to maturity. As favoured son and potential world-ruling cakravartin, he was a cossetted child, and indulged young man. Figuratively it was a life of 'wine women and song'; a life which emphasised personal pleasures, and which sought to avoid the realities of everyday existence. It was a life of delusion, not in accord with the harsh nature of ordinary people's lives.

Then, quite abruptly, this pampered prince was forced to reflect about the deeper meaning of life. The story relates that on successive days, he met in the street the human faces of old age, of sickness and of death; and, on the next day, a beacon to a different way of life, in the form of a wandering holy man. Just when these 'divine messengers' caused the prince's life to be disturbed, we do not know for sure. Tradition would have it that the prince had been so sheltered, that he was totally unaware of old age, sickness and death until the age of twenty-nine. Complete oblivion to these universal truths until adulthood, seems unlikely, suffice to know that the prince became deeply troubled by life's existential questions.

SIDDHARTHA AND DEVADATTA

A constant acquaintance of Siddhartha during his early life was his cousin Devadatta. There are numerous accounts in the literature of their uneasy relationship. Devadatta, whose name means 'god given', had a jealous disposition which was stimulated by his perception of the young prince's privilege and which in later life culminated in serious conflict between the two.

The Injured Goose

The difficulties between the two cousins are said to have started from a childhood episode. An arrow fired by Devadatta injured a flying goose, which landed in the garden of Siddhartha. The young prince removed the arrow, treated the wound and refused to release the bird to Devadatta. The dispute was sufficiently vehement to involve city elders, who ruled in favour of Siddhartha. It is said, that Devadatta never forgave this slight. Some accounts of this incident say the bird was not a goose, but a Sarus crane, a bird whose ancestors still frequent the wetlands around Kapilavastu.

Hastigarta

When Siddhartha was seventeen he was engaged in athletic contests with other young notables. On winning one contest, cousin Devadatta was jealously enraged. On meeting a caparisoned elephant that had been sent to return the prince to the city Devadatta 'punched and kicked the elephant to death'—thus blocking the south gate of the city. Nanda, Siddhartha's younger brother pulled the body aside, only to have Siddhartha pick up the animal and hurl it beyond the city moat. On landing, the elephant carcase gouged the ground, to create Hastigarta—'the ditch of the fallen elephant'.

It's a good yarn, but details of the story are not credible. A more likely interpretation is that the tale is a later addition to the canon to further discredit Devadatta after his attempts at schism and assassination of the Buddha. Nevertheless, this event was recognised very early in Buddhist history, with the construction of a small stupa, the remains of which used be located near the Kapilavastu museum. Now, the stupa has been 'flattened' and there is nothing to see.

Devadatta became a disciple of the Buddha on Gautama's first return visit to his home town after enlightenment. He remained a member of the Buddha's community until they were both old men. For the most part he was regarded as a good and diligent monk but Devadatta continued to harbour a resentful attitude towards the Buddha. This led him to directly challenge the Buddha's authority by leading a splinter group of five hundred monks to found a separate community. This was the most serious issue faced by the Buddha in his forty-five years of ministry. Later still, Devadatta tried several times to kill the Buddha, although some scholars suggest that these attempted homicides might have been another later invention to further discredit the already sullied monk. The schism and assassination attempts are thought to have happened in Rajgriha.

Problems With a Girl

It could not have helped their relationship, when the two cousins competed for the same girl. Yasodhara was Siddhartha's cousin, daughter of his mother's brother, a princess from the nearby tribe of the Koliya people. As you would expect, like many another princess, she was beautiful, and sufficiently wise, to choose Siddhartha as her husband and thus enter world history.

A difficulty with this standard version is that we have little factual evidence about Gautama's wife. Even her name is uncertain. The earliest accounts refer to her as 'Rahula Mata'—Rahula's mother. It is the later texts which have named her Yasodhara.

Siddhartha's Marriage to Yasodhara

Like most young men Siddhartha married and had a child. He may, in fact, have had several wives as was the custom for men of his class.

Whether Yasodhara did choose her husband we do not know. At that time, women had little independence, so it is not unreasonable to speculate that she had little say in the choice of her princely spouse. Later, her faith in him as a reliable husband was to be sorely tested when he left her on a spiritual quest.

Siddhartha's Departure from the Palace

Whatever Gautama's domestic situation, to call his first-born son Rahula (fetter) indicates that the prince found family life constraining. Driving his dissatisfaction was the deeper angst of unsatisfied spiritual needs. Why is there sickness? Why old age and why death? And what was the solution to the apparent inevitability of human suffering? And, particularly for his time and culture, how could he escape the endless round of life, death and rebirth?

Unlike most fathers, and in non-exemplary style, he left his family and his life of privilege to pursue a spiritual path. All Buddhist traditions relate that one night, at the age of twenty-nine, the prince resolved to abandon the palace and his family. It was a critical moment in his life, and indeed, for all Buddhist history. To reinforce the drama of this event, the literature provides a vivid last-minute punctuation.

Just at the moment of departure, Mara the Lord of Desire, appeared before the young prince. Gautama could have remained comfortable, a member of the upper class; living a life of relative ease to become a ruler, a man of influence and power. Mara, the seducer and supreme king of attachment to all things of the material world, questioned the departing prince:

> *Why leave this life of comfort—why abandon a loving wife and new-born son? Why not stay and become ruler of the world? Why, not indeed!*

Both knew that the prince was leaving for a life of hardship and self-denial that would be long and difficult. A life which in the end, offered only a possibility that Siddhartha would break the bonds of attachment and become enlightened. Such life-changing decisions are not easy for anyone, but Siddhartha had extra to lose. To abandon his newly created family was bad, but the insult to his noble father and to his clan was probably worse. Leaving them was a public rejection of much that his family and society held dear. It says a lot for Siddhartha's sense of spiritual unease, that he was able to push aside the enticements of Mara, and leave. For Siddhartha it was surely something he had pondered for years.

Mounted on his white horse Kanthaka, accompanied by his groom Channa, Gautama left the city via the east gate, Mangaladwara—the 'lucky gate'. Riding eastward the two men reached the banks of a river where the prince dismounted, removed his robes, cut his long hair and commenced his six year quest for enlightenment. This ultimately led him to become 'the Buddha'—'the Enlightened One'—and the rest, as they say, is history. His wife Yasodhara and his son Rahula subsequently became members of the Sangha and eventually monastics.

GAUTAMA THE ASCETIC

Gautama had become a shramana, a wandering spiritual seeker, dependent on what he could glean from begging to survive. Within the Ganges valley at the time, there were several groups of shramanas who followed specific meditation teachers. Gautama studied initially with one teacher then another, mastering what was taught, but remaining unsatisfied with what they offered. Possibly two years were spent in this endeavour, before Gautama decided that only by following his own path would he find the peace of realisation that he sought. With five companions, he then spent several years practising extremes of self-mortification before recognising that self-denial was also a dead end. On the banks of the Niranjana river at Bodhgaya, he took food and chose to follow the Middle Way.

THE BUDDHA RETURNS TO KAPILAVASTU

Early sources relate that the Buddha revisited Kapilavastu four times following his enlightenment.

On the first occasion, a year following his enlightenment he received a somewhat rocky reception. It had been seven years since the prince had fled the city unannounced. 'The Great Departure', was surely a surprise to both his wife Yasodhara and his father Suddhodana. So, it is not unremarkable that some resentment still vibrated in the family, especially as there had been no chance to socialise with this newly-enlightened person, or to hear him teach.

During this first visit, the Buddha with his accompanying monks, stayed at Nyagrodha Grove, about five kilometres south of the city. The next morning while on his begging round in Kapilavastu, father and son met in the street. Suddhodana exclaimed angrily *'How can a Sakyan beg in the streets, barefoot and wearing rags?'* In response, the Buddha clearly expressed opposition to his father's views. The Buddha's realised state had dissolved for him, all issues of caste and position in society. So, he could declaim *'I am not of the Sakyan lineage, but of the Buddha lineage. I beg because that is what Buddhas do'.*

Yasodhara also had cause for complaint. After being abandoned, her husband did not return for years. For most of that time Siddhartha lived as a solitary ascetic in jungle areas, remote from Kapilavastu. During that period, it is likely, that Yasodhara had little or no knowledge of her man, until he became a public teacher after his enlightenment at Bodhgaya. She must have been a tolerant woman. After a seven year gap, they met for the first time at Kudan, five kilometres from her home at Kapilavastu. Siddhartha was now the Buddha, the Fully Enlightened One. Despite her reasonable grievance, it is unlikely that Yasodhara berated her wayward husband. It is much more probable that she celebrated his gift to her, and to the world, of an enlightened Great Teacher.

A more positive initial response came from other friends and relatives. The Buddha's cousins Ananda, Anuruddha and Devadattta all became disciples, along with his former groom Chandaka. Ananda was a particularly important addition. Later when the Holy One was fifty-five, Ananda became his personal assistant. For the remaining twenty-five years of the Buddha's life they were constant companions and best friends. The only condition made by Ananda, in taking up this position, was that he should be present whenever the Buddha gave a teaching. This constancy and his phenomenal memory made him the Buddha's most reliable recorder.

It is said that Ananda could recite 'word perfect' every discourse the Buddha had ever delivered. Other members of the Sangha helped, by committing to memory specific teachings. Thus, a collective memory was passed on to subsequent generations. In our computer world, memory is something digital—a machine skill. That is a very recent change in the human experience. Although the 'sayings of the Buddha', were not written until several hundred years after his death, it is not unreasonable to view many of the written records as the Buddha's actual words. Early in the development of the Buddha's Sangha, individual monks, additional to Ananda, were given the task of committing to memory specific discourses of the Teacher. These were later written into the Buddhist records. Such phenomenal memory still exists in the contemporary world—the Manaschi reciters of the Manas epic of Kyrgyzstan, being a good example.

Later, when the Buddha's father, Suddhodana, was dying at the age of ninety, the Buddha again revisited his former home. Suddhodana died and, in the tradition of all good Hindu sons, the Buddha lit the cremation fire of his father. The Buddha visited twice more. His last visit was after the destruction of Kapilavastu by King Vidudhava of Shravasti.

KING VIDUDHAVA AND THE DESTRUCTION OF ANCIENT KAPILAVASTU

The Buddha preached a doctrine of non-violence. Despite having the respect of many contemporary kings, he was not always successful in maintaining peace. His attempt to deflect the vengeance of Vidudhava against his own Sakya clan is a poignant example.

To the north west of Kapilavastu, several days distant, was the capital of the Kosala people, Shravasti. Before Siddhartha was enlightened, King Prasenajit of Shravasti requested as bride, a princess from his neighbour. The Sakyas of Kapilavastu were proud and had little respect for the citizens of Shravasti or their King. So instead of a princess they sent a beautiful slave girl, deceitfully calling her royal. This lie and the pride which drove it, was to ultimately cause their destruction.

The King and new Queen of Kosala gave birth to a son, prince Vidudhava. His name means 'precious jewels', appropriate for any baby, but not a sobriquet that fitted his adult conduct. As a youth he was sent to

Kapilavastu for training and while there as a student, the young Vidudhava discovered the truth of his humble origins. The day after a formal reception, one of Vidudhava's retinue noticed palace staff ritually cleaning the seat on which the prince had sat and cursing his master as a slave. Only then did the full story emerge.

Returning home to Shravasti in fury, Vidudhava was further enraged when his father, King Prasenajit, hearing the story, stripped him and his mother of all royal privileges, and reduced them to the status of slaves. Not surprisingly, Vidudhava vowed revenge on the Sakyas, and harboured resentment towards his father.

The Buddha was a friend of King Prasenajit. They were the same age and Prasenajit admired the virtuous life of Gautama and his followers. The Buddha pleaded on behalf of the demoted queen and prince. His successful intervention enabled the queen to be restored to the palace and Vidudhava to be made commander of the Kosalan army. The story, and its deeply negative karma, continued to role forward. Vidudhava never forgave these insults from his father, nor the original deceit of the Sakyas. Later, when he became King, by overthrowing his father, Vidudhava sought revenge on the Sakyas, who had outraged him. On several occasions, the Buddha was able to deflect his anger.

Hearing that King Vidudhava and army were en-route to Kapilavastu, the Buddha contrived a meeting. The story relates, that although comfortable, shaded seating was available, Gautama chose to seat himself in semi-sunshine under a withered tree. The King was sufficiently surprised to remark *'There are plenty of green and umbrageous trees; why do you not sit beneath one of these, instead of under this withered one with dried leaves...?'*

To which the Buddha responded *'My honourable tribe is like branches and leaves; these being about to perish, what shade can there be for one belonging to it?'*

Vidudhava was sufficiently moved by the Buddha's concern for his clan, to withdraw his army, but his resentment towards the Sakyas persisted.

Custom of the time is said to have demanded that an army withdraw if it met a religious sage en-route to battle. At that time, as now, there were numerous mendicants wandering the roads of India, so successfully reaching a battle ground would have been a matter for congratulation. In any event, it is said that the Buddha was able to deflect Vidudhava on two subsequent occasions. With his fourth attempt, Vidudhavu was successful. He attacked Kapilavastu, killed most of the Sakya clan and burnt the city.

SAGARWA

At the time of Vidudhava's assault, many citizens fled Kapilavastu city a few kilometres northwards, to the woody region of Sagarwa. Here they were slaughtered. The sources vary as to how many died, varying from nine thousand to many more. There must have been a significant massacre. Xuanzang's account is at the high end:

> To the north-west of the city there are over 100,000 stupas; this is the place where the Sakya clan was all slaughtered for its wantoness. King Vidudhava. subjugated the Sakya clan, enslaved their whole clan, seized 99,900,000 men, massacred them one after the other and piled up the bodies like a haystack. So much blood flowed that it formed a lake. The gods were alarmed by the humans, and later collected the bones and buried them.

An estimation of ancient Kapilavastu's size suggests that a lower, rather than higher number is more likely. Some accounts relate that the Sakyas offered little resistance as they had adopted the non-violence teaching of the Buddha.

A poignant twist to the story was the fate of 500 Sakyan women who were selected to join Vidudhava's harem. Proud of Sakyan heritage, they rejected Vidudhava not because of their honour but because of his low birth. Not surprisingly, 'The King was filled with rage and ordered that all the women be killed. At the King's orders the executioners cut the sinew of their arms and legs and threw the women into a ditch.'

In any event, the attack by Vidudhava did not completely wipe out the Sakya clan. After the Buddha's death the Sakya clan were allocated a one eighth share of his relics. Despite the recent war, they still had sufficient energy and resources to erect a stupa to honour The Great Teacher's relics. The location of that stupa remains uncertain.

OTHER BUDDHAS OF THE KAPILAVASTU REGION

Buddhist cosmography divides time into six great eons, or kalpas. Our current era is the Bhadrakalpa—the 'Fortunate age' or 'Era of stability'. During this era it is believed that a sequence of five Buddhas have come, or will come, to help all sentient beings. They come as humans, and at specific times when their presence will be most beneficial. Each birth marks a change in world order.

Collectively these historical Buddhas are known as Manusi, or human Buddhas. Four have come, during this current kalpa, with one still to

157

arrive. What's fortunate for the modern pilgrim visiting Tilaurakot, is that most of most of the Manusi-Buddha activity happened in the Kapilavastu region.

- **Krakuchhanda**—the first Manusi-Buddha, was born in Gotihawa, Tilaurakot district, Nepal.

- **Kanakamundi**—the second, was born in Niglihawa, Tilaurakot district, Nepal. His name derives from the legend, that at his birth 'gold showered from the sky'.

- **Kasyapa**—the third, was born in Varanasi, India.

- **Sakyamuni**—the fourth and current Buddha, was born in Lumbini, Nepal.

- **Maitreya**—the fifth, and last Buddha for this kalpa, is yet to come.

THE 'REAL' LOCATION OF KAPILAVASTU—NEPAL OR INDIA?

To this time, there is considerable debate about the location of the Buddha's home town. Most authorities agree that the evidence favours here, the Nepal site, as ancient Kapilavastu. However, fifteen kilometres away, across the Indian border is the site of Piprahwa, thought by others to be the site of Gautama's early life.

Major evidence in favour of the Nepal site is the location of two stupas belonging to the Buddha's parents; a surrounding moat and brick walls of a city; an eastern gate from which Prince Siddhartha left of a life of religious exploration; and its correct orientation to other sites as mentioned by the Chinese pilgrims.

Additional scientific evidence has more recently come to hand. In 1997 a UNESCO sponsored excavation was undertaken by the University of Bradford. Beneath the ruins, underground sonar revealed an extensive system of roads suggestive of a large settled population and formal excavation brought ancient treasures of Siddhartha's time to the surface. In 2000 the same group found carbon-14 evidence reliably proving that the Tilaurakot-Kapilavastu site had been continuously settled throughout the 5th and 6th centuries BCE.

In addition, an Italian group from the University of Naples found 110 previously unknown sites in the region between Lumbini and the Banganga river. Their area of exploration was not Tilaurakot, but it is very close, and helps confirm that during the Gautama's time the whole Tilaurakot region had significant lay habitation. No similar claim can be made for the Piprahwa-Ganwaria site on the Indian side of the border which is essentially a religious site.

The most compelling evidence in favour of the Indian site at Piprahwa occurred during the 1970s excavations. First to be excavated, were two soapstone relic caskets which are ancient, and arguably contain bone fragments of the Buddha. Those relics are now on display in the National Museum in New Delhi. More compelling evidence, was an impressive number of clay seals bearing inscriptions to the effect that they were owned by 'The community of Buddhist monks of Kapilavastu'. Archaeologists and Buddhist scholars continue to argue about the relevance of these details. A definitive decision favouring the Nepal or the Indian site is years away. Such finality would require extensive excavation on both sides of the border, and may never happen, given the potent politics involved.

Today's Tilaurakot– Kapilavastu region

The dense forest, which delayed exploration a hundred years ago, has been replaced with ordered fields of rice. Places of historical interest are widely scattered. To visit these sites in the sequence listed below is a practical way to tour the region.

ABOVE
The Buddha receives a robe from Yasodhara, at Kudan.

KUDAN—NYAGRODHA

Roughly a year following enlightenment, the Buddha resolved to visit Kapilavastu. He and his entourage of 300 monks stayed at the Nyagrodha Grove. Suddhodana had initially resented Siddhartha taking up a religious life, but gradually he accommodated this choice although it was in conflict with the prevailing responsibilities of a Sakyan son. After the Buddha had been several days at Nyagrodha, his father Suddhodana, although ailing, travelled the five kilometres south from the city, to make peace with his son. The place where they reconciled is now called Kudan.

Three Sakya monuments were built at Kudan. The first was a monastery to house the Buddha and his entourage. These very early Buddhist monasteries would have been made from wood or bamboo. Dense groves of bamboo were common then, as were groves of banyan trees. (Ficus bengalensis or nyagrodha). Nowadays, the three main monuments of Kudan are encircled by aged mango trees.

Nyagrodharama monastery is the largest visible monument, facing you directly at the gate. It was built to celebrate the union of father and son and to accommodate the Buddha's entourage. Later, during Mauryan times, the wooden structure was replaced with a brick building. In later centuries futher renovations were made by Sunga, Kushan and Gupta rulers. Many of these early bricks are elaborately incised and are still in situ along the lower courses. A steel walkway gives access to the top, where a flattened spot has been claimed by a small Shiva lingam, housed in its encircling yoni.

To the right is, the second stupa is where Prajapati, the Buddha's step-

RIGHT
The 'Gate of Great Departure', Kapilavastu.

mother, gave the Buddha a golden robe and where the Buddha's wife Yasodhara invited him for a meal at the Kapilavastu palace. At the base of the stupa, is a contemporary plaque showing Prajapati donating the robe. Near the stupa's front, are two bricks recording the paw-prints of a long-dead dog and the finger marks of its (possible) owner.

To the left is the third stupa. The highest of the three, it is crowned by a skinny, brick temple to Lord Shiva. The stupa records the ordination as a novice, of eight year old Rahul, the Buddha's son. This initiation was carried out by the monk Shariputra. Rahul would have been excited to meet his father. Given the circumstances, it must have been an anxious encounter for an eight year old. He was about to meet, effectively for the first time, a father who had abandoned both his family and his princedom, and who, in childish eyes, must have seemed a god. His anxiety could not have been helped by a demand placed on him by his mother.

Dutifully, and with a significant display of Sakyan courage, Rahula demanded of the Buddha *'Give me my inheritance.'* In response, the Buddha requested Shariputra to *'...please give Rahula whatever I have in this lifetime'.* By which he meant that Rahula was to be ordained as a novice monk. Just what happened next is not clear. It seems there was objection to Rahula being taken away from the family home, but the Buddha was adamant that Rahula be taken into the order with Shariputra and Maudgalyayana as his tutors. Later the Buddha was to agree that children could not become novices without permission of their parents.

GOTIHAWA

The narrow access road to Gotihawa gets little traffic. Not many pilgrims visit despite it being only three kilometres from Kudan. The local people are welcoming, and their children don't beg. Their homes open immediately to the street to give a glimpse of rural life.

NOTE: only smaller vehicles can traverse this road. If you are in a large bus, jeeps can be hired from Kudan.

Gotihawa, was birthplace to the first Manusi-Buddha, Krakuchhanda. Ashoka left an inscribed pillar here, with an impressive lion-capital that was seen by both Faxian and Xuanzang. Now, only the lower metre stands upright in a small, brick pond. Three other small fragments of Ashoka's column lie abandoned in Gotihawa. Their antiquity is reflected in local lore. The Sanskrit for Gotihawa means 'broken pieces', and, the remaining upright fragment is known in Nepali as 'Phutesvara Mahadeva', the Broken Lord. A joint Nepalese/Italian group in 1994 found Gotihawa to be one of the oldest sites in the area. Their carbon-dating of charcoal at ca. 800 BCE confirms that humans were here long before the Buddha was born.

THE ROYAL STUPAS AT KAPILAVASTU

Heading north to Kapilavastu, it is best to first drive around the fence which defines the main site, to the stupas of Suddhodana and Mayadevi, father and mother of Siddhartha. Here In unfenced farmland, the base of two large brick stupas lie exposed, a metre below ground level. When excavated, each contained a Gupta-period terracotta seal with their respective names. Suddhodana's seal was discovered in the larger one.

THE MAIN TILAURAKOT–KAPILAVASTU SITE

Returning to the main entrance, what's immediately striking is the relative lack of excavation. The broad brick walls, which encompassed the city, have sunken, lie in curves and are overgrown with trees. The moat which provided protection to these walls is only observable with the eye of faith. Between each excavated site the brush and trees grow so densely that you cannot see from one region to another. When the Buddha lived, the houses here were built of timber, or wattle and daub. The brick remains we see are additions by dynasties that followed the Sakyas of Buddha's time. However, few historians doubt that underneath these bricks lie the byways of Siddhartha's youth.

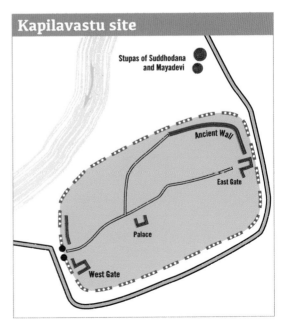

Kapilavastu site

Stupas of Suddhodana and Mayadevi

Ancient Wall

East Gate

Palace

West Gate

On entering, West Gate is to the right. Low brick walls define the entrance way and rooms for guards. Centrally within the complex, is the Palace. With low brick walls and large rooms, its significance can only be inferred.

161

Most noteworthy is The Gate of the Great Departure, or Managalad-wara—the lucky gate, lying to the east of the town. It was from here that the twenty-nine year old prince rode out to change himself and the world. A hundred metres beyond the gate is a stupa commemorating Siddhartha's horse Kanthaka. Legend relates that Kanthaka had the sole life-purpose of carrying the future-Buddha out of the world to luxury towards enlightenment. When this task was complete, the horse died before he could return to the palace.

From the Managaladwara, it is possible to walk along the top of the recently excavated city wall, then back to the entrance by a forest path. En-route is the Smaimai temple. A Hindu shrine so aged, that its bricks have been entwined, and become part of, the overshadowing tree. In centuries past, the bricks of Buddhism have been taken to complete a tiny shrine to a local god. Around the shrine are a herd of black elephant statues, protectors of the deity within.

THE TILAURAKOT—KAPILAVASTU MUSEUM

Near the main entrance to the site is a small museum. Only visit if time and enthusiasm permit. One tiny room has a range of dusty cabinets with terracotta pottery, seals and toys, along with a few coins of Sakya times.

NIGLIHAWA

Eight kilometres to the north-west is the Niglihawa, the birthplace of Kanakamuni, the second of the Manusi-Buddhas. Two fragments of an Ashokan column are here protected by a shelter. They are thought to have been brought here from some other place in the distant past. Both have an inscription. The smaller piece, projecting a metre from the ground, records in Brahmi script, that Ashoka visited twice. This inscription is similar in style to that of the Lumbini Pillar making it likely that they were carved by the same hand. Ripu Malla's 1312 inscription is on the larger portion of column, which lies on its side. The two incised birds are much later additions. When Xuanzang visited Kapilavastu in the 7th century, he found the pillar erect, bearing its lion capital. The exact location of the pillar at that time, and the capital have been lost to antiquity.

The base which supported the column has not been found, so it is likely that Niglihawa is not the original location of these two fragments. In 1904, General Khadka Shamsher Rana drew attention to the Shiva lingam worshipped in the Towleshwar Mahadev temple in downtown Tilaurakot. He suggested this was not only the missing lower fragment of the Kanakamuni Ashokan Pillar, but also its original location, as it stands atop a mound which the General surmised was an old stupa. Today, religious sensibilities, prohibit examination of the Towleshwar Temple linga.

In 1895, Dr. Führer read the Ashokan inscription on Niglihawa column, and realised that the Kapilavastu of Siddhartha's youth must lie nearby. Anxious that he should be first to discover Kapilavastu he falsely claimed the presence of a large stupa and numerous other ruins around the Niglihawa site. This lie ultimately helped to bring about his downfall.

SAGARWA

Down a dusty trail, four kilometres from Niglihawa is the place where the Buddha's relatives were massacred by the vengeful Vidudhava. For two seasons in 1897–98, Dr. Alois Führer excavated here. He found a multitude of small votive stupas to the slain. Today, there is no sign of these stupas and the Lumbu Sagar (long-lake) is no longer filled with Sakyan blood.

It's a quiet place. At the lake's western end are the remains of the large stupa investigated by General Khadga Sumsher Rana and later by Anton Führer. Now it is a three metre mound, with loose bricks sprinkled over the surface allowing a view over the lake. In the land between was the location of Führer's eighteen votive stupas.

SARAKUPA

It was not uncommon during ancient times for the most suitable suitor to be chosen by some form of martial arts contest. Legend relates that the young Siddhartha won the hand of princess Yasodhara by his skill at archery. The prince's arrow was so powerful that it pierced the iron target and flew another twelve kilometres. At the end of its flight there was sufficient energy bring forth a fountain of clear water. The place where the arrow landed was known as Sarakupa—'the arrow fountain'. The water was, and is, renowned for its health giving qualities.

Today's village is called Dharmapaniya—'religious water'. Driving from Tilaurakot, it lies thirteen kilometres west of the Lumbini Garden, two hundred metres off the northern side of the road. Only the memory of the legend exists today.

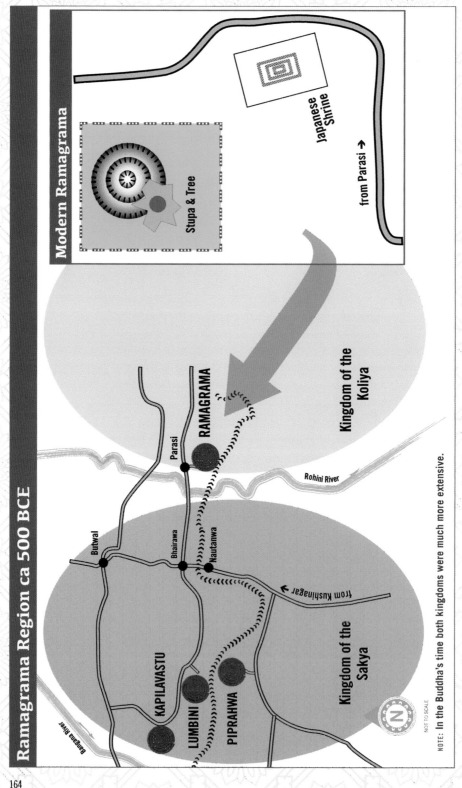

Modern Ramagrama

Stupa & Tree

Japanese Shrine

from Parasi →

Ramagrama Region ca 500 BCE

Kingdom of the Koliya

RAMAGRAMA

Parasi

Butwal

Bhairawa

Nautanwa

Rohini River

from Kushinagar →

KAPILAVASTU

LUMBINI

PIPRAHWA

Kingdom of the Sakya

Banganga River

N

NOT TO SCALE

NOTE: In the Buddha's time both kingdoms were much more extensive.

CHAPTER FOURTEEN

Ramagrama

FOR Buddhists, Ramagrama is important because it is one of the original eight stupas to receive relics of the Buddha. When Emperor Ashoka set about redistributing those relics, the Ramagrama Stupa was the only original one he did not open. Although extensive excavation was carried out here by Nepalese archaeologists in 1997 the earliest section of the stupa was not touched, so it presumably contains relics of the Buddha placed here very soon after his death.

ABOVE
**The Ramagrama
Stupa.**

During Buddhist times the Koliya people were friends and neighbours of the Sakyas from Kapilavastu. The legend of Koliya origins demonstrates charming naivety. Four brothers married four sisters. In due course the senior sister developed leprosy and went to live in the forest. Here she was joined by the King Rama of Varanasi who was also afflicted with the same disease. One day, while sitting under a kolam tree (Haldina cordifolia) pondering their ill fortune, they were miraculously cured of leprosy. Their descendants became the Koliya people, named after the tree and the city was called Ramagrama after the king.

The state of Koliya was mostly known as Devadaha (God's Lake). The Koliya people lived across the Rohini River from the Sakya, about fifty kilometres east of Kapilavastu. The ruling families of the two clans, as Kshatriya, or warrior caste, were conscious of status and purity of blood line and regularly intermarried. The Buddha's mother Maya, stepmother Prajapati, and his wife Yasodhara all came from Devadaha, the capital city. The site of Devadaha has not been identified, but it is thought to be near the modern Nepalese city of Butwal. Excavations at nearby Bhavanipur, by Nepalese archaeologists in 2011–13 have so far not found relics earlier than the 10th century.

THE BUDDHA AND DEVADAHA

During his secular life as a young man, it is likely that Siddhartha Gautama came to visit relatives at Devadaha. As a teacher, the Buddha came here several times. The Devadaha Sutra preached here, clarifies the

Elephants lustrating the Ramagrama Stupa. Sanchi East gateway, Ashokan, 3rd century BCE.

importance of karma in relation to current suffering. Gautama delivered this teaching in response to the Jain belief that all pain and pleasure experienced now is determined by past action. This implies that no current action will influence the experience of pleasure or pain. The Buddha pointed out, that if that were so, why should the Jains become free of pain when they cease their self-abusive activity? As the Buddha demonstrated, the present experience of pleasure and pain is a combination of both past and present actions and it is not due to past karma alone.

On one occasion, because of a prolonged drought, there was a dispute between Sakya and Koliya about distribution of water from the Rohini River. As the armies gathered to battle there was loud disputation until the Buddha arrived from Vaishali. Some accounts have him flying in to dramatically calm the situation by hovering over the disputed water, and then admonishing *'It is not fitting that because of a little water you should destroy kshtriyas who are beyond price.'* Eventually, a compromise was reached and peace restored.

BUDDHA'S RELICS—RAMAGRAMA—ASHOKA—AND THE CHINESE PILGRIMS

Shortly after the Buddha's death, the Koliya's obtained a one eighth share of his relics. These were placed in the Ramagrama Stupa, making it one of the original Mahastupas. When Ashoka came to the region to open this stupa he was astonished to find Ramagrama protected by a giant naga (snake deity).

In a much more loquacious style than usual, Faxian tells of Ashoka's visit. He relates that, beside the stupa was a large pool *'...and in the pool a dragon, which constantly kept watch...'* The dragon was able to dissuade the Emperor from opening the stupa to remove the precious relics.

'*Afterwards*' Faxian says '*the ground all about became overgrown with vegetation, and there was nobody to sprinkle and sweep; but a herd of elephants came regularly, which brought water with their trunks to water the ground, and various kinds of flowers and incense, which they presented...*' at the stupa.

The story of elephants protecting the Ramagrama Stupa was well known long before Faxian. The 1st century eastern gateway of the Great Stupa of Sanchi has a herd of ten elephant offering flowers to the Ramagrama stupa. Later, this story of the Emperor's visit, and why he did not open the stupa was related to Xuanzang.

ARCHAEOLOGICAL INVESTIGATION AT RAMAGRAMA

Dr. Hoey identified the site in 1898 but apart from recording the dimensions of the stupa carried out no further investigation. It remained for a group of Nepalese archaeologists to systematically investigate the stupa and a nearby monastic complex that had been described by the Chinese pilgrims. They established there had been several phases of construction from the Mauryan period. The clay mound comprising the core of the stupa was not touched, so if Buddha relics are here, they remain undisturbed. The size and regular rebuilding of this stupa from Mauryan to Gupta times is indication of its perceived importance over hundreds of years.

Today's Ramagrama

A visit to Ramagrama is a journey to rural Nepal. There are few ancient monuments, but it's a chance to meditate on a good story and experience quiet charm. If time permits, don't miss Ramagrama. Little traffic follows the road running eastwards from Bhairawa to the tiny village of Parasi. The boundary between Sakya and Koliya territory is the second small river you cross, the Rohini. From Parasi a rough trail runs another two kilometres to Ramagrama.

It's appropriate to first visit the new Japanese shrine two hundred metres before the stupa. An infant golden Buddha holds aloft a single finger to indicate the primacy of the Buddha Way. Your view of the main stupa is shielded by trees until you arrive. It sits, a mound of dense grass, seven metres high. There is no sign of ancient bricks except at the base of an impressive tree which stands on the southern slope. Closer investigation reveals three different types of tree growing from the same site. It would be nice to report that one of them is the original healing kolam tree, but they are different species. The extensive excavations of recent years lie protected beneath a grassy sward. Sadly, there are no herds of elephant bearing flowers.

Piprahwa Indian-Kapilavastu

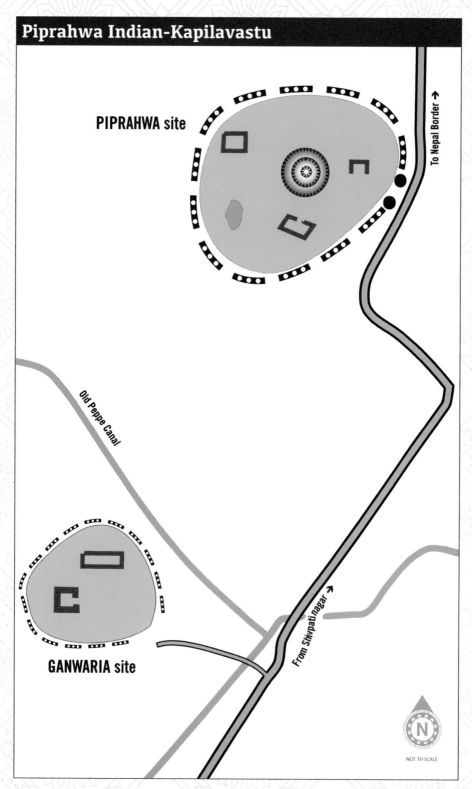

PIPRAHWA site

To Nepal Border →

Old Peppe Canal

GANWARIA site

From Shivpatinagar →

N

NOT TO SCALE

CHAPTER FIFTEEN

Piprahwa
Indian-Kapilavastu

THE 'REAL' LOCATION OF KAPILAVASTU—AGAIN

There is considerable dispute about whether the
Nepalese or the Indian site is the location of ancient
Kapilavastu. The debate is muddied by the fervent
patriotism of journalists and archaeologists of both
nations, with each group vying to prove that the
Buddha grew up on Indian or Nepalese soil. Gautama
Buddha would probably be amused by the current controversy as to which modern nation 'owns'
Kapilavastu, seeing it as an example of attachment,
and potent source of negative karma. What makes
the current nationalistic claims more ironic is that the
present-day border between the two contesting states,
Nepal and India, was drawn in 1815 at the Treaty of
Sugauli. In that treaty, Nepal lost more than a third of
its territory. Using the old boundary lines, the Buddhist sites of Piprahwa, Kushinagar and Shravasti are
well within Nepalese territory—even Delhi.

ABOVE
The 'Relics'
Stupa, Piprahwa.

THE CHINESE PILGRIM—FAXIAN AT TILAURAKOT—PIPRAHWA

An English version of Xuanzang's *Record of the Western Regions* was
published in 1884, followed by Faxian's *A Record of Buddhistic Kingdoms* two years later. These two works were scrutinised meticulously by
all involved with Buddhist exploration. Their inconsistency about the
location of Kapilavastu created difficulties, which continue to simmer to
this day.

What does not help is that the, usually consistent, Fa Hsien and Xuanzang seem to have visited two sites. Faxian probably went to Piprahwa
and Xuanzang to Tilaurakot, now in Nepal. These two places are about
fifteen kilometres apart in direct line; the region is flat; and in their time,
covered by dense jungle. Given that each man's Indian travels were separated by more than two hundred and thirty years, their lack of congruity
is understandable. In fact, it is surprising that there are not more differences in their published accounts. It is likely that both Chinese pilgrims

believed they were at 'ancient Kapilavastu' and, like modern tourists, that's what they were told.

A feature of both accounts is the fact that neither Chinese pilgrim mentions the presence of a relic-bearing stupa at their respective Kapilavastu. The Sakyas were given an eighth share of the Buddha's relics after his death. These were enshrined in a stupa of their home town, and later this stupa was opened by Ashoka for the second distribution of the holy relics. The whereabouts of this stupa remains uncertain, but some evidence suggests it may be Piprahwa.

THE PEPPÉ DISCOVERIES AT PIPRAHWA

In 1898 William Claxton Peppé was manager of the Birdpur estate just south of the Nepal border. His father had started the project fifty years before in what was swampy jungle, notorious for malaria. The hard work of clearing the forest and draining swamps resulted in a model property fifty square miles in area, famous for the production of high quality rice. Peppé, a Scots-educated engineer, was friendly with Hoey and Smith and their enthusiasm for Buddhist discovery. And, he would have been aware of Dr. Führer's work in nearby Nepal.

ABOVE **W.C. Peppe c1884, about fourteen years before his excavations.** Photographer unknown, courtesy Neill Peppé.

The surrounding region was flat, except for numerous artificial mounds, known as kot, the Sanskrit term for fort. A particularly large one sat on Birdpur land, a few kilometres from the homestead, close to the Nepal border. It was logical for Peppé to suspect this as being an ancient Buddhist stupa and he was advised on how to excavate this by his good friend Vincent Smith. Preliminary work over several months had cleared the mound of scrub and loose bricks to reveal a symmetrical stupa forty metres in diameter. On the 18th of January 1898, Peppé's workers cut a trench through its centre and at the depth of around twenty feet, made a remarkable discovery.

At the centre of the stupa, about seven metres below its apex, they uncovered a polished sandstone coffer resembling a giant shoe box, more than 1.3 metres long. The main coffer had been carved from a single piece of stone weighing 680 kilograms (1500 pounds). The lid, which was cracked into four sections, fitted the underlying casket so well that it had not collapsed. Inside were five lidded containers of differing shapes, each about the size of a jam jar. Four were of made of steatite (soapstone) and one of rock crystal.

Each was found to contain, scores of tiny beads, jewels, gem stones, pearls and fine gold plaques, some 1,200 in total. Mostly the gems had been cut to resemble six or eight pointed flowers. Similar ornaments have been found in other Buddhist monuments, but not of this quality, nor in such numbers. That this had been a site of great veneration was further confirmed by the notable size of the enclosing coffer, and the fact that it was made of stone from the same quarry as Ashoka's columns.

ABOVE
The Piprahwa stupa during the 1898 excavations
Photographer unknown, courtesy Neill Peppé.

The containers had originally been confined inside the coffer, within wooden boxes which on examination crumbled to dust. Amidst the excitement of finding such a profusion of tiny treasures, Peppé initially overlooked that scattered amidst the crumbs of wood, and the loose jewels, were fragments of bone. These bone and wood fragments were separated and kept separately. As evidence accumulated over succeeding days and years, the bone pieces came to be regarded (arguably) as actual relics of the Buddha.

The validity as to whether or not the bone remains might be those of the historical Buddha was based on a line of script scratched on the lid of one steatite container. All experts agree that the script is Brahmi, similar to the Ashokan inscriptions, and the language was archaic Maghadi, a form of Pali. That the writing seemed to have been done with an amateurish hand, was to become a debating point. The day after the discovery, Peppé had provided copies of the inscription to Dr. Führer, at that time at Sagarwa, and to Vincent Smith at Gorakhpur. These earliest transcriptions by Peppé contained minor errors which served to confuse the translators but they were in agreement that the inscription suggested the bones were those of the historical Buddha.

Within a month, early versions of the translation were published in the Indian press to great excitement, within and without India. Unfortunately, at the time, and even to this day, experts differ as to the translation, but a generally accepted modern rendition is:

This receptacle of relics of the blessed Buddha of the Sakyas (is the pious gift) of the brothers of Sukirit, jointly with their sisters, with their sons and their wives.

Recognising the significant nature of his find, William Peppé agreed to hand over the discoveries to the Indian Government, retaining about one sixth of the small gem stones for his family. In August 1898, the coffer, with its four steatite and one crystal containers, along with the majority of the beads, gems and gold leaf plaques were given to the Superintendent of the Indian Museum in Calcutta, where they remain to this day.

Whether Peppé had discovered 'genuine relics', was open to question. However, no such doubts troubled the international Buddhist community of the time, who immediately sought to have the remains transferred to a Buddhist country. Because of their significance, it was agreed by the Viceroy of the time, Lord Elgin, that they should be given to the King of Siam. At Gorakhpur, in February 1899 they were given to the King's representatives and taken with great ceremony to Bangkok. There, they were once again divided. Two portions for Burma went to the Shwe Dagon Pagoda in Rangoon and the Arakan Pagoda in Mandalay. Three went to Ceylon: the principal portion to Anuradhapura; and the other two for distribution to five separate sects in Kandy and Colombo. The residual relics from Piprahwa, along with some of the gemstones and jewels were enshrined in the Golden Mount Pagoda in Bangkok.

THE SHRIVASTAVA DISCOVERIES AT PIPRAHWA AND GANWARIA

For five years, from 1970 K.M. Srivastava, an archaeologist in the Archaeological Survey of India (ASI) carried out a series of excavations at Piprahwa, and nearby Ganwaria. Digging at the centre of the main stupa, he went below the level at which Peppé had discovered the massive coffer. About forty centimetres further down he found two soapstone containers of similar size and composition to those found by Peppé. One contained ten charred-bone fragments, the other twelve. The containers were accompanied by red-pottery dishes, most of them damaged. Srivastava dated these findings to *'fifth-fourth century BC',* about the right time-line for the Buddha.

During that first season Srivastava also determined that the Piprahwa stupa had been built in three phases. The first, a mud stupa, he dated around the time of the Buddha's death. The second, distinguished by well-fired large bricks, was early-Mauryan, within the reign of the Emperor Ashoka, around 200 BCE. And the third construction period he assigned to the reign of the Kushans, three hundred years later, about the start of the Common Era.

Srivastava carried on excavating ruins close to the stupa. He concluded that these were remains of monasteries that, like the stupa, had several stages of construction before being destroyed by fire and abandoned around 300 CE. In 1973, great excitement resulted from the discovery of terracotta seals which carried Kushan-period Prakrit script. Thirteen of them read *Of the Community of Buddhist monks of great Kapilavastu.* Another group of twenty-two had parts of a more extensive message indicating that the Kapilavastu monks had the patronage of the Kushan king, Kanishka or his successor, Huvishka. These important findings, of relics and inscribed sealings, were not initially made public, presumably because of rivalry within the ASI.

The next set of ruins to receive Srivastava's attention was the nearby complex known as Ganwaria. Almost a kilometre square, he found here numerous burnt-brick buildings and shrines, along with artefacts of Kushan times. The largest structures had been monasteries, similar in size and construction to those near the Piprahwa stupa. However, there was no trace of surrounding walls or extensive lay habitation.

It was not until 1976, that Srivastava eventually had opportunity to claim publically that he had settled '..*the location of ancient Kapilavastu, which had been eluding the archaeologists for more than a hundred years*.' A tidal wave of support from the Indian media followed. It was obvious, as far as the Indian press were concerned, that Gautama Buddha had grown up 'as Indian'.

There was similar journalistic enthusiasm about the relics. As they had been found beneath those of Peppé, it was immediately assumed that they must be older. And, it was only a short imaginative stretch to claim that these relics must be remains of the Buddha Sakyamuni. Buddhist scholars, were mostly less impressed. Western experts were unhappy with how Srivastava dated his relic chamber to the Buddha's time. Additionally, they pointed out that the soapstone containers found by Peppé and Srivastava were essentially identical in form and of a type that matched others found throughout the sub-continent, and were of a style that not in production prior to the 1st century BCE. In their view, if the bones found by Peppé, or by Srivastava were to be genuine they must have been repackaged by Ashoka and again repackaged a couple of centuries later.

None of these doubts were of concern to Asian Buddhists who mostly agreed with the 'genuine' interpretation, and were delighted when the Indian Government allowed them to be taken with great ceremony to Sri Lanka, Mongolia, Singapore, South Korea and Thailand. Today, the caskets and relics found by Srivastava are on display in the National Museum in New Delhi labelled as '..*the holy relics of Lord Buddha*.'

BELOW
Boy monk at Piprahwa.

Given the significance of Srivastava's findings, the nationalistic claims and the media hype, it is not surprising that controversy immediately erupted. The Nepalese were particularly miffed by the way India had claimed territorial rights over the early part of the Buddha's life. Rights, which they felt were much more justly theirs.

Nepalese experts, along with other international critics, pointed out that Srivastava had ignored the glaringly obvious fact that Piprahwa-Ganwaria was a monastic rather than a residential site, and, that it lacked the protective walls required of ancient Kapilavastu. In contrast, the Nepal site had all these features, along with evidence of an extensive network of buried roads and appropriate radio-carbon dating. The critics felt that Srivastava's terracotta inscriptions only affirmed that during Kushan times the monasteries of Piprahwa were part of the Kapilavastu monastic community, and they did not mean the monks occupied the ancient city of Gautama's childhood.

Non-Indian critics proposed an alternative scenario. As the two sites in contention, were only fifteen kilometres apart, they suggested that ancient Kapilavastu had been located on the Nepal side near modern Tilaurakot. Five hundred years after the Buddha's death, ancient Kapilavastu had expanded their monastic community to include the present locations of Piprahwa and Ganwaria which the archaeological evidence showed to be monastic and not residential. QED: or so it might seem, but the controversy continues to inflame passions on both sides of the border and beyond.

THE PIPRAHWA DECEPTIONS

In 2001 detailed accusations were made on the internet that the inscription on the Peppé container was a forgery. This claim was made by an independent English researcher, Terry Phelps. He also avowed that the inscriptions on the Ashoka pillars at Lumbini and Nigliva had been faked by Dr. Führer. The breadth of these accusations created much interest. At the heart of his claims about Piprahwa was the presence in the region of the well-known forger, Dr. Anton Alois Führer and that the inscription on the Peppé container seemed done by an amateur.

At the time of the Peppé excavation at Piprahwa, Dr. Führer's various forgeries and deceptions had not been revealed to his colleagues. Although each had understood the significance of Peppé's discovery, other duties had prevented both Führer and Smith from coming to view the findings for several days. The evidence shows that Dr. Führer had no opportunity to inscribe the vase. He had only one brief opportunity to view the inscribed container and at that time he was accompanied by others. Others present around the time of the Peppé excavation had no reason to embark on falsification. The senior ICS officers, Smith and Hoey lacked any rational motivation to involve themselves in conspiracy and the suggestion that W.C. Peppé might have tampered with the container ignores his lack of skill in ancient Brahmi script and his own complete lack of incentive for such an act.

In 2006 a conference of international experts was convened at Harewood House, Yorkshire, in an attempt to sort out whether the Piprahwa inscription was a forgery or part of some wider conspiracy. It was convened by Charles Allen, the noted historian on matters Indian, author of 'The Buddha and Dr. Führer', and supporter of the authenticity of the Peppé discovery. If the inscription was a forgery, which individual had the unsupervised opportunity, the skill and the motivation to carry such a deception? At its conclusion, one expert summed up the majority view of the conference as follows *'In short, it is hard to imagine that Führer, or anyone else for that matter, could have created such a convincing forgery.'* The conspiracy advocates, continue to think otherwise.

It would be nice to have conclusive proof one way or the other. But such finality is difficult, especially when the topic is so distant in time, and so charged with political and religious heat. Further excavation would be helpful in resolving the dilemma. Archaeological investigation continues at Nepal-Kapilavastu and, following a gap since 1977, was restarted at Piprahwa in 2012.

During his life, the Buddha attempted to mediate in many disputes, at times successfully and others less so. This dispute he would probably greet with wry exasperation. As in the case of the wounded soldier, what does it matter where the arrow came from?

It is the view of this author that Nepal-Kapilavastu is where Gautama lived his first twenty nine years. But for many others, Piprahwa is the Buddha's old home town. The experts and others less qualified, continue to argue. Uncertain? Well, you are not alone.

Today's Piprahwa

Travelling from Lumbini, and allowing for border-crossing, it will take about three hours to reach the small town of Shivpatinagar. Here, is a comfortable and convenient stopover, the Royal Retreat. A former hunting lodge, it was built in the 1840s in the jungle area known as the Terai. At that time the region had numerous tiger and other wild animals. The tiger have long retreated but some of their relatives are displayed on the

BELOW
Remains of the West monastery, with the 'Relics' stupa in the distance. Piprahwa.

walls of the lodge. The trophies, spacious rooms and furniture to match
are a glimpse of an era long gone.

THE PIPRAHWA SITE

Despite exaggerated claims, Piprahwa is important in the history of
Buddhism. It has a fair claim to have been the repository of The World
Honoured One's 'genuine' relics. And, as W.C. Peppé showed, the stupa
and the relics he discovered, were so highly regarded to be showered with
exquisite treasures.

So that you do not forget, the ASI signs welcome you to 'Kapilavastu'.
It's a lovely place, quiet and understated. Gently rolling lawns and flower
beds surround the excavations. A large lotus pond, and flanking mango
trees give an impression of a classy, if somewhat eccentric golf course.

THE EASTERN MONASTERY

To the right on entry, are walls of an expansive monastery with 31 cells
facing a central courtyard. Here, Srivastava found evidence of four separate construction phases, and in 1973 the inscribed sealings. The longer
inscription on twenty-two of them stated:

> Om of the community of monks of Kapilavastu in the monastery of
> Kanishka (or Huvishka).

THE PIPRAHWA STUPA

Directly ahead is the brick stupa unearthed by Peppé in 1898. It rises in
three gentle terraces to a height of around seven metres. The trench cut
by Peppé and reopened by Srivastava seventy years later is not apparent.
Two small viharas and a couple of low stupas complete the ensemble.

THE GANWARIA SITE

A kilometre to the south, are the remains of Ganwaria. Each monastery resembles what you have seen at Piprahwa. Spacious brick cells for individual monks look out to a central courtyard. For their time, they must have been comfortable and quiet. Warm in winter, cool in summer and without the animals and bustle of village life.

BIRDPUR HOUSE

A more contemporary ruin, is Birdpur House, a few kilometres to the south-west. When in 1842, the father of W.C. Peppé came to India he chanced to meet and marry a widow of the Birdpur estate near to the Nepal border. The first estate house was single storeyed, with a roof of thatch. As fortunes improved, the house became spacious, two storeyed, with expansive gardens and colonnaded entrance way. Descendants of the W.C. Peppé lived here until their land was nationalised by the Government of India shortly after independence in 1947. For some years, following, the house was used as an Inspection Bungalow for visiting officials, before being abandoned. It is now used by the Irrigation Department for their offices.

ABOVE
Birdpur House today.

BELOW
Birdpur House, painted in 1943 by Elfie Peppé.
Courtesy Neill Peppé.

Shravasti Region

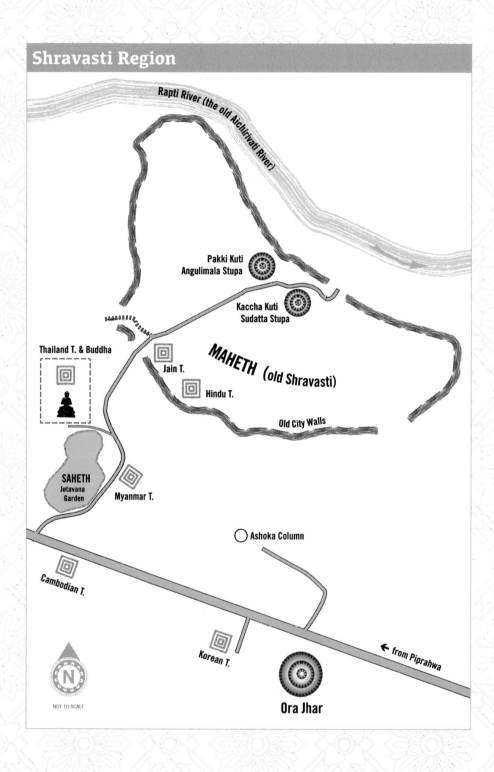

Rapti River (the old Aichirvati River)

Pakki Kuti
Angulimala Stupa

Kaccha Kuti
Sudatta Stupa

Thailand T. & Buddha

Jain T.

MAHETH (old Shravasti)

Hindu T.

Old City Walls

SAHETH
Jetavana
Garden

Myanmar T.

Ashoka Column

Cambodian T.

← from Piprahwa

Korean T.

Ora Jhar

N

NOT TO SCALE

CHAPTER SIXTEEN

Shravasti

THE BUDDHA AND SHRAVASTI

DURING the Buddha's lifetime Shravasti was the largest town in the Gangetic plain. It was capital of the Kosala kingdom, one of the mahajanapada—'great footprint of the tribe'. Wealthy citizens and the King, provided support for the Buddha and his growing Sangha so that it was appropriate to spend rainy seasons here, particularly during the latter part of his life. It was here that many of the great teachings of Buddhism were offered for the first time. And, although the Buddha was not given to miracles, it is here where he performed several of the most famous.

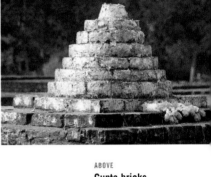

ABOVE
Gupta bricks adorned with gold foil. Gandhakuti monastery, Saheth.

The Buddha first came to Shravasti in the third rainy season after his enlightenment, and he visited regularly for a total of twenty five seasons in all. Buddhist literature is filled with descriptions of events and teachings which took place during the many seasons Sakyamuni lived here. There were two very active monasteries here during the Buddha's lifetime. Jetavana vihara, for monks, was built by the wealthy merchant Sudatta, while the equally rich lay-woman Visakha built the Purvarama vihara for nuns. Buddhist nuns had a strong presence in Shravasti. Numerous tales relating to Buddhist women are sited here at Shravasti. On a less positive note, it was from Shravasti, during the latter part of the Buddha's life, that a devastating attack was launched by King Vidudhava, against the Buddha's own clan, the Sakyas.

PRASENAJIT—THE KING OF KOSALA

During most of Gautama Buddha's preaching lifetime the king of Kosala was Prasenajit. As absolute ruler of a rich kingdom he led a luxurious lifestyle but, in keeping with the times, was threatened by intrigue both from within the court and without. The two most powerful kingdoms were his own, Kosala, and that of his brother-in-law, the kingdom of Magadha. For most of Prasenajit's life there was uneasy peace between him and Bimbisara of Magadha, but after his death Kosala was conquered by Bimbisara's son, Ajatasatru.

Prasenajit was exactly the same age as the Buddha. Initially he was wary of the Buddha's abandonment of property, of caste, and of ritual, seeing such a lifestyle as a threat to his own class and to the Brahminic duties demanded of him as king. His attitude changed as the Buddha's support in Shravasti expanded to include Mallika, the king's principal wife and other rich merchants. It was a support base Prasenajit could not ignore, especially after the wealthiest man in the kingdom, Sudatta, gifted Jetavana vihara to Gautama. Eventually Prasenajit was won over by the Buddha's style of teaching and his practical advice, which carried no hidden agenda and was without courtly subterfuge. The King became an enthusiastic supporter, frequently seeking to meet with Gautama whenever the monk was in town or when their paths crossed. This reflected the King's deep affection of the Buddha but did not lead him to ruling Kosala according to Buddhist principles.

THE DOWNFALL OF PRASENAJIT

There were many within Shravasti who required little stimulus to plot against the king. In the style of many autocrats, he controlled opposition with a combination of secret police, torture and execution. Two events however, which ultimately led to his downfall and death, happened years before and were prompted by his own direct actions. There is little doubt that the story is genuine. It is a tale of an ageing king, family betrayal and death, that Shakespeare would have recognised as befitting the stage.

When his son Vidudhava was revealed to be the son of a slave-wife of Prasenajit, the King had both stripped of their royal titles and reduced to slaves. This was patently unjust, particularly for the prince, who had been completely unaware of his humble origins. The Buddha's intervention allowed both the royals to be reinstated, but the resentment which seethed within Vidudhava was to inspire serious trouble later.

At another time a worthy official, who had been appointed by Prasenajit to root out corruption in the court, was falsely accused. The King had him executed, only to later learn that the official had been framed, and that he had killed an innocent man. In a clumsy attempt at restitution, Prasenajit appointed the dead man's cousin, Digha-karayana, to be a senior general in his army. The General, was not impressed with how his relative had been treated, nursing his resentment against the king for a future time.

The negative karma of these two episodes came together years later when the Buddha became unwittingly involved in the downfall and death of his friend, the King. The date is not certain, but it was within the last few years of the Gautama's life, when both men were almost eighty years of age.

Prasenajit was travelling in the Sakya region on business. Hearing the Buddha was nearby, he went to visit. Finding the Holy One relaxing in a small house, he left his ceremonial sword and turban outside, to be

guarded by General Digha-karayana. These items were his royal 'badge of office', the symbols of state. Seeing opportunity to revenge the death of his relative, Digha-karayana rode quickly to Vaishali with sword and turban. Here he and Prince Vidudhava, implemented a coup. The reign of King Prasenajit of Kosala was over.

Emerging from the Buddha's residence, Prasenajit found himself with only a single horse and one servant as retinue. Realising what had happened, he set off to Magadha to seek refuge from his nephew, King Ajatashatru. Rajagriha was several days away. Arriving in the night, when the city gates were closed, the king housed at a humble inn. That night he died. Ajatasatru was furious that his uncle had been so badly treated, but as murderer of his own father he was not in a strong position to accuse Vidudhava of disloyalty. Uncomfortable peace prevailed between the two kingdoms.

Meanwhile, responding to his own psychological imperative, Vidudhava beat the drums of war. He had never forgiven the slights he'd experienced as a youth in Kapilavastu, and vowed to expunge Sakyan pride forever. His armies set forth to teach the Sakyans a lesson about honesty.

SUDATTA—THE RICH MAN

A notable citizen of Shravasti was the wealthy merchant Sudatta who had become a follower of the Buddha in Rajgriha. Xuanzang describes Sudatta as: *'...a man of humanity and talent. He had amassed great wealth, and was liberal in its distribution. He succoured the needy and*

181

Laying bricks of gold in Jetavana's garden. Plaque, Kolkata Museum, Gupta 3rd century CE.

destitute, and had compassion on the orphan and helped the aged.' As the richest man in Shravasti their relationship illustrates Gautama's attitude towards wealth. Having grown up privileged, and a member of the warrior caste, the Buddha was as comfortable in the company of kings and merchants as he was with farmers or beggars. In political terms, his constituency were all members of society from the highest to the lowest.

Unlike many shramana groups, Gautama and his monks did not lead lives of extreme austerity nor did they enrich themselves with fees for performance of ritual. As social campaigners they led lives of moderation avoiding both self-indulgence and self-denial. It was by teaching and by example that the Buddha helped his followers deal with the practicalities of their everyday lives.

If his monastic community was to flourish, support from rulers and wealthy members of the laity was essential. Monks were required to abandon material possessions, but no such implication was placed upon lay members of the Sangha. By teaching that there was nothing inherently wrong with wealth, providing it was acquired in a moral way, the Buddha gained the attention of the privileged. And, by demonstrating how attachment to that wealth caused unhappiness and a failure to develop spiritually, he earned their respect and support. The Buddha's teaching was, and is, for all people, regardless of their financial status. To live a virtuous life in harmony with reality depends on your state of mind, not the depth of your pockets.

THE JETAVANA VIHARA—THE JETAVANA ANÁTHAPINDIKA ÁRÁMA

Early in the Buddha's teaching period, while on a visit to Rajgriha, Sudatta asked him to visit Shravasti, six hundred kilometres to the northwest. Gautama agreed, providing a monastery would be available for the Sangha.

Sudatta and Shariputra, the foremost disciple, were sent off to find something suitable. An area of parkland owned by Prince Jeta, son of the Kosala king looked ideal, but Jeta insisted that to buy the land would require '...*covering the whole area with gold coins*'. Responding to this, perhaps metaphorical, request, Sudatta showered the area with gold coin to '...*the value of eighteen crores*', or 180 million golden coins. Such flamboyance was artistically appealing, so many subsequent seals and stone carvings depict the covering of Prince Jeta's field with gold coin.

Accounts of this incident vary. In one, Prince Jeta noted that, although he had sold the field, the trees were not covered with gold coin, and they thus belonged to him. Soon however, he had a change of heart, and donated all timber for construction of the monastery required by the Buddha.

In another story, Jeta claimed back for himself a small area that Sudatta had been unable to cover with coin. On this site Jeta built an elaborate gateway, spending all the gold coin he had earned from the sale.

Despite his purchase of the Prince Jeta's grove, Sudatta still had sufficient money left over to build other shrines, wells and monasteries. Because of his generosity he became known as Anathapindika, 'the Incomparable Bestower of Alms to the Poor'.

Whoever paid the money, the vihara (monastery) of Jetavana must have been very grand. In the Pali literature it is almost always referred to as—Jetavane Anāthapindada ārāma—meaning: 'in Jeta Grove, Anathapindika's Monastery'. This joint-name was the Buddha's suggestion, so that the generosity of the two initial donors might be recorded and perhaps with the hope that others might follow their example. It is possibly the world's first example of 'naming rights'. Subsequently, as supporters, if not devotees, both Prince Jeta and his father Prasenajit, built numerous temples and monasteries for the Buddha.

GANDHAKUTI—THE BUDDHA'S HUT

Gandhakuti (Fragrant Hall) was the Buddha's preferred place of residence while at Shravasti. Initially it was a wooden, thatched wall structure which in Gupta times was enlarged to become a brick walled monastery. Tradition relates that it was from here that the Buddha emerged to walk the jewelled rainbow and perform the 'pair' and 'great' miracles.

THE FIRST BUDDHA STATUE?

For a period of three months after the Great Illusion miracle, the Buddha is said to have visited his mother Maya Devi, in the Heaven of Trayastrimsa. King Prasenajit responded to this absence by commissioning the construction of a statue of the Holy One. Buddhist legend relates that this 'first statue of the Buddha', carved from sandalwood was placed in Gandhakuti.

For historians, when the 'first' image of the Buddha was made is still a matter of debate. Most scholars are of the view that representations of the Buddha in human form were not made until around 100 CE, during Kushan times, three hundred years later. However, a less popular opinion favours an earlier date because of stories similar to this.

Faxian relates that when the Buddha next came to visit Gandhakuti, the statue came out by itself to greet him. Faxian saw a statue, but by Xuanzang's time in the seventh century, the temple was in ruins and the statue gone. Walking, talking or otherwise, the statue seen by the Chinese pilgrim was probably not fashioned during the Buddha's time.

THE ANANADABODHI TREE

When at Shravasti during the rainy season, Gautama stayed for about three months. He was a well-known, popular personality, revered by many citizens. When the Buddha was absent, his devotees were distressed by their lack of contact. Anathapindika, asked the Buddha to provide some permanent reminder for times when he was away. The Buddha requested Ananda to bring a branch of the Bodhi tree from Bodhgaya and plant it. Some accounts say that the sapling was conveyed by magical powers from Bodhgaya, others relate that a cutting was brought from the Bodhi-tree at Anuradhapura, Sri Lanka. Today, a descendent of this tree looms large at the centre of the Jetavana garden.

THE USE OF MIRACLES

During these times, miracles and paranormal powers generally, were used to demonstrate the superiority of one religion over another. By such means, royal patronage might be secured, the already-convinced further educated, and the obtuse induced to change their view. Buddhist scriptures say that miracles were a form of skilful means, used reluctantly by the Buddha. However, after being repeatedly challenged to demonstrate the validity of his teaching, he occasionally agreed to a 'conjurer's contest'.

The Great Illusion and The Pair Illusion are episodes, usually located at Shravasti, although the texts vary as to exactly what happened and where the miracles took place. For this reason, Shravasti is remembered amongst Buddhist-Olympians as the place where Sakyamuni defeated the holders of other doctrines. Some records suggest this was accomplished by miracles, others by debate. It may have been both.

A common account, relates that the Buddha was challenged by leaders of Jain and other philosophic schools to demonstrate his miraculous ability. King Prasenajit had a special hall constructed to hold the thrones of seven religious leaders. On the appointed day six of the leaders took their thrones while the Buddha flew to his. He then warmed up the audience by causing the hall to be destroyed, only to be magically rebuilt as a magnificent palace, adorned with a giant tree, resplendent with fragrant blossoms and fruits.

ABOVE
Bowls of marigold offerings. Gandhakuti Monastery, Shravasti.

THE PAIR ILLUSION

The next day, in the morning he caused a jewelled walk to extend from the eastern to the western rims of the world. That evening he emerged from the Gandhakuti to descend the jewelled walk in the midst of a vast heavenly assembly. Along the jewelled walk, he performed 'The Pair Illusion'. From the upper part of his body there emitted flames, and from the lower, water. He alternated water and flames and at the same time a 'Buddha-counterpart' appeared. This counterpart stood, walked and lay down like a mirror image.

THE GREAT ILLUSION

Gautama then performed 'The Great Illusion' in which a lotus rose from the ground on which the Buddha sat. He then multiplied himself endlessly 'to fill the sky', with thousands of his counterparts actively preaching the Dharma. In both painting and sculpture, the 'Pairs illusion' and, particularly that of the 'Great Illusion' became favourites of Buddhist artists. The miracles may be interpreted literally or as a metaphor, representing the universality of all Buddhas, and the presence of Buddha-nature in all and everything.

THE MIRACLE OF THE MANGO

The location is uncertain for another famous miracle. Either King Bimbisara of Rajagriha, or King Prasenajit of Shravasti, wanted the Buddha to perform a mango-related miracle near the gates of the city. The Buddha agreed, so the King sent forth 'the Crier of Truth' each day for a week, to tell the citizens that a miracle was to happen.

In the Shravasti version of this miracle, the Buddha arrived at the appointed spot to find all mango trees in the area had been cut down by schismatics, who opposed him. As sign of solace and respect, Ganda, the local gardener, offered Gautama a mango fruit to eat. When he was finished eating the Buddha asked Ananda to have Ganda plant the seed.

Immediately on planting, the seed split and a mature tree, *'fifty cubits high'*, instantly appeared, laden with fruit.

ANGULIMALA

Angulimala (the finger-garlanded) was a notorious local bandit who wore a necklace of human fingers collected from each of his victims. The story of his notoriety, and eventual redemption through the Buddha's intervention, is as gripping as any opera—soap or classical. It expounds the Buddhist view that even the most reviled person is not beyond redemption. And, that reformation can more readily be achieved through compassion than through punishment. For Gautama, *'...Not by hatred are hatreds ever pacified...They are pacified by love'.*

Angulimala is described as:
'...brutal, bloody-handed, devoted to killing and slaying, showing no mercy to living beings. He has turned villages into non-villages, towns into non-towns, settled countryside into unsettled countryside.'

He was not a man easily ignored. According to the story, Angulimala was acting under an oath to collect a thousand fingers. His Brahmin guru had demanded this vow from his student, whom he falsely believed had seduced his wife. Acting under orders, Angulimala *'...became a highwayman, killing travellers who passed through the forest. When the people of the kingdom began to avoid the roads, he entered the villages and dragged people from their homes. He never took clothes or jewels from his victims, only fingers.'*

Such a bizarrely disruptive individual was clearly unacceptable, so King Prasenajit of Vaishali, determined to have Angulimala killed. Hearing of this royal edict, Angulimala's mother set off to warn her son, not believing that she might become a target. Apprehending that if he met Angulimala that day he might avert matricide, Gautama went out onto the highway.

Angulimala was only one finger short of his avowed total. Seeing his mother approaching Angulimala believed that completing his vow was more important than quality family time. He set about to murder his mother. Before he could act, he spied the Buddha walking along a nearby road. A compassionate flicker in the killer induced him to switch target from mother to Buddha. Calling out, he ran towards the Buddha with sword raised. The Buddha walked on, ignoring the threat of assassination. Despite running as hard as he could, and demanding that the Buddha stop, the killer could not catch up with Gautama. Commenting on their relative states of mind the Buddha said *'I am always standing still; but you are not standing still yourself.'*

Eventually they spoke. In a moving exchange, the Buddha confronted Angulimala with the enormity of his actions and their consequences. Angulimala expressed genuine regret and desire for reformation. Casting aside the necklace, he threw himself at the feet of the Buddha and begged to be admitted as a member of the Sangha. Impressed with his sincere yearning for reformation, the Buddha agreed.

Angulimala did become a monk, but had to endure the karmic consequences of earlier deeds. The irony of his reformation made him an object of ridicule. When begging for alms he was spat upon and stones were thrown. With time, he became an enlightened and respected member of the community—an example of the universal human potential for spiritual progress, regardless of background. Angulimala wrote this verse:

Who checks the evil deeds he did?
By doing wholesome deeds instead,

He illuminates the world
Like the moon freed from cloud.

On a later occasion he was distressed by observing a woman in agony from obstructed labour. The Buddha suggested he return to the woman and say *'Sister, since I was born into this noble life I do not recall intentionally killing a living being. Through this act of truth may there be well-being for you and for your child.'* Reciting such an 'act of truth' was a potent declaration in the Buddha's world, akin to a magical mantra. Mother and child are reported to have survived. To this day, in some Buddhist traditions, this verse is still recited at the time of a woman's delivery.

Angulimala's conversion had wrought in him a different view of reality, turning him from a life of negative activity to a way that was compassionate and nurturing. His remains are said to be buried in the Pakki Kuti stupa in the old section of Shravasti town.

THE LADY VISAKHA—PURVARAMA MONASTERY

One of the Buddha's most active supporters in Vaishali was the wealthy businesswoman Visakha. Daughter of a Buddhist family, she was married at a young age to a wealthy Brahmin. Her father-in-law, Migara disapproved of her support for the Buddha but Visakha's wisdom and patience eventually led him to become a Buddhist follower. There are numerous stories of her ready wit and able character. With her wealth she built the Purvarama Monastery outside the eastern gate of Jetavana. Here the Buddha spent six rainy seasons.

DEVADATTA'S DEATH

There are several versions of how Devadatta died. One has its finale at Shravasti. Devadatta became mortally ill. Repenting of his assaults on the Buddha, and realising that his end was near, he instructed his disciples to carry him to Jetavana so that he could see the Buddha one last time. It is said, that when the Buddha heard of this he predicted that Devadatta would not succeed in seeing him.

As the party neared Jetavana the disciples put down Devadatta's litter to bathe in a lotus pond. The traveller rose from the litter but when he placed his feet upon the ground they sank into the earth, to be slowly followed by his legs and torso. Before he was completely swallowed by the earth, Devadatta managed to cry out and take refuge in the Buddha. The place where this took place is believed to be the swampy area behind the old Burmese monastery, north-west of the modern entrance to the archaeological park.

ASHOKA AND THE CHINESE PILGRIMS AT SHRAVASTI

In 249 BCE, the Emperor Ashoka came here as part of his pilgrimage to Buddhist holy places. At the eastern gate of 'The Shrine of the Garden of Gold', Jetavana he erected two pillars, each '70 feet high'. Faxian noted Ashoka's pillars in 407 CE, commenting: *'On top of the left pillar is a wheel and on the top of the right one is a bull. The water in the pool is clear, the trees and plants luxuriant, and flowers of many colours make a lovely sight, so beautiful to behold that it was named the 'Shrine of the Garden of Gold'.*

The pillars and capitals of Jetavana, have not been found. Faxian commented that Buddhism had declined in the old city, but that Jetavana was still occupied by monks who expressed delight that *'..men from such a far-off country should come all this way to seek the Dharma!'*

Two hundred and thirty years later Xuanzang found Jetavana deserted and the main city in ruins. However, shortly after his visit, archaeologists have confirmed, that the Jetavana monasteries were restored and new buildings constructed. As a Buddhist community, it continued to flourish right up until the twelfth century, before being enveloped by jungle.

Today's Shravasti

Three hours from Shivpatinagar, by a good road, is Shravasti. For much of the way, a phalanx of trees, arch over to shade your journey. There are numerous groves of mango, along with plantations of teak. The rest is rice paddy and untidy villages, with increasing fields of sugar cane as you approach Shravasti.

ORA JHAR

On the left, a kilometre before the main site, a forty metre mound rises from the plain. The name has a local meaning which approximates 'basket shaking', referring to the place where labourers clean their baskets when returning to their homes at end of day. The sides of the mound, are now a jumble of ancient bricks, overgrown with weeds. At the top, are remaining brick walls of a minor monastery. A small plinth, which was probably the place for an ancient Buddha statue is now enlivened with a modern white Burmese Buddha and a flutter of Buddhist flags.

This stupa must have been important to warrant such a massive enterprise. Excavation in 2000 revealed the remains of a brick stupa believed

Sri Lankan
pilgrims, beneath
Buddhist flags.
Ananda Bodhi
Tree Shrine,
Shravasti.

to be built by Ashoka. Local accounts suggest that Ora Jhar is where the Buddha performed his miracles of 'The Pair' and 'The Great', and relate that this is where he departed for Trayastrimsa heaven.

MAHETH—OLD SHRAVASTI CITY

The archaeological site is split in two, now known as Saheth and Maheth. It is a good idea to start your tour in Maheth, the ancient capital of the Kosala kingdom. There is less to see here. Making Mahet your first site, will allow more time at Saheth, which has more monuments dating to the Buddha's lifetime.

At Maheth, near the northern ramparts of the old city, are two important sites, adjacent to each other. From their summits you get an impression of the size of ancient Shravasti. The old mud walls are still visible, enclosing a space two kilometres long and one across. This is now a tangle of scrub-filled ruins, which just a lifetime ago was dense, virtually impenetrable forest.

To the north, out of sight, flows the Rapti River. Its waters drain the Annapurna region of Nepal two hundred kilometres away. In Buddha times it was called the Achiravati, or 'pure water' river which flowed close to the old walls of Shravasti.

KACHCHI KUTI—THE STUPA OF SUDATTA

On the right of the road is the most important site, the stupa of Sudatta, the rich merchant who paid for the gift of the Jeta grove to the Buddha and who supported him in many other ways. The earliest remains here date to Kushan times, at the start of the Common Era. Other additions were made later. The current name of the site is inappropriate. It refers to the bricks used in the construction of a modern Hindu shrine on top of the stupa. Kachcha is mud, thus Kachchi Kuti is 'the house of mud'. It was the generosity of the fabulously wealthy Sudatta which made the Buddha's

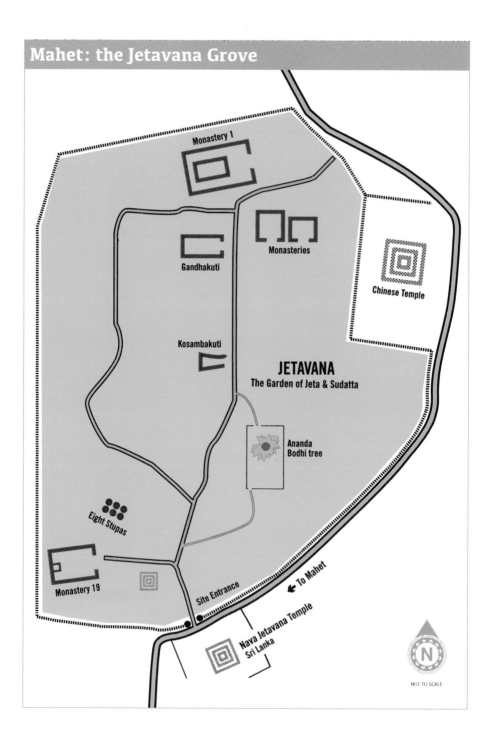

Mahet: the Jetavana Grove

Monastery 1

Monasteries

Gandhakuti

Chinese Temple

Kosambakuti

JETAVANA
The Garden of Jeta & Sudatta

Ananda
Bodhi tree

Eight Stupas

Monastery 19

Site Entrance

← To Mahet

Nava Jetavana Temple
Sri Lanka

N

NOT TO SCALE

residence in Vaishali possible. 'Mud house' does not seem an appropriate memorial to the man who covered Prince Jeta's Grove with gold.

From the top of Kachchi Kuti you can look directly down the old 'main street' of Shravasti southwards to the great mound of Ora Jhar. Street and stupa are in line, their conjunction cannot be accidental.

PAKKI KUTI—THE STUPA OF ANGULIMALA

Across the road is the stupa described by Faxian as the place where Angulimala was cremated. The low tunnel, which passes through from side to side was dug by the Archaeological Survey of India to assist drainage. It is not 'Angulimala's cave' despite local claims.

Xuanzang came to Maheth as did Cunningham, following the trail of the Chinese pilgrims. Cunningham first identified the Maheth site in 1863. Thirteen years later he and Hoey excavated here and at Saheth. Their explorations confirmed the twin sites as the Shravasti of Buddha's time.

The Chinese pilgrims described this stupa as the 'Hall of the Law' presented to Lord Buddha by King Prasenajit. That name used by the Chinese does not seem to fit other evidence. Pakki, however, means 'hard', an appropriate descriptor of Angulimala's steely personality.

Saheth—the Jetavana grove

Two kilometres back down the road is the Saheth archaeology site—a delightful garden, of lawn, brick and flowers, deserving successor to the mango grove of Prince Jeta. In this area the Buddha spent twenty five rainy seasons. If the 'garden' of the Buddha's time was as pleasant as today, it is understandable why he so favoured this place.

BELOW
The stupa of Angulimalla – Pakki Kutti, Mahet.

ABOVE
**The Eight stupas,
Sahet garden,
Shravasti.**

MONASTERY #19

On the left just after entering the site is monastery '#19', which had cells
for twenty one monks. It was first built in the 6th century and rebuilt
to the same plan five or six hundred years later. Buried in a clay case
beneath one cell was a copper-plate inscribed with the date of burial,
equivalent to the 23rd of June 1130 CE. It records the gift of six surrounding villages, as well as their annual revenue, to the monks residing
at Jetavana. Some nearby modern villages still bear these ancient names.
Also uncovered was a terracotta plaque depicting the Buddha receiving a
bowl offering from a monkey.

THE EIGHT STUPAS

Nearby, like displaced chessmen, the Eight Stupas, sit awaiting play. They
were probably built to commemorate revered monks. A seal discovered in one stupa, dates to the 5th century. These are not in any sense
'maha'—or great stupas. They are round, truncated and 'finger size'. Their
flat tops are often adorned with petals, sprinkled by pilgrims.

THE BODHI TREE—ANANDA'S TREE

Further along the path, on the right, is the Bodhi Tree commemorating
that planted by Ananda when the Buddha was absent from Shravasti. It

was a reminder to the citizens of the Buddha's continued presence in all things, despite him being absent in body.

When Shravasti was abandoned around the 12th century CE, the tree planted by Ananada from seed brought from the Bodhgaya tree, was overgrown and its location ultimately lost. Today's tree is impressively two metres in diameter. Unlike Bodhgaya, this tree is accessible to visitors. Enclosed by a distant iron railing festooned with flags, the tree stands undecorated, except when a national group temporarily wrap the trunk with golden cloth. Those same groups often lay flower mandalas on the brick platform below.

KOSAMBAKUTI—A BUDDHA RESIDENCE IN SHRAVASTI

The main path leads on to Kosambakuti, one of the places favoured in Jetavana for the Buddha to reside. Sometime, around the 1st century CE the monk Bala donated a large sandstone image of the Buddha to this place. It was found by Cunningham and donated to the Calcutta Museum. Given that it was a place favoured by the World Honoured One, it is surprising that Kosambakuti receives so little attention from modern pilgrims. What you see are flower-strewn brick foundations, which replaced the wood-thatch shelter of the Buddha.

GANDHAKUTI—THE BUDDHA'S FAVOURITE SHRAVASTI RESIDENCE

Centrally sited in Jeta's Garden, one hundred metres further is Gandhakuti—'the Fragrant Hut'. Wherever the Buddha resided, his disciples

BELOW
Gandhakuti monastery, Shravasti.

would offer flowers, sandalwood and perfume. Hence all houses where the Buddha lived were called 'Gandhakuti'. Later the name came to refer to any shrine where an image of the Buddha was placed. The Buddha lived here for more than twenty rainy seasons. His presence is still felt in the devotion of Buddhist groups from all lands, coming here to bow their respects to the World Honoured One.

LEFT
Seated Buddha statue and the Thai Mahamongkolchait temple, Shravasti.

The Gandhakuti here at Shravasti was the Buddha's first permanent residence. The original building was probably a simple wood or bamboo structure. Faxian tells that it subsequently became a seven-storyed building filled with offerings, banners and canopies. One day a rat took a lighted lamp-wick in its mouth, ignited a banner and burnt the entire structure to the ground. Later it was rebuilt with only two storeys.

Other nearby places

Many nationalities have built individual temples and residence halls for their monks. Japanese, Korean, Thai, Burmese, Sri Lankan and Nepalese signify the spread of the Buddha's teaching.

NAVA JETAVANA TEMPLE

Across the road from the main entrance to the archaeological park is a modern Sri Lankan temple—Nava (new) Jetavana Vihara. The temple is home to relics of the Buddha and, on its walls, are thirty- one contemporary Buddhist paintings, mostly depicting events of the Buddha's life while he was residing here in Shravasti.

THE MAHAMONGKOLCHAIT TEMPLE

Open daily 2–5pm. No cameras or cell phones allowed.

Most recent, and most obvious on the skyline, is the 111 metre tall spire of the Thai Mahamongkolchait temple. The '111' height is a deliberate comment on the three strengths, and the three gems, of Buddhism—the Buddha, the Dharma and the Sangha.

Beside the temple spire, facing down a long avenue of mango trees, is the golden statue of Lord Buddha, in Sukhothai style. Sitting serenely on a triple golden throne, his 39 metre height is another reminder of Buddhism's three wheels.

PURVARAMA—THE MONASTERY OF LADY VISHAKA

A kilometre due east of Jetavana, is the village of Purvarama which contains the remains of Lady Vishaka's monastery. There is not a great deal to see, except a fragment of an Ashokan pillar, here reverenced as a Shiva lingam. Purvarama is most easily reached by taking the dirt road which heads directly north near Ora Jhar for a few hundred metres, then head west for another short distance.

Sankasya

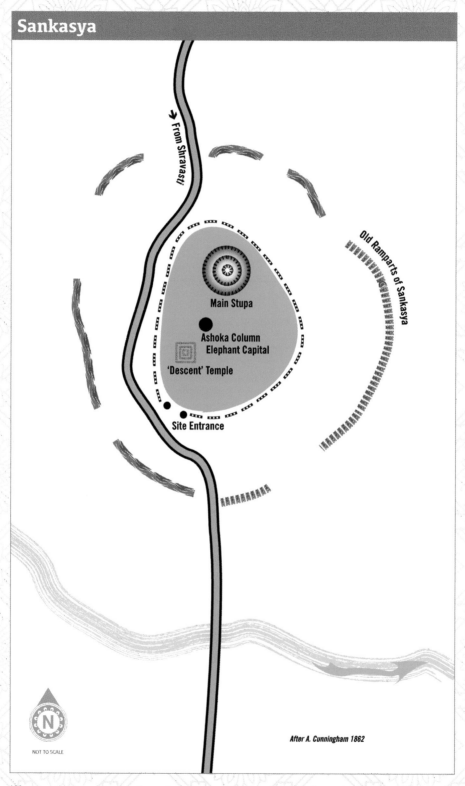

From Shravasti

Old Ramparts of Sankasya

Main Stupa

**Ashoka Column
Elephant Capital**

'Descent' Temple

Site Entrance

N

NOT TO SCALE

After A. Cunningham 1862

CHAPTER SEVENTEEN

Sankasya

SANKASYA is the least visited of all important Buddhist sites. It has received little attention from archaeologists, so there is not a lot to see, but there is a rich history to reflect upon. It was here that the Buddha descended from the heaven of Trāyastrimśa with the principal Vedic gods, Indra and Brahma as attendants. With this symbolic act he demonstrated the superiority of his doctrine. In recognition of this event, Ashoka raised a column with an elephant capital.

THE GREAT DESCENT FROM TRAYASTRIMSA HEAVEN

Gautama's mother Maya Devi, died six days after giving birth. After death, she is believed to have ascended to Trāyastrimśa Heaven. In Buddhist cosmology, Trāyastrimśa is located on the summit of Mt Sumeru, the most central, and greatest of the world's mountains. Although remote, it is still connected to earth so that those who dwell there are still involved in earthly affairs, unlike more distant heavens. Early Buddhists adopted the earlier Vedic beliefs about this heaven. The name literally means 'the heaven of the thirty three', in reference to the gods who dwell there. However, that number does not limit the heavenly gods to a few score. Trāyastrimśa was populated by a whole pantheon of gods, with Indra and Brahma the most important.

ABOVE
**Monks at the
'Descent' shrine.
Pala dynasty
ca. 900 CE,
Sankasya.**

Immediately after the Miracles of Shravasti, the Buddha disappeared, unannounced, to the heaven of Trāyastrimśa. Here he preached the Dharma to his mother, and other gods, for the entire three months of the rainy season. This was the only time during his ministry that he was absent from his disciples and lay followers. It is an immutable demand of all Buddhas, those of past eras, as well as our current historical Sakyamuni, that they should resort to the 'Heaven of the Thirty three', after they perform their greatest miracles. The Buddha was always reluctant to be 'a conjurer', seeing miracles as a distraction from the reality of daily existance. He had however performed great miracles at Shravasti and to fulfil the cosmic imperative, went to Trāyastrimśa heaven.

As time passed, the Buddha's disciples, back at Shravasti, became increasingly distressed by his unexpected absence. Many feared that the Buddha had gone forever. Responding to their queries, Maudgalyayana, who himself possessed great magical abilities, travelled to the Trāyastrimśa heaven to beg the Buddha to return. The Buddha informed Maudgalyayana that he would return to earth in seven days, specifying the site of Sankasya and suggesting that those who wished to see him should gather there. On learning that the Buddha was to leave the heaven, Indra:

...created three ladders, one of gold, one of jewels and one of silver. The feet of these ladders rested against the gate of the city of Sankasya, and their tops against the summit of Mount Sumeru.

On the appointed day the Holy One's personal disciples and a crowd of the faithful gathered at the base of the steps. Facing towards the east, the Buddha descended the middle jewelled stair; Brahma on one side, descended the silver ladder carrying a parasol to protect the Buddha; and Indra on the other, descended the golden stairs, holding a white choury (a yak-tail fly-whisk, a symbol of royalty). During the Buddha's time, the dual cult of Indra and Brahma was common religious practice. By enlisting the Vedic gods as attendants, the Buddha, made obvious his spiritual dominance over the ancient religion.

The trio were accompanied by other gods. Above, the sky was filled with a heavenly host singing praise and showering flowers. As he came down, the Buddha performed another miracle. He made visible, to all present, the wondrous spectacle of the gods in the heavens and the disturbing vision of those beings who were suffering in the hells below the earth. The records vary as to who walked on the right or left of the Buddha; on what they carried; and the composition of the ladder-stairs; but all scriptures are in agreement that on that day, there was visual conjunction of the heavens, of the earth and of the hells. So that:

...the gods saw the humans, and the humans saw the gods and all living beings in god, human and hell realms saw each other.

Because all beings could see the various realms of existence and, could experience the Buddha descending in glory from Trāyastrimśa :

...there was not one who did not want to be the Buddha... ...At that time, of all the devas, humans and beasts, even down to the tiniest red or black ant, who saw the Buddha, there was not one among them who did not desire Buddhahood.

The Great Descent of Buddha from Trāyastrimśa Heaven happened on the full moon day in October, sixteen years after his enlightenment, at Sankasya, on a day of great pomp and celebration.

UTPALA THE NUN

In the group preparing to welcome the Buddha's return to earth was the nun Utpala. As one of the foremost nuns in the Buddha's community, renowned for her beauty and psychic powers, she was particularly desirous of being the first to greet him. Realising, that women would be pushed to the back of the crowd, she miraculously transformed herself into a cakravartin—a world conqueror—complete with chariot and attendants. This transformation made obvious to the crowd that she was now, both important and a man. She was ushered to the front row and was indeed the first to greet the Buddha on his return.

With a chariot and four horses
created by supernormal power,
I worshipped at the feet
of the Buddha, saviour of the world.

Some records suggest that the Buddha was responsible for her transformation and others say she was rebuked by the Buddha for being so forward.

ASHOKA, THE CHINESE PILGRIMS AND SANKASYA

Ashoka came here as part of his pilgrimage in 249 BCE. Later, both Faxian and Xuanzang each found a thriving community of about a thousand monks and nuns at Sankasya and noted the presence of numerous stupas and monuments.

Seven hundred years after Ashoka, Faxian reported that the emperor sought to find out how deeply into the ground the triple ladders had penetrated. His workers dug to the water table but failed to find the bottom of the ladders. He goes on to relate how the emperor then built a large temple and erected a column: '...*on top of which he placed the figure of a lion.*' On the four sides of the pillar, which was a clear and transparent as glass, images of the Buddha were carved.

Faxian does not say that he personally saw any trace of ladders, but he did comment how Ashoka's lion helped resolve a land dispute between the monks and a community of Brahmins.

...both sides took an oath that if the place did indeed belong to the monks, there should be some supernatural proof of it. When these words had been spoken, the stone lion on top of the nearby Asoka pillar gave a great roar. Witnessing this, their opponents were frightened, bowed to the decision, and withdrew.

Xuanzang, who visited in 636 CE, definitely saw impressive replicas of the ladders which he found lined up from north to south, facing towards the east. He said:

Some centuries ago the ladders still existed in their original position, but now they have sunk into the earth and have disappeared. The neighbouring princes, grieved at not having seen them, built up

ABOVE
**The Sankasya
Stupa, with tiny
votive stupas
at its base.**

*of bricks and chased stones ornamented with jewels, on the ancient
foundations to resemble the old ones. The present stairs are more
than 70 feet high with a Buddha Vihara on top enshrining a stone
statue of the Lord. The statues of Brahma and Indra stand on top of
the right and left stairs respectively, and they are represented in a
descending position.'*

It was from Sankasya, that Xuanzang collected a large silver statue of the
Buddha descending the heavenly staircase to take back to China.

Today's Sankasya

It takes serious dedication to reach the site of the Buddha's descent from
heaven. By Indian standards the region is remote, 'a no place' with narrow roads and few people. Although the site is under the 'protection' of
the Archaeological Survey of India, there has been little restoration, excavation or signage. Here, the pilgrim, to borrow a term from the Raj, is
'out station'. To drive from Shravasti to Sankasya takes six to eight hours.
Going on to Agra is four to five hours, with an extra three onwards to
Delhi.

Unfortunately, nothing remains of Xuanzang's giant stairs with the triple
statues. It is not unreasonable that traces are buried nearby, as numerous
mounds lie unexplored, and the Ashokan pillar, has yet to be found.

LARGE STUPA

There is a twenty metre high stupa of ancient bricks. On top is a more recent Hindu shrine. It is not clear if this is a stupa raised by Ashoka, or raised later as no excavation has been done. Contemporary pilgrims are prevented from climbing to the summit of this stupa. This does not stop groups of devotees offering flowers and candles at the base.

BELOW
Ashokan elephant capital, Sankasya.

THE ELEPHANT CAPITAL

On display is an elephant capital which sits at ground level on a modern base, facing away from the stupa. What has happened to the lion capital and pillar described by Faxian, is unknown.

The elephant, like a zoo inmate of yore looks out through the bars of an iron cage. His imprisonment suggests Lord Ganesh down on his luck. In size and de-meanour, the statue has the appearance of an Ashokan emblem, but lacks the finesse of other more famous Ashokan capitals. It does not help that time has removed his trunk. Ashoka's capital deserves to be housed better. It is not a good look.

THE PALA SHRINE

Nearby, under a large banyan tree is a tiny brick shrine housing a magnificent stele from Pala times. Behind iron doors, the stele encapsulates the story of Sankasya. Emerging from the rock, in almost full round, are the Buddha, Brahma and Indra caught in the moment of their arrival back to earth. Each stands erect in the instant of walking forward from the ladders, which are depicted on the stone behind. Centrally is the Buddha. To his left is Brahma carrying an umbrella that shelters the Holy One. To his right is presumably Indra. In the accounts, Indra carries a yak-tail fly whisk, but here he is equipped with the Buddha's begging bowl. Each image was once dark rock. Now they are of golden hue, with their details blurred from innumerable gold-leaf donations.

ABOVE
Indra, the Buddha and Brahma descend from Tráyastrimsa heaven, Sankasya.

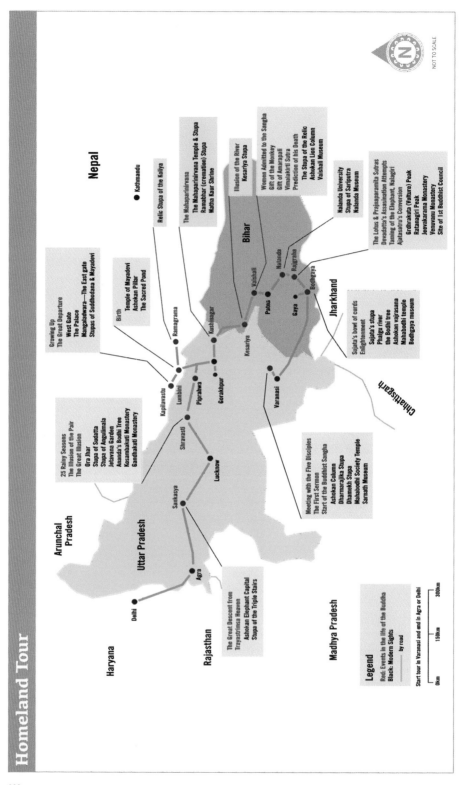

Homeland Tour

NOT TO SCALE

Nepal

Kathmandu

Relic Stupa of the Koliya

The Mahaparinirvana
The Mahaparinirvana Temple & Stupa
Ramabhar (cremation) Stupa
Matha Kaur Shrine

Illusion of the River
Kesariya Stupa

Women Admitted to the Sangha
Gift of the Monkey
Gift of Amrapali
Vimalakirti Sutra
Prediction of his Death
The Stupa of the Relic
Ashokan Lion Column
Vaishali Museum

Bihar

Nalanda University
Stupa of Sariputra
Nalanda Museum

The Lotus & Prajnaparamita Sutras
Devadatta's Assassination Attempts
Taming of the Elephant, Nalagiri
Ajatasatru's Conversion
Grdhrakuta (Vulture) Peak
Ratanagiri Peak
Jeevakarana Monastery
Venuvanu Monastery
Site of 1st Buddhist Council

Birth
Temple of Mayadevi
Ashokan Pillar
The Sacred Pond

Growing Up
The Great Departure
West Gate
The Palace
Mangaladwara—The East gate
Stupas of Suddhodana & Mayadevi

Ramagrama

Kushinagar

Vaishali

Nalanda

Rajgraha

Patna

Gaya

Bodhgaya

Jharkhand

Kesariya

Kapilavastu

Lumbini

Piprahwa

Gorakhpur

Varanasi

Chhattisgarh

Sujata's bowl of curds
Enlightenment
Sujata's stupa
Phalgu river
the Bodhi tree
Ashokan vajrasana
Mahabodhi temple
Bodhgaya museum

25 Rainy Seasons
The Illusion of the Pair
The Great Illusion
Ora Jhar
Stupa of Sudatta
Stupa of Angulimala
Jetavana Garden
Ananda's Bodhi Tree
Kosambakuti Monastery
Gandhakuti Monastery

Shravasti

Lucknow

Meeting with the Five Disciples
The First Sermon
Start of the Buddhist Sangha
Ashokan Column
Dharmarajika Stupa
Dhamekh Stupa
Mahabodhi Society Temple
Sarnath Museum

Sankasya

Arunchal
Pradesh

Uttar Pradesh

Agra

Dehli

The Great Descent from
Trayastrinsa Heaven
Ashokan Elephant Capital
Stupa of the Triple Stairs

Haryana

Rajasthan

Madhya Pradesh

Legend

Red: Events in the life of the Buddha
Black: Modern Sights
——— by road

Start tour in Varanasi and end in Agra or Dehli

0km   150km   300km

'Homeland' Tour

············

THIS section suggests how to spend your time on a daily basis. The number of days proposed, make for a non-rushed tour. If time is no object, extra days could usefully be spent at, Varanasi, Bodhgaya, Rajgir, Kushinagar, Lumbini and Shravasti. Each day outlines a sequence of visits that link to the overall historical Buddhist focus of the tour, although not everything suggested is Buddhist. From a timing perspective, it is what works, and in the opinion of the author, is what's likely to be of interest to any serious traveller.

ABOVE
The Pragbhodhi hills, near Bodhgaya.

Travel time

It is assumed that travellers will have their own car, van or bus. The times given are generous estimates for driving between sites in a bus—but road and traffic conditions can double, or treble, the time-estimate given. It is a good idea to seek local advice about road conditions on a daily basis, especially when travelling through Bihar.

The hotels suggested are good value in terms of location, quality and price at the time of writing. However, all things change, so travellers are advised to check and make their own decisions.

Tour summary: Accommodation

Day	Overnight	Suggested hotel	Day	Overnight	Suggested hotel
1	Varanasi	The Taj, Varanasi	10	Kushinagar	Residency, Kushinagar
2	Varanasi	The Taj, Varanasi	11	Lumbini	Buddha Maya Garden
3	Bodhgaya	Lotus Nikko, Bodhgaya	12	Lumbini	Buddha Maya Garden
4	Bodhgaya	Lotus Nikko, Bodhgaya	13	Shivpatinagar	Royal Retreat
5	Rajgir	Centaur Hokki, Rajgir	14	Shravasti	Lotus Nikko, Shravasti
6	Patna	Hotel Maurya	15	Sankasya	Residency, Sankasya
7	Vaishali	Residency, Vaishali	16	Agra	numerous options
8	Vaishali	Residency, Vaishali	17	Delhi	numerous options
9	Kushinagar	Residency, Kushinagar			

Homeland of the Buddha Tour

DAY 1 ARRIVE VARANASI

Evening | River boat tour; evening aarti ceremony at Dashashwamedh Ghat.

DAY 2 AT VARANASI

Early Morning | Dawn boat tour on the Ganges river.

Morning | Walk in the old city; Bharatmata Temple; VHU museum.

Afternoon | Sarnath: (10km from Varanasi city to Sarnath.) The Mahabodhi Society Temple; Sarnath main site; Sarnath museum.

DAY 3 VARANASI TO BODHGAYA

5hr (Time your departure to allow for a full afternoon in Bodhgaya.)

Morning | Sasaram: Sher Shah Suri's tomb (2 hrs from Varanasi).

Afternoon | Bodhgaya: Sujata's Stupa; Temple of the Kushi Grass; the Mahabodhi Temple.
(5km out of town is the stupa of Sujata.)

DAY 4 IN BODHGAYA

Early Morning | the Mahabodhi Temple.

Morning | Bodhgaya: the 'Great Buddha' statue; Japanese Temple; Bhutanese Temple; Archaeology museum

Afternoon | Bodhgaya area: Dhungeshwari Cave; the Mahabodhi Temple (2nd visit)

DAY 5 BODHGAYA TO RAJGIR

2hrs.

Morning | Modern Rajgir: Chariot grooves; Venuvanu grove; Ajatasatru's Stupa; Japanese Temple.

Afternoon | Ancient Rajgir: Bhimbisara's jail; Ratanagiri Peak; Vulture Peak.

DAY 6 RAJGIR TO PATNA

(Rajgir to Nalanda 1hr ; Nalanda to Patna 3hrs.)

Morning | Nalanda: Nalanda University; Nalanda Museum.

Afternoon | Kumrahar (on the outskirts of Patna)

DAY 7 PATNA TO VAISHALI

2hrs.

Morning | Patna–Golgarh; +/- Buddha Ghat; Patna Museum.

Afternoon | Vaishali: Ananda's Stupa; Ashokan Pillar; tank of the monkeys.

DAY 8 AT VAISHALI

Morning | Stupa of the Relic; Vaishali Museum; Peace Pagoda; Amvara village.

Afternoon | Free time.

DAY 9 **VAISHALI TO KUSHINAGAR**

(Vaishali to Kesaria 1.5hrs; Kesaria to Fazilnagar 4hrs; Fazilnagar to Kushinagar 0.5hrs)

Morning | Kesaria: the main stupa; Fazilnagar: the stupa of Cunda; Kushinagar: the Ramabhar Stupa.

Afternoon | Kushinagar: Parinirvana Temple; Museum; Matha Kunwar shrine.

DAY 10 **AT KUSHINAGAR: DAY TOUR TO GORAKHPUR AND KABIR'S TOMB AT MAGHAR**

(Kushinagar to Maghar 1.5hrs; Maghar to Gorakhpur 0.5hrs; Gorakhpur to Kushinagar 1hrs)

Morning | Maghar: the twin tombs of Kabir.

Afternoon | Bauddha Museum (Gorakhpur); Parinirvana Temple (Kushinagar).

DAY 11 **KUSHINAGAR TO LUMBINI**

(Kushinagar to Sunauli 3hr; Cross India–Nepal border 1.5hr; Bhirawa to Lumbini 1hr)

Afternoon | Tour Tilaurakot sites: Kundan; Gotihawa; Kapilavastu; Niglihawa; Sagrahawa; Dharampaniya.

DAY 12 **AT LUMBINI**

Morning | Buddha Maya Temple

Afternoon | German, Tibetan, Japanese and Burmese temples at Lumbini.

DAY 13 **LUMBINI TO SHIVPATINAGAR**

(Lumbini to Ramagrama 1.5hr; Ramagrama to Bhairawa 1hr; Cross Nepal–India border 1.5hr; Sunauli to Shivpatinagar 2hr)

Morning | Visit Ramagrama site.

Afternoon | Visit Piprahwa site; Birdpur house.

ABOVE
Young nuns from China and Taiwan, Bodhgaya.
FACING PAGE
Flower and water offering, Bodhgaya.

DAY 14 **SHIVPATINAGAR TO SHRAVASTI**

3hrs.

Morning | Ora Jhar; Mahet site (Kacchi Kuti and Pakka Kuti).

Afternoon | Sahet site #19 Monastery; 8 Stupas; Bodhi tree; Kosambakuti; Ghandakuti; Thai temple.

DAY 15 **SHRAVASTI TO SANKASYA**

6-8hrs.

Afternoon | Sankasya site.

DAY 16 **SANKASYA TO AGRA**

4hrs.

Evening | The Taj, sunset visit.

DAY 17 **AGRA TO DELHI**

2.5hrs

Morning | Agra Fort, Itamadu-ud-dhaula; the Taj second visit.

Afternoon | Drive to Delhi.

205

Glossary

Aarti ceremony *lit.* Towards the love of God—the fire ritual performed at the end of Hindu rites.

Abhaya mudra *lit.* Fearless gesture—made with the arm raised to the shoulder and the palm turned outwards. It symbolises reassurance, protection and the dispelling of fear.

Ahimsa *lit.* Do no harm—the practice of nonviolence and the positive effects which come from that.

Ajatasatru Son of King Bimbisara of Magadha, who killed his father and ultimately became a supporter of the Buddha.

Akbar The third, and greatest, of the Mughal Emperors.

Amrapali Famous courtesan of Vaishali who donated land to the Buddha and became an ardent supporter.

Anagarika Dharmapala Sri Lankan Buddhist activist who founded the Mahabodhi Society, a major aim of which was the restoration of Indian Buddhist sites to the Sangha.

Ananda Cousin and favourite disciple of the Buddha, renowned for his memory.

Anandabodhi tree At Shravasti—a descendent of the Bodhi tree from Bodhgaya.

Anathapindika (Sudatta) 'the Incomparable Bestower of Alms to the Poor'—a rich disciple from Shravasti. He paid for the Jetavana monastery at Shravasti.

Angulimala The finger-garlanded—a notorious murderer of Shravasti, ultimately a disciple of the Buddha.

Ashoka The third and most famous emperor of the Mauryan dynasty. In later life a strong supporter of Buddhism, who erected stone pillars at important Buddhist sites.

Atisha Bengali Buddhist teacher 980–1054CE—he studied at Nalanda and, from Tholing, was the main proponent of the second development of Buddhism in Tibet.

Banyan tree Ficus bengalensis or nyagrodha—the national tree of India.

BCE Before Current Era (an alternative to BC)

Beglar, Joseph English photographer and Arch.Soc.India assistant, during the Bodhgaya excavation in the 1880s.

Bharhut A famous Mauryan stupa—its finely carved railings are on display in the Kolkata Museum.

Bhimbisara King of Magadha during the Buddha's lifetime. A good friend of the Buddha, he was killed by his son Ajatasatru.

Bhumisparsha mudra The 'earth-witness' position in Buddhist iconography—the Buddha touches the ground with his right hand, to confirm his right to Enlightenment.

Bihar State of modern India, the region where Buddha spent much of his life.

Bodhi *lit.* Wisdom, enlightened.

Bodhi tree A type of banyan fig, Ficus religiosa—specifically the tree, or one of that tree's descendants, under which the Buddha became enlightened.

Brahma The Hindu god of creation—one of the Trimurti (three forms of God) the others being Shiva and Vishnu.

Brahmi script An early form of written Sanskrit, used in Ashokan edicts.

Buchanan, Dr. Francis Explorer of early Buddhism—in 1797, the first to use the word 'Buddhism' in print.

Buddha—*lit.* One who has awakened.

Buddha Purnima—(Vesak) the day of Buddha's birth, enlightenment and death.

Chakravartin World Ruler

Carlleyle A.C.L. Assistant to Alexander Cunningham—responsible for the excavation of Kushinagar.

CE—Current Era (an alternative to AD)

Chakra Wheel

Chakravartin 'Wheel turner'—world conquering monarch.

Chandragupta Maurya The 1st emperor of the Mauryan Dynasty.

Chandaka (Channa) Siddhartha's groomsman.

Choury A yak-tail fly-whisk—a symbol of royalty, usually white.

Chunar Source of the sandstone used by Ashoka for his columns.

Cunningham, Alexander Explorer of early Buddhism—First Director of The Achaeological Survey of India.

Darshan—*lit.* Sight—a Hindu belief that merit can be obtained by proximity to a temple deity or other noted person or place.

Devadaha Capital of the Kolliya kingdom—home of the Buddha's mother, Maya Devi.

Devadatta Cousin and disciple of the Buddha. He led a schism against the Buddha and is reputed to have instigated several assassination attempts on the Buddha.

Dharampaniya 'Religious water'—the modern name for Sarakupa, the place where Siddhartha's arrow landed.

Dharma The law, the teachings.

Dharmachakra Wheel of the law (teachings).

Dhungeshwari A hill-cave complex near Rajgir where Gautama practiced austerities for several years, also known as Pragbodhi (before Buddha).

Enlightenment The state of being of the Buddha—a potential for all humans.

Fa Hsien Chinese traveller to India in search of Buddhist scriptures.

Fazilnagar The modern name for Pava, where the Buddha took his last meal.

Gandhakuti 'The Fragrant Hut'—the name given to all residences of the Buddha.

Gandhara Region of ancient Pakistan/Afghanistan—home of the Kushans and origin of the Graeco-Roman form of Buddhist art.

Gautama Clan name of Siddhartha.

Ghat Step

Golghar *lit.* Round house—a famine relief structure in modern Patna.

Gotihawa Birthplace of the first Manusi Buddha.

Grdhrakuta *lit.* Vulture Peak—in Rajgir. The place where many Buddhist sutras were first delivered.

Great Illusion A miracle at Shravasti—where a myriad of Buddhas appeared In the sky.

Gupta Empire ca. 320–550CE—a 'golden age' of artistic creation in north India.

Hamsa *lit.* Goose—a symbol of fidelity in Buddhist art.

Haribala 5th century Buddhist monk who donated the 'reclining Buddha' statue in Kushinagar.

Hastigarta Elephant ditch—a site near Kapilavastu where Gautama threw an elephant killed by Devadatta.

Indra Leader of the gods in Hindu heaven.

Jain Reformist religion of ancient India.

Jeta Prince Jeta—Owner of Shravasti land that was used for the first Buddhist monastery.

Jetavana Vihara Monastery at Shravasti—paid for by Sudatta. Here, the Buddha spent 25 rainy seasons.

Jivaka Physician of Rajgraha who treated the Buddha's injured leg.

Kalinga Early Indian state which opposed Ashoka.

Kalpa An aeon of time.

Kanakamundi The second Manusi Buddha of this kalpa, who was born in Niglihawa.

Kanishka 3rd Emperor of the Kushans and strong supporter of Buddhism.

Kanthaka Siddhartha's horse.

Kashi *lit.* 'Light'—ancient name of Varanasi.

Kashyapa—Mahakashyapa An early disciple of the Buddha.

Kasyapa The third, Manusi Buddha of this kalpa, who was born in Varanasi.

Krakuchhanda The first Manusi-Buddha of this kalpa, who was born in Gotihawa.

Krishna An avatar of Vishnu.

Kshtriya The warrior caste of the Hindu caste system.

Kumrahar Site of Ashoka's palace at Patilaputra (Patna).

Kudan Site where, after enlightenment, the Buddha first met his father, wife and son.

Kusa grass A tall grass (Desmostachya bipinnata)—used by the Buddha as a seat during his Enlightenment.

Kushan Empire 1st–3rd century CE. It dominated much of central Asia and north India.

Licchavi Clan Occupied a region north of the Ganges with their capital at Vaishali.

Lotus Sutra Important Mahayanist Sutra which expresses that: all people can become Buddha; that faith and devotion are important to achieve this; and that the Buddha is the unifying vehicle in attaining enlightenment.

Lumbini Birthplace of the Buddha.

Magadha One of the mahajanapada, or main fledgling states—it dominated north India following the Buddha's death.

Magadhan A common dialect of Sanskrit in the Buddha's time.

Maha Great

Mahabarata *lit.* 'Great Bharat' (or Great India)—one of the greatest Sanskrit epics. It details the war between the Kaurava and Pandava families. Written around the 9th century BCE, allegedly, by Lord Ganesh.

Mahakasyapa (Mahakassapa) 'Great Kasyapa'—one of the Buddha's foremost monks. Convenor of the First Buddhist Council, which defined the sutras a year following the Buddha's death.

Mahanjanapada 'Great footprint of the tribe'

Mahant Abbott of a Hindu community

Mahaparinirvana 'Great Final Cessation'—the death or cessation from the round of rebirth.

Mahastupa 'Great stupa'—one of those which contained relics of the Buddha after the original distribution.

Mahavira *lit.* Great Hero—The 24th and last, Tirthankara of the Jain religion, effectively the founder of Jainism and a contemporary of the Buddha.

Mahayana *lit.* Great Vehicle—the main Buddhist sect of China, Korea, Japan and Vietnam. As distinct from the Hinayana 'Lesser' or Theravadan sect.

Maitreya The fifth, and last Manusi Buddha for this kalpa, who is yet to come.

Managaladwara *lit.* Auspicious gate—the eastern gate of ancient Kapilavastu from which Gautama set forth on his Great Renunciation.

Mandala Cosmic diagram, used in Tantric Buddhism—a visual depiction of the relationship between various deities and their powers.

Mango miracle At Shravasti -The Buddha had a fully grown mango tree appear.

Manjusri The boddhisattava of wisdom

Manusi Buddhas Human Buddhas of this kalpa.

Mara The Great Temptor and Lord of Illusion.

Mathura North Indian city famous for its school of Buddhist art.

Maurya The first dynasty to control most of India.

Mayadevi Mother of the Buddha.

Megasthenes Seleucid (Greek) ambassador to the Gupta court, the compiler of 'Indica', an account of many aspects of Indian society and nature.

Maudgalyayana (Moggallana) One of Buddha's foremost disciples.

Mucalinda A naga who protected the Buddha after his enlightenment.

Mudra Hand gesture

Naga Snake-like; being common in Buddhist and Hindu cosmology.

Nagarjuna Noted south India Buddhist philosopher whose thinking consolidated Mahayanist doctrine.

Nalanda Foremost Buddhist university which flourished from ca500-1100CE.

Niglihawa Birth place of Kanakamundi—the second Manusi Buddha of this kalpa.

Nirvana A state of mind which is beyond sorrow.

Nyagrodha tree Ficus bengalensis or nyagrodha, a type of banyan tree.

Pair Illusion Miracle at Shravasti where the Buddha appeared with his 'double'.

Pakki Kuti Shravasti stupa containing Angulimala's remains.

Pala dynasty 750-1170CE—rulers of eastern India who were strong supporters of Buddhism.

Pali A mixture of 3rd c. BCE, Prakit-languages of eastern India that were compiled in written form in the 1st c. BCE, in Sri Lanka.

Parinirvana Beyond nirvana—beyond the realm of birth and rebirth.

Parvarti The spouse of Lord Shiva.

Pataliputra Capital of the Mauryan empire, nowadays modern Patna.

Patna Formerly Pataliputra.

Pava Home of Cunda, the blacksmith who served the Buddha his last meal, now the village of Fazilnagar.

Peepal tree (Ficus religiosa)—the tree under which the Buddha became enlightened, a species of fig.

Peppé, W.C. The Scottish planter who discovered possible Buddha relics at Piprahwa.

Pitha *lit.* Seat—refers to the seat of the Buddha.

Piyadesi The name used by Emperor Ashoka.

Pragbodhi *lit.* Before Buddha—a hill-cave complex near Rajgir where Gautama practised austerities for several years—also known as Dhungeshwari.

Prajapati The Buddha's milk-mother—sister to his birth-mother Maya and the first member of the female Buddhist Sangha.

Prajnaparamita sutra The Perfection of Wisdom Sutra—an important Mayahanist sutra.

Prakit Any one of several popular languages derived from Sanskrit. eg. Magadhan

Prasenajit King of Shravasti and follower of the Buddha.

Pravartanamudra The hand gesture indicating 'setting in motion the wheel of the doctrine'.

Rahula *lit.* Fetter—the son of Siddhartha and Yasodhara.

Rajgir Formerly Rajgraha—capital of the Magadhan kingdom during the Buddha's lifetime.

Ratnadadhi *lit.* Jewel Ocean—one of the library buildings in Nalanda University.

Ratnagriha *lit.* Jewel Seizing—the shrine at Bodhgaya where the newly enlightened Buddha is said to have spent the fourth week after enlightenment.

Ratnaranjaka *lit.* Jewel Delighter—one of the library buildings in Nalanda University.

Ratnasagara *lit.* Jewel Sea—one of the library buildings in Nalanda University.

Rummindei Previous name of

Lumbini, birthplace of the Buddha.

Ryot A peasant.

Sagrahawa Site of the massacre of the Sakya clan by King Ajatasatru of Kosala (Shravasti).

Sakya Clan name of the Buddha.

Sakyamuni Sage of the Sakya—the fourth Manusi and current Buddha, who was born in Lumbini.

Sal tree (Shorea robusta)—the Buddha died between two sal trees.

Samsara Everyday reality.

Sanchi Site of an important Ashokan stupa.

Sangha The religious community—later extended to involve religious and lay people.

Sanghamitta (Sangamitra) 'Friend of the Sangha'—daughter of the Emperor Ashoka who went as a missionary to Sri Lanka.

Sarakupa 'The arrow fountain'- where the arrow of Siddhartha landed. The modern village of Dharampaniya.

Saria Relics of the Buddha.

Sariputa A disciple of the Buddha.

Seleucid Empire Founded by Seleucus Nikator after the death of Alexander the Great.

Sher Shah Suri A Pathan from Afghanistan who defeated the Moghul ruler Humayun and briefly ruled India.

Shikara The spire of a Hindu temple.

Shiva The Hindu god of Creation and Destruction.

Shravasti Capital of the Kosala kingdom—ruled by King Prasenajit during the Buddha's lifetime.

Sudatta (Anathapindika) A wealthy disciple of the Buddha from Shravasti. His funds paid for the Jetavana monastery at Shravasti.

Suddhodana Father of Siddhartha and ruler of Kapilavastu.

Sujata The milkmaid who gave the starving Siddhartha a bowl of curds.

Sutra A discourse of the Buddha.

Tantric Buddhism A form which uses ritual and identity with tantric deities to achieve enlightenment.

Tathagata—'one who has thus come'—a term used by the Buddha when referring to himself.

Taxila Important ancient city in NW Pakistan.

Theravada *lit.* Way of the Elders— the main Buddhist tradition in Sri Lanka, Thailand and Cambodia. Also called (disparagingly) Hinayana.

Tholing Buddhist kingdom in western Tibet.

Tirtha A ford.

Tirthankara *lit.* Ford-builder—a term applied to Jain saints.

Trāyastrimśa Heaven 'The heaven of the thirty-three'—presided over by Indra, where the Buddha went for three months following the Great Illusion of Shravasti.

Trimurti *lit.* 'Three forms'—the three Hindu gods, Brahma, Shiva and Vishnu.

Utpala A nun who (as a man) was first to greet the Buddha on his descent from Trāyastrimśa Heaven.

Uttarapatha The north road—an important highway in Buddhist times.

Vaishali Capital of the Licchavi republic, a town frequently visited by the Buddha.

Vajrasila *lit.* Diamond seat— the enlightenment seat of the Buddha at Bodhgaya.

Venuvanu The bamboo grove in Rajrgraha used by the Buddha.

Vesak (Buddha Purnima)— the day of the Buddha's birth, enlightenment and death.

Vidudhava Son of King Prasenajit of Vaishali Responsible for the

Sakyan massacre at Sagarwa.

Vihara Monastery.

Vikramshila An important Buddhist university, contemporaneous with Nalanda.

Vimalakirti Friend and lay disciple of the Buddha, said to be as deeply enlightened as the Buddha.

Visaka The Indian calendric month roughly corresponding to April/May—the month of the Buddha's birth, death and enlightenment, in the Theravadin tradition.

Vishwa Shanti Universal peace.

Xuanzang Chinese pilgrim who went to India to find Buddhist scriptures— his eighteen year journey was recorded in *Record of the Western Regions*, a document used extensively by early European explorers and romanticised as 'Monkey' in book and television.

Yashodhara Wife of Siddhartha and mother of Rahula—subsequently she became a Buddhist nun.

Acknowledgements

Charles Allen for advice about images of the early explorers.

Tim and Pauline Evill for use of their Buddha statue for the cover images.

Samantha Gilchrist: Senior Librarian at the University of Glasgow, for help beyond the usual discovering photos of Laurence Austine Waddell.

Sheila Middleton for images of her grandfather, Dr. William Hoey (M.A., D.Lit., Q.U.I. and M.A. Oxon.)

Neil Peppé, grandson of W.C. Peppé for details of his family's involvement with the archaeology of Piprahwa and images from that time.

Bibliography

As this is a book for the general reader, notes and references within the text are not included. For this work, the original texts have been consulted together with numerous web resources which are not listed here. Books regarded as most useful to the general reader interested in travel to the Buddhist regions are marked * to ***.

Allen, Charles, *The Buddha and the Sahibs*, 2002 ***

The Buddha and Dr. Fuhrer, 2008 ***

Aitken, Molly Emma (ed.), *Meeting the Buddha, on Pilgrimage in Buddhist India*, 1995 *

Armstrong, Karen, *Buddha*, 2000 ***

Bashmam, A.L. (ed.), *A Cultural History of India*, 1975 *

Bauddh, Shanti Swaroop, *In the Foot-steps of the Buddha*, 2008

Bauddha, Jugal Kishore, *Rajagraha, The Historic Capital of Magadha* 2009 *

Beal, Samuel (Trans.), *Buddhist Records of the Western World* (Hiuen Tsang) 1994 ***

Bidari, Basanta, *Lumbini, A Haven of Sacred Refuge*, 2002 *

Kapilavastu, The World of the Siddhartha, 2004 *

Blomfield, *Vishvapani, Gautama Buddha*, 2011 ***

Dhamikka, Ven. S, *Middle Land Middle Way*, 2008 **

Eicher Goodearth Publications (pub.), *Walking with the Buddha, Buddhist Pilgrimages in India*, 1999 *

Gosh, A., *Nalanda*, 1959 *

Rajgir, 1975

Grousset, Rene, *In the Footsteps of the Buddha*, Trans. 1971 **

Huntington, John, *Sowing the Seeds of the Lotus: A Journey to the Great Pilgrimage Sites of Buddhism, Orientations*, pt.1 (pp. 46-62); Feb. 1986, pt.2 (pp. 28-44); March 1986, pt.3 (pp. 32-47); July 1986, pt.4 (pp. 28-41); Sept. 1986, pt. 5 (pp. 46-59) ***

Keay, John, *India, a History*, 2000 *

Legge, James (Trans.), *A Record of Buddhist Kingdoms*, 1886 *

Mahajan, Jagmohan (ed.), *Ganga Observed, Foreign Accounts of the River*, 1994

Majupuria, Trilok and Indra (eds.), *Holy Places of Buddhism in Nepal and India,* 1986 **

Muthiah, S (ed.), *Where the Buddha Walked*, 1990

Nhat Hanh, Thich, *Old Path White Clouds*, 1991 **

Rai, Hari D., *Lumbini, The Supreme Pilgrimage*, 2010 *

Singh, Rana B.P., *Where the Buddha Walked*, 2003 **

Snellgrove, David (ed.), *The Image of the Buddha*, 1978 *

Wriggins, Sally Hovey, *Xuangzang, A Buddhist Pilgrim on the Silk Road*, 1996 ***

FACING PAGE The 'Big Buddha', Bodhgaya.

ABOUT THE AUTHOR

John McKinnon has visited the holy Buddhist
places numerous times since the 1960s. For more
than twenty years he has been a practitioner of Zen

Buddhism. As a young man,
he lived in the Mount Everest
region, where he was the first
doctor at Khunde Hospital. It
was in Khunde that he developed
an interest in Buddhism.
Returning to New Zealand,
John trained and practiced as an
ophthalmologist. Since those early
years he has been continuously
involved with Sir Edmund
Hillary's development work in Nepal.

John's wife Diane, was a constant companion
during that time. With her extensive knowledge of
Nepal, Diane became a guide for trek-groups in the
Himalaya, later starting her own company, Footprints
Tours Ltd. Using her detailed interest in Asian
textiles she took groups to visit the craftspeople of
Asia. John often joined these groups to commentate
on regional history and the art of Buddhism.

Homeland of the Buddha brings this
lifetime experience of Asia into focus as a
practical, informative guide to the major
Buddhist sites of India and Nepal.

Printed in Great Britain
by Amazon

33170248R00117